KU-681-190

CARL ROGERS

By the same author

*Psychologists on Psychology*
*John B. Watson: the founder of behaviourism*
*Broadmoor*
*Piaget: critique and reassessment*
*Testing Psychological Tests (with Douglas Shelley)*
*Essential Psychology*
*The Development of Play*
*The Development of Imagination (with Stephen MacKeith)*
*Being A Man*
*Forgotten Millions*
*Soviet Psychiatry*
*Body Language in Relationships*
*How to Succeed in Psychometric Tests*
*Alter Egos*
*The Secret Life of the Mind*

# CARL ROGERS

## A CRITICAL BIOGRAPHY

David Cohen

Constable · London

First published in Great Britain 1997
by Constable and Company Limited
3 The Lanchesters, 162 Fulham Palace Road
London W6 9ER
Copyright © David Cohen 1997
The right of David Cohen to be identified as the author
of this work has been asserted by him in accordance with
the Copyright, Designs and Patents Act 1988
ISBN 0 09 477010 7
Set in Linotype Sabon 11pt by
Rowland Phototypesetting Ltd,
Bury St Edmunds, Suffolk
Printed in Great Britain by
St Edmundsbury Press Ltd,
Bury St Edmunds, Suffolk

A CIP catalogue record for this book
is available from the British Library

To my son, Reuben,
with love

# Contents

# Acknowledgements

Many people and institutions have helped in the writing of this book. The Library of Congress houses 140 boxes of Rogers' papers as well as some objects, such as one of his bank books and some of the medals that he was awarded. This is a veritable treasure trove of material. The Manuscripts Division of the Library of Congress was very gracious. The Library also has many of the films and tapes Rogers was involved in making.

I am also grateful to the librarians of the following collections for ferreting out material on Rogers: the University of Chicago Library, the University of Wisconsin Library, the University of Ohio Library, the University of California Library, Columbia University Library and Rochester Public Library. Nel Kandel of the Carl Rogers Memorial Library in La Jolla also offered valuable assistance. Stephen White, Director of Information of the British Psychological Society, was also helpful.

I am also grateful to Barbara Temaner Brodley and Tony Merry for useful information. Rogers engaged in something of an intellectual duel with the physicist Richard Feynman. I am grateful to Jeremy Webb of the *New Scientist* for giving me considerable help with understanding Feynman's history and character. I have also drawn on material for an interview I did with Rogers' old personal friend, Dr Karl Menninger, that was published in the *New Scientist* in the 1970s. I discussed many aspects of Rogers' work with Dr James MacKeith of the Denis Hill Unit at the Royal Bethlem

Hospital. Rogers does inspire fierce loyalty and there were a few people I would have wished to talk who declined to do so and I am very sorry that was their decision.

My biggest help and sternest critic has been my son, Reuben, who helped me ferret out material in the Library of Congress. I know that he thinks I have at times been a shade severe with my subject.

In finishing the book I was greatly helped by the comments of my editor at Constable, Carol O'Brien, as well as of Anne Charver, who did the copy-editing and helped put the bibliography into good order. Julia Ross read and commented on the manuscript. She has also had to live with me – and the project – for much of the past two years. She gets a gold star for patience and good humour. As with all books, responsibility for the mistakes is mine.

## How I want to be in our relationship.

I want to express my feelings as they occur. I realize I have not been good at this. My way has been to withdraw, to clam up, for fear of hurting (Ex. Her saying this trip all her idea.)

I want to feel OK about keeping a part of my life separate from our relationship. I don't want complete togetherness. It is not healthy or good for me.

I want to share when I want to share, & not feel I must share.

I want to let Helen know when, in response to her behavior, ~~makes~~ I feel guilty. Too often she is able to bring about guilty feelings in me by a word, an inflection. (An example "I guess I can hold out that long".)

I want to have more respect for Helen's ability to take care of herself, to engage in an independent life.

Currently, I feel I can only escape from ~~her smothering~~ what I experience as a kind of smothering control by getting away. I don't want to have to get away.

A page from Rogers' many manuscript notes in the Library of Congress

NOTE ON SPELLING

Rogers' books and articles were published with American spellings, for example *Client-Centered Therapy, Counseling and Psychotherapy*, but rather than switch constantly between client-centered and client-centred, counseling and counselling, English spelling has been used throughout this biography.

# 'Almost a God'

The archives of the Library of Congress hold a photograph of Carl Rogers taken when he was about 55. He is sitting at a table with a number of other professors. All the men are wearing suits and look conservative. Rogers seems younger than the others; his long, lean face is a little drawn. He looks intense, as if he were paying complete attention to what is being said in the room. Or perhaps one sees that, because everyone who knew Rogers felt he was such a wonderful listener. Well into his eighties, he could make people feel they had his complete attention. He could give 'unconditional positive regard', a phrase he used to describe one of his key concepts.

Psychologists are often cynical about the greats of their discipline but many individuals who met Rogers said he made them feel, not important, but accepted. He saw them and did not judge them. He didn't just hear what people said but he heard *them*. He could be totally attuned to another human being. When he looked back on his career, Rogers was amazed his ideas should have touched and affected so many people. The modesty seems engaging.

Rogers did not become well known until he was in his forties after he had published his second book, *Counselling and Psychotherapy* (1942), which outlined the fundamentals of non-directive therapy. The book sold far better than its publishers expected. Rogers offered a number of radical ideas that had a great impact on personality theory and the development of psychotherapy. Therapists should not act as if they were magicians whose techniques could lay bare the mind and soul; they should not tell 'ignorant' patients what their problem really was. The therapist was more a facilitator, a midwife who would help the 'client' to produce his or her own insights. Switching from talking of 'patients' to talking of 'clients' was not just cosmetic. Rogers 'empowered' those he treated. Second, he offered hope. He argued most of us have a tendency to 'self-actualise', to grow, to make the best of ourselves. Where Freud was a Central European pessimist, Rogers was a Midwestern optimist.

After 1942, Rogers' books and ideas reached a wide audience. In a letter to his eldest brother, Lester, Rogers listed his sales figures. They were impressive. He had sold hundreds of thousands of copies; he had been translated into over 20 languages, including Japanese, which delighted him as he was the first Western therapist to make an impact there. From 1942 until the year of his death, Rogers continued to publish and influence. He came to believe his therapeutic techniques could help resolve political conflicts and he was brave enough to go into hostile territory such as South Africa to assist radicals there. At one time there was talk of his being a candidate for the Nobel Peace Prize.

Rogers is one of the pioneers of humanistic therapy but, in one crucial way, he differed from other humanist therapists such as Fritz Perls, the creator of Gestalt therapy, and Abraham Maslow, who popularised the concept of 'peak experiences'. Rogers was always interested in research. He did not think therapy was so precious it was above being studied by conventional empirical methods. From the age of 13, he saw himself as a scientist. He pioneered the recording of therapy sessions and he was the first therapist who tried to prove in any scientific sense that psychotherapy works. In various forms, this project lasted 25 years. Just what Rogers did prove remains a matter of controversy to this day.

In the 1960s Rogers' fame and his positive attitude to science led to an extraordinary contract. He was hired by Caltech (the California Institute of Technology) to act as a consultant. The Provost was worried that Caltech's brilliant physicists, chemists, mathematicians and physiologists were feuding and failing to agree on the future of the institution. Caltech's students were wilting under examination stress. The Provost feared hot-heads would start sit-ins and demonstrations like students at lesser campuses. He recruited Rogers to spend two days a month counselling the scientific elite so that they could learn to improve their human relationships. The men he was to work with included Richard Feynman, the Nobel prize-winning physicist, and Roger Sperry, who did the pioneering studies on the differences between the right and the left hemispheres of the brain. Rogers eventually persuaded 18 of the high-flying faculty to take part in a two-day encounter group. As they were all hard-nosed scientists more used to observing distant galaxies than their own complexes, it was a tribute to his reputation that they came at all.

Rogers was also an excellent debater. He had public debates with theologians including Paul Tillich and Martin Buber, author of *I and Thou*. Rogers had been rather shy as a young man but he had mastered this and turned himself into an effective speaker. His most famous debate was with the behaviourist B. F. Skinner in 1956. That was seen as a great confrontation between scientific and humanistic psychology. Rogers also debated with the radical psychiatrist R. D. Laing. Their relationship was marred by a dispute over money because Rogers had put up $2000 to help book the London Hilton as a venue for the debate and Laing, who was broke, refused to repay the money.

The students of the 1960s loved Rogers. He caught the radical mood well. From the 1920s, he had been interested in new approaches to education. One of his heroes was the philosopher John Dewey, who believed a good education should be more than intellectual; it should make a person truly open to experience. Rogers was almost lyrical about the student movement of the 1960s; he did not condemn the use of mind-bending drugs and thought 'flower power' a lovely idea. As an old man, he may even have dabbled in drugs himself. Rogers also became one of the most influential advocates of encounter groups. His wife Helen sniped that some people saw him as 'almost a God'.

Even when he was 70, Rogers was tremendously energetic. He set up encounter groups bringing Ulster Catholics and Protestants together in the hope of working through their ancient hatreds. He wrote perceptively about the ageing process.

Rogers was one of the most influential psychologists of the century. If he was not a pioneer in quite the same league as Freud, Pavlov or the behaviourist John B. Watson, he was one of the major figures in the development of psychotherapy. His ideas helped fashion Western fascination with psychology and therapy. It has become part of our life and language. We talk about our complexes, our repressions, our conflicts. We try to work out if we're growing, becoming the person we want to be or if we should go to the shrink for a personality make-over. A thousand therapies bloom, from AA to Zen. It has been estimated that over 250,000 people work as therapists and counsellors in the UK alone. In America, the figure is closer to 700,000. Then there are meta-counsellors who only treat other counsellors. Rogers played a large part in making people feel that going into therapy could be a positive experience rather than a cause for shame. Any course in psychotherapy has to cover his ideas. Many of his books are still in print and read widely.

There has been no previous critical biography of Rogers although there are two useful books that incorporate much biographical material. The first is Howard Kirschenbaum's *On Becoming Carl Rogers* (1979) which was 'authorised'. Rogers read it before publication. In some ways, however, it is an extended interview with Rogers, in which he reviewed his career. Kirschenbaum was a devoted admirer and very rarely challenged what Rogers said about himself or his work. Rogers' daughter, Natalie, feels it is the last word and needs no revision. However, the book does not deal with many influences on Rogers or with how his ideas are now perceived. It also avoids a number of painful episodes that Rogers may well not have wanted made public while he was still alive. Letters that Rogers himself kept reveal that sometimes other people saw incidents very differently – and they sometimes felt hurt or betrayed by him.

The second useful book is Brian Thorne's *Carl Rogers* (1992). This is part of a series on key psychotherapists. Thorne devotes the opening chapter to Rogers' career and then goes on to analyse his ideas and their subsequent influence. Thorne is much more critical than Kirschenbaum of Rogers' ideas, but his biographical chapter is just a 20-page introduction.

## Unconditional impersonal disregard

I first got to know about Rogers when I was a student in the 1960s. He seemed a breath of fresh air. Even though the psychology degree course at Oxford was largely experimental, we were taught Rogers' ideas by a young post-graduate, Brian Little, who was something of a fan. Little wrote to Rogers asking for detailed information about one of Rogers' papers. He expected a letter back from his hero but, instead, he got a duplicated sheet with 13 or 14 different boxes on it. Each box covered a particular contingency. If you wanted details of research findings, there was an address you could write to for reprints. If you wanted to invite Carl Rogers to address your college, he was probably booked up for the next few years, but there was an address you could write to. If you had psychological problems, Dr Rogers regretted but he didn't have any more time for new clients. The letter was astonishingly cold and pompous.

We were surprised, as the letter was the very opposite of everything Rogers stood for. It seemed to be a classic of unconditional negative – and impersonal – disregard. Where was the caring, the acceptance, the valuing Rogers was famous for?

Looking back, I have no doubt that we felt particularly insulted because as Oxford students, we were convinced we were special. Some of our teachers, such as the ethologist Niko Tinbergen and the social psychologist Michael Argyle, were themselves world famous. We were not to be palmed off.

I started this biography with a little scepticism, therefore, and also with questions born of writing a book of 13 interviews with famous psychologists, *Psychologists on Psychology* (1977). As I interviewed these psychologists, I found they often acted as if their theories of human nature applied to everyone apart from themselves. B. F. Skinner, for example, argued that free will was an illusion. We are all conditioned and shaped by the rewards and punishments we have received. Yet he talked about his ideas and feelings and how they influenced his work, and gave every impression of exercising free choice. Many biographers of psychologists have had to confront this paradox: the mismatch between the ideas of psychologists, the lives they lead and the way they 'explain' their lives. Nina Sutton in her recent book *Bruno Bettelheim* (1996) complains that, at times, she seemed to be writing the biography of two different individuals. She struggled to reconcile the 'good' Bettelheim, the survivor of concentration camps who developed new therapies for treating autistic children, with the 'brute' Bettelheim who had beaten these same children. Alan Elms in *Uncovering Lives* (1994) wrestles with a number of similar cases.

Rogers offered not only a theory but what seems to be an ethic. We should be open to experience; we should hear what others are trying to tell us. He was not shy about exposing some of his own personal problems. He wrote about his troubled relationship with his parents. He confessed to a personal crisis in the 1940s when he had completely gone off sex for a year. He explained, without being specific, how he had mismanaged one schizophrenic client: the therapeutic relationship was a fiasco which ended up with him literally on the run and close to a breakdown.

Rogers wanted people to know about these failures and conflicts. He left the Library of Congress 140 boxes of his papers as well as tapes and films he was involved in making. Some of what they reveal is at odds with the public image of Rogers. Rogers, however, placed no restrictions on these papers. They are in the public domain by his own wish. That seems a very admirable attitude and I have relied heavily on them.

Twentieth-century lives are full of subversive discoveries – Perls slept with his patients, Jung flirted with Fascism, Heidegger was a passionate Nazi, Sartre exploited young women and was beastly to de Beauvoir, Bettelheim was brutal. One view is that it doesn't really matter, provided their ideas are important. More than most modern thinkers, however, Rogers made accepting the feelings of other people a central feature of his philosophy. A biography cannot evade the question of how well he managed to practise what he preached.

Rogers insisted his 'learnings', a favourite phrase of his, had enabled him to grow throughout his life, to 'become Carl Rogers'.

The evidence he left shows him in a different light – as a muddled human being. Being a great therapist did not stop him being confused and, at times, cruel. He could often hurt people badly, and hurt them more than he let himself realise. One of those who was most affected was his wife, Helen.

## Questions of principle?

By the late 1960s, Rogers was conflicted about his marriage. He felt he had missed out on the joys of the sexual revolution. In a photograph taken at the time, Helen looks like a nice white-haired old lady. She's plump and wearing a frumpish dress with spots; Rogers, on the other hand, still looks attractive. He was often surrounded by young men and woman who regarded him as a guru. In the days of 'make love not war' Rogers was all too aware of how few women he had made love to, and he rather fancied being open to some new sexual experiences. Sometimes when he was unfaithful, he insisted on telling Helen because they had to be honest with each other. She stopped sleeping with him for a while and he claimed that this justified his infidelities. She had broken their sexual contract.

Helen fell seriously ill in the early 1970s, which put great pressure on Rogers who had to be her main carer. He did not abandon her but, in the interests of honesty, he told her that he was very attracted to a young woman he had met, Bernice Todres. This new love did not mean he loved Helen less. It was just different.

There were also several cases where questions were raised about Rogers or his students publishing confidential details about patients without their permission. The most obvious instance was personal. Although he invented fictitious names for the couple, Rogers published details of his daughter's marriage to Larry Fuchs as a key case history in *Becoming Partners* (1972). When Fuchs wrote to ask why and to say how shocked he was, Rogers did not reply. Fuchs wrote a second letter. Again, Rogers did not reply.

In another instance it is much easier to understand what seems to be a betrayal of trust. As Rogers knew, in 1972 his son David was unhappy in his marriage. David's wife, Corky, was very neurotic. She drank a great deal. She took large doses of Seconal. Rogers had spent hours on the phone trying to help her so he knew how fragile she was. When David decided to leave her, Rogers went to see a divorce lawyer and counselled his son with infinite guile. David should apply for a temporary job in California. As it was temporary, there would be no reason for Corky to come and live in California. After six months David would have established residence in California and could file for divorce there, which would ensure that Corky did not get the marital home. David followed his father's master plan. Soon after he filed for divorce, Corky killed herself.

In the 1970s Rogers took to heavy drinking. His daughter, Natalie, wrote to him saying it was not surprising he was putting on weight if he consumed over half a bottle of vodka a day. She warned him he was starting to smell and that this would not make him very attractive at a time when he wanted to find new sexual partners. She begged him to look at why he was drinking so much but found her father, the perfect listener, did not hear what she said.

I'm aware I may sound judgemental myself but I would suggest that is a peril of biographies. One can hardly fail to confront the differences between the public stance and the private behaviour. Rogers was an immensely influential psychologist, but he was also very human, ambitious, aloof, unsure of himself in social situations, competitive, unforgiving and a little surprised by his success. He was also a man who could never forget his past. As an old man he was still apt to blame his parents for having made him feel that he did not deserve to be loved. To understand Rogers one has to understand his roots.

# 1

## The Boy Who Went to China,

## 1902–1924

In 1871, after Chicago suffered a terrible fire, many of its rich moved out to a village called Oak Park. By 1902, the year Carl Rogers was born, Oak Park had 10,000 citizens. Ernest Hemingway, who grew up there at the same time as Rogers, was acerbic, describing it as a place of 'wide lawns and narrow minds'. He often talked about writing a novel about its suburban snobberies but refrained as he couldn't do it without hurting people.

Nearly everyone who met Rogers as an adult was struck by his personal qualities. He could accept people as they were; he did not judge them. Yet Rogers came from a family where judgements were constantly being made. He came from a community which was as carping as it was nominally Christian. One Church looked down on another; there were controversies about whether it was decent to let young people learn how to dance. Rogers said his parents were 'masters of subtle emotional control'. They had strict rules, rules the children were meant to know without being told. His mother Julia preached the need to 'keep the standards high'.

Admittedly much of what we know of Rogers' childhood comes from his own writings and interviews. No one seems to have asked him why his brothers and sister gave a rather different account of the family atmosphere. His sister Margaret, for example, compiled a family history that stressed how loving their mother was. In one letter Margaret noted the day that would be 'dear mother's 109th birthday'. Rogers, however, stuck to his version in many papers, books and speeches. His parents were loving but controlling. Everything was on their terms, according to their rules. At first, Rogers complained in private but, eventually, when he was famous and felt it important for people to understand what had shaped him, he complained in public. He judged his parents as he never judged his clients. To be a hurt child who becomes a healer is a seductive narrative about one's life.

Rogers' father, Walter Alexander Rogers, was the son of a train conductor. Walter was born on 19 January 1868. He went to the University of Wisconsin, studied engineering and became president of the local YMCA. In 1888, Walter graduated with special honours in mathematics. He stayed at the university for another year and specialised in research on how to strengthen cement. Before he finished his second degree, Walter left to work for the Wisconsin Central Railway. Over the next ten years, he became an expert in bridge building and, eventually, assistant engineer for the Chicago, Milwaukee and St Paul's Railway. Assistant meant deputy chief; it was a very senior job and Walter supervised the building of much of the elevated track in Chicago.

Walter had known Julia, the girl who would become his wife, from childhood. Julia was a bit of a tomboy. One of her uncles called her Boy Jim and that turned into the nickname Dim. But Julia was far from Dim. She was ambitious, went to college and completed two years of study before she and Walter married in 1891.

Once they were married, Julia left college and concentrated on running the home. She was 29 when Carl Rogers was born. His earliest memories suggest she was already set in her personality and attitudes. God was a constant, dominant presence in her house. Every day, there were family prayers; every meal, grace was said; every Sunday, the main family outing was to church. Rogers remembered for the rest of his life two phrases Julia wove into their prayers. She would often repeat, 'Come from among them and be ye separate' and 'All our righteousness is as filthy rags in thy sight, O Lord.' When he wrote a chapter for *A History of Psychology in Autobiography* (1965) Rogers argued these two phrases revealed much about his mother. The first 'expressed her feeling of superiority, that we were of the elect'; the second emphasised that the family might enjoy worldly success but, in the sight of the Lord, they were still, at best, 'unspeakably sinful' (p. 344). In all his writings about his childhood, Rogers said nothing kinder about her.

Margaret Rogers recalled other favourite sayings of Julia's, however. Sometimes Julia would say, 'My child, if the Lord had wanted everyone just like you, He would have made them so.' Both children agreed that Julia believed in hard physical work. 'Scrubbing floors will cure most ills' was another favourite motto, as was the more uplifting 'keep the standards high'. Margaret wrote that Julia's hands were tender, beautiful and that they gave her 'so much love'. When she had nightmares, her mother comforted her, sitting by the side of the bed and quoting Joshua 1:9, 'Be strong and of a good courage.' But Carl never saw his mother in such a sweet, soft light.

Carl Ransom Rogers was born on 8 January 1902. When he was born, Margaret was five years old. There was also an elder brother, Lester, who was nine years old, and another brother, Ross, who was three. Carl was born just after his father gave up his safe job with the Chicago railroads and went into business with Onward Bates, an older engineer. The two men founded the Bates & Rogers Construction Company. Their accountant also had a memorable name, Noble Judah! The three had useful contacts; Walter had published articles in the *Wisconsin Engineer* and in the *Railway Review* and he had a reputation as an expert in cement. Onward Bates fell ill soon after the company started, which put considerable pressure on Walter. But the business soon prospered.

Rogers described himself as a sickly child who was prone to burst into tears. He was so often ill that his parents told him they were afraid he would die young. There was nothing wrong with his brain, though. He started to read very young. By the time he was four, Julia and Walter were proud of their son who could understand books of Bible stories specially adapted for children.

When Carl was five years old, the family moved to 547 North Euclid Avenue in Oak Park. Oak Park had become as smart and snobbish as Hemingway suggested. In 1899, its voters rejected an invitation from Chicago to join the city. There was enough wealth locally to attract the architect Frank Lloyd Wright to move there in 1899. He soon had a number of clients, so Oak Park became an important, if unlikely, site for the development of modern functionalist domestic architecture. A few buildings might be modern; not many attitudes were.

In 1901, Oak Park made itself even more exclusive by seceding from the neighbouring township of Cicero because Cicero teemed with 'low life'. Many blue-collar Catholic immigrants who liked a drink lived there. Walter and Julia never drank. In Oak Park, even such relatively liberal churches as the First Congregational Church were puritanical. Its pastor, Dr William E. Barton, believed that death was a positive spur to moral development as it made the living reflect, day in, day out, on the rewards of Heaven and the punishments of Hell.

The first day Carl went to school, the head teacher was told the new boy could read. The head was so impressed he decided Carl should go straight into the second grade. Carl was relieved because the first-grade teacher looked so fierce. The second-grade teacher, Miss Littler, seemed much nicer and he developed a crush on her, a crush that gave him the courage to defy his parents for the first time. Miss Littler asked him to stay behind after school to help tidy up the classroom. Julia's rules were clear. Her son had to come home the moment school was over. No dawdling, no chatting with friends, no games in the street. Carl didn't care. He helped Miss Littler clear up.

In everything he wrote about his childhood, Rogers' ambivalence about his parents shines through. Though there were 'good family times' with lots of humour, there was often a surprising edge to so-called family fun. The fun and laughter were often 'biting'. Rogers once claimed he was teased 'unmercifully', another time that the teasing was 'merciless'. In 1965, he revealed some of the reasons. First, he was something of a 'bookworm'; secondly, he was extremely absent-minded. His brothers and his parents called him 'Professor Moony' after a famous comic-strip character. Rogers was nervous for the rest of his life about his poor memory. He took copious notes. His papers at the Library of Congress are full of jottings and scribbles, some on tiny, flimsy bits of paper. He was making sure he didn't forget. Rogers said he did not realise until he was an adult that such teasing 'was not a necessary part of human relations'.

Rogers came to believe being teased made him very shy. He would often complain he was inept in social situations partly because he did not know what to say. Siblings do often tease each other. It is also not unusual for small children to use humour to get away with bad behaviour (Cohen 1985), but it is less normal for parents to tease their children a great deal. Little research has focused on parents who use humour and mocking and on the effect that has on their children. Some psychologists and psychotherapists such as Erik Erikson suggest that constant mockery is bound to damage a child's self-esteem (Erikson 1972). To a surprising extent, Rogers wrote as if he had been a victim in his childhood.

A number of times Rogers' brothers and sister countered that he exaggerated and even distorted his childhood. In the early 1970s, Lester said Carl was being unfair; their upbringing had been loving and an excellent preparation for life. Rogers did not change his story. A revised version of his chapter for *A History of Psychology in Autobiography* was published as 'Personal Growth' in the book *Twelve Therapists* (1972). The only difference between the two versions is that the word 'unmercifully' is set in italics in the first version and is in ordinary type in the second. In 1982, at his 80th birthday party, Rogers gave a paper in which he again complained about his parents.

His relationships with his brothers were also not easy. Rogers felt Lester was too old for them to play together though the young Carl 'hero-worshipped' him. Ross, just three years older than Carl, could play with him, but Ross seems to have provoked intense jealousy. Carl was sure Walter and Julia loved Ross more. He even developed the theory that he, Carl, had been adopted. In 1908, in a world where most middle-class children lived in stable families, fantasies of being adopted were not common. Rogers didn't dare ask his parents for many years if he was really their son. Those fears were perhaps triggered by the arrival of two younger brothers, Walter (born in 1907) and John (born in 1908). Unlike Lester, they never intimidated him.

As Rogers describes his parents, it is perhaps not so strange that he should have felt unable to talk to them about such bizarre fears as whether he was adopted. 'Masters of the art of subtle and loving control' do not like being interrogated. David, Rogers' son, remembered that in the 1930s when he was a child, the great therapist did not encourage his children to talk about 'bad' feelings. Upset children were expected to go into their bedrooms, cool off, come out when they felt better and be cheerful, smiling and polite. Those were the rules. Was Carl Rogers as a parent repeating patterns he had learned as a child?

Rogers' parents certainly did have some curious restrictions. In high school Rogers was again expected to come home as soon as lessons finished. He had chores to do. His parents disapproved of activities outside the family circle. The outside world, the fleshpots of Cicero, were packed with wicked temptations. When Carl first made friends with a girl called Helen Elliott at Oak Park, they took to riding their bicycles back from school together. That way Carl was not late back home and Julia did not learn of this friendship. She would certainly not have approved. The Rogers family did not dance, did not attend movies, did not play cards, did not smoke, did not drink and absolutely did not show any interest in relationships with persons of the opposite sex. Julia punished her children by withdrawing affection and approval. Rogers once said Julia could be withering as ice.

The Hemingways are an interesting contrast. The Hemingways also went to church every Sunday and said grace before every meal. Hemingway's father believed drink and cigarettes were sinful. Though their family was as religious as the Rogerses, Ernest and his sister Marcelline were allowed to attend school dances and to go to a local dancing academy run by Miss Belle Ingram. Carl never had such freedom.

Much later in his life, Rogers recalled an image that illustrates some of this cramped youth. He spoke of seeing spindly, sick potato plants that had been left in a dark corner of a dank cellar. Their shoots struggled to find the light. He wrote as if he identified with that need to grow out of the dark.

As Walter's business became more successful, he spent longer away from home. The company started to get business as far north as British Columbia. As a result, Julia was challenged less and less in her views and she became more and more fundamentalist.

Rogers shared this intensely religious, 'we are the elect' upbringing with many leading psychologists of his generation. David McClelland, professor of psychology at Harvard and author of *The Roots of Consciousness* (1964), explained his history to me (1977), a history he felt was typical. He was the son of a minister, a young man 'rebelling against the Church but who also had become tremendously interested in psychological things because they were so involved in religion.' Psychology, like theology, tried to seek 'reasons for doing things.' McClelland knew that I would be talking to B. F. Skinner and added that Skinner himself had been attracted by psychology partly because he was so opposed to his family's doctrinaire, fundamentalist religion. The behaviourist John B. Watson was brought up by a fanatically religious Southern Baptist mother, Emma Roe, who warned him the devil was out day and night to ensnare him. Emma Roe drummed this into him so hard that, as an adult, Watson hated to sleep without a night light to protect him.

There is another way of looking at McClelland's observations, though. At a time when children were expected to obey and conform, maybe it made it easier to rebel if parents were seen as religious bigots, fundamentalists for whom the Word of the Lord was the only word.

The first real conflict between Carl and his parents came over books. By the time he was eight, his reading habits seemed unsavoury to them. Uplifting Bible stories didn't interest him any more. He adored frontier stories about cowboys and Indians and other penny dreadfuls. Walter and Julia tried their best to get him to give up these sinful texts but Carl would go into his room, open the latest version of Billy the Kid and escape into a world of his own. The problem became worse when they left Oak Park.

The Bates & Rogers Construction Company flourished, which allowed Walter to buy a farm with over 200 acres of land at Wheaton, outside Chicago. At first the family went there only at weekends but, in 1911, they moved permanently from North Euclid Avenue. They weren't just moving up in the world, according to Rogers. His parents 'were concerned about the temptations and evils of suburban and city life and wished to get the family away from these threats.' Carl liked the farm even though it meant changing schools. He had to travel two hours every day but he was still expected to get home as soon as possible to do chores on the farm. As a result, he could get to know his schoolmates only 'in a very surface fashion'. He felt 'decidedly different and alone'. He had no close friends; he was never part of a gang. He argued later that this isolation made him hungry for intimate contact with people and that it was probably one of the reasons that made him want to become a therapist.

One curious story about the farm again shows how different Rogers' memory was from that of his siblings. Margaret remembered their father's birthday in 1911 when his friends turned up with a gaggle of cows, goats, chickens and horses as presents. The animals would help stock the farm. They were nice gifts and they don't suggest Walter was seen as a cold man cut off from his community. Rogers never mentioned this story. For him, the farm was a place where he fought his first bitter fight with his father.

All the children were expected to work on the farm. Carl had to get up at five o'clock every morning to milk a dozen cows. The physical effort meant his arms were often asleep during the school day and he could never get them quite free of a prickly feeling. Carl took care of all the pigs and, in the summer, he drove the cultivator. His father gave him a cornfield at the far end of the farm to look after. It was the boy's responsibility to make sure the machine worked and to fix it if it went wrong. Carl didn't like being made to work so relentlessly. In retrospect, Rogers thought he might have benefited from having real responsibility, but at the time he saw it as another sign of his parents' lack of love. Like many children who are – and who feel – teased and unhappy, he took refuge in his imagination and in the woods.

The woods – or the forest, as he called it – that surrounded the farm were the perfect setting for fantasies. Fantasies about frontier life, fantasies about cowboys and Indians, fantasies about excellent adventures. The influence of these fantasies can be seen in Rogers' earliest surviving writing. In 1913, aged 11, he produced a newspaper called 'The Chickville Times'. Written in his curvy handwriting, it was lurid and funny. Headlines told of hens on the run from prison, of the arrest of a delinquent Blacktail and of the adventures of Mr Peckadone and Mr Badpeck. The paper had endless puns and one grisly illustration. A man in silhouette holds an axe over a chicken he's about to kill. We do not know how Walter and Julia reacted to 'The Chickville Times.' A year later, however, they seem to have been very worried about their son.

In 1914, Rogers was 12. In the middle of the academic year, Walter decided to take him on a three-week trip while he visited various construction jobs in the South and East. Special permission had to be obtained from the school. None of Carl's brothers had ever been taken on such a journey. Everything suggests that such a break with convention was a reaction either to a crisis or persistent anxiety. Carl wasn't shaping up as well as Lester, Ross and Margaret. Lester was a model son and had already decided to be an engineer. Ross was doing well at school. Margaret was dutiful and devout. But Carl was a problem.

As a 12-year-old, Carl did not realise how strange it was for him to be taken on this expedition. In 1965, Rogers suggested his father wanted to show him a slice of real life to jolt him out of his perennial dreaminess. The school insisted Carl write a long essay about the experience.

Father and son took the train to New Orleans on 10 December 1914. They got to the city late at night and put up at the Hotel Grunewald. In the morning, before they had their breakfast, Walter took his son for a walk down to the wharves. They looked at the ships and the construction of the harbour. Then Walter had business to attend to. Carl noted that the old French quarter 'is very picturesque in spite of its dirtiness'. The harbour with its 'immense warehouses' made a big impression. Seven German ships were interned because of the war. The next day was a Sunday so they went to church and on to a smart restaurant called the Louisiana. Walter did not miss opportunities to instruct his son. Carl learned that many graves in New Orleans are above ground because the ground is so wet that four feet below the surface 'you strike water'.

On 17 December they went to the Newport News Shipyard where they saw three warships under construction, including the 'superdreadnought *Pennsylvania*'. Carl was impressed by the 14-

inch-thick armour-plating on the hull. Walter had enough sense to know his son had to enjoy the trip if it was to be a positive influence. That wasn't easy; the boy often had to wait and wait while Walter had business meetings. So Walter tried to compensate with such treats as meals in smart restaurants and exciting little expeditions. In Virginia, they went walking on the sand dunes at six in the morning and then back for breakfast. In Norfolk, at Billups Restaurant, Carl discovered oysters. 'You can have raw oysters, fried oysters, roast oysters or oyster stew but that is all,' he wrote. It was the best line of his required essay on the trip. Father and son went for breakfast after their walk and then returned at 4.30 p.m. for another oyster feast.

From Norfolk, they took the train to New York where Walter had business with the president of the Erie Railroad. They went to another smart restaurant, Delmonico's, and then toured Wall Street and the Battery. They nearly missed their train home. In his essay Carl calculated they had travelled through 16 States and done 3200 miles.

Unlike 'The Chickville Times,' the school essay is very dry – a list of places, hotels, restaurants and shipyards. It conveyed no emotion, not even a conventional sense of contact with his father. No line said that he and his father had fun together. If it was meant to be a bonding experience, the essay showed no trace of it – nor did the autobiographical chapter Rogers wrote over 50 years later; rather he highlighted a few picturesque moments. He recalled: 'I came back thrilled by the chanting Negro workers on the New Orleans docks and with a passionate taste for raw oysters' (Rogers 1965). Memory or embroidering the past? In his schoolboy essay, Rogers admitted nothing so emotional. The 12-year-old boy could not let himself go.

It was neither his parents' anger nor the trip with Walter that persuaded Carl to drop the penny dreadfuls and the fantasies of cowboys and Indians. At the age of 13, Carl made a discovery, a discovery he believed shaped the rest of his life – the discovery of bugs. Carl became an avid reader of Gene Stratton Porter who was well known for her *Girl in the Limberlost* books, which featured large night-flying moths. Carl started to look for them in the woods and he was very persistent. He wrote, 'I was in responsive mood when I discovered in the woods ... two lovely luna moths,' which had just emerged from their cocoons. He got more books on moths. He hatched eggs. For the first time in his life he observed behaviour, and reality became more interesting than fantasy. Carl turned into something of a local expert on these moths. Neighbours would bring large or unusual bugs for 'Professor Moony' to examine.

Rogers always believed his fascination with moths primed him to become a scientist. 'In my own small and specialised field I became something of a biologist,' he wrote. This new interest was respectable and should have brought him closer to his parents – especially to his father, who was interested in science and in 'scientific agriculture'. But it didn't work out that way.

At first Walter had seen the farm as a hobby but he also wanted it to be profitable and to be a model of scientific agriculture. He often invited teachers from the University of Chicago to come out and advise on the latest methods to boost yields or produce wonder seeds. Listening to Walter and his friends talk didn't enthuse Carl. Again, it was a book that changed his attitudes – not people. One day Carl picked up a recent agricultural text, Morison's *Feeds and Feeding*, which contained descriptions of egg and milk production, of fertilisers, of different kinds of seeds and soils. It was better than bugs. Rogers said Morison gave him 'a thoroughgoing feel for the essential elements of science'. Morison taught him the basics of complex subjects such as the correct design of experiments, the rationale of control groups and the statistical analysis of results. Rogers believed much of his approach to psychology stemmed from Morison.

Rogers came to see the Morison episode as significant, as proof of his isolation. He had been brought up in such a way that he found it easier to 'listen' to a book than to turn to his father, his mother or to other people for help or inspiration.

Carl decided to try some of Morison's ideas, sent off for some seeds and tested various varieties. He worked methodically, which impressed his father, so Walter did something very generous. He gave Carl and his younger brother, Walter, some land on which to experiment. The five acres would be their own little farm to run as they liked. The boys were organised and motivated. They bought seeds, grew produce and sold it in one of the local markets. Carl was the prime mover but his father's generosity did not make Carl feel he could confide in him.

Rogers told another story to make the point that he was so shy and insecure that he buried himself in books even when it would have been much easier to discuss issues. Walter gave the apprentice farmers 11 lambs which were too young to sell. Instead of asking his father or any of the farmworkers for advice, Carl sent off for the Department of Agriculture publication on how to raise lambs. When it came to killing the lambs, Carl sent off for a new pamphlet, the official guide to slaughtering. It advised using a heavy mallet to stun the lamb but Carl was sure a baseball bat would do as well. The result was a bloody farce, literally. The poor lamb wasn't knocked out and had to be hit a second time. Brother Walter couldn't bear the sight of its fractured skull as its brains were oozing out over the barn floor. Carl stayed calm and pounded the animal again with the baseball bat. Walter and John were still screaming. Carl then stuck the animal with a knife.

That first summer the five acres flourished. But then, according to Rogers, his father acted harshly. Walter had seen how his sons enjoyed the experiment and how competent they had been, but now he wanted his land back. Carl felt angry and hurt. The farm was a hobby for his father; there was no financial necessity. Carl protested, argued, reasoned and even wept. His father was being unreasonable. But Walter would not change his mind and took the five acres back. Carl promised himself never again to let himself be dominated by his strong parents.

It has to be asked why, given the enormous impression this row made on Carl, there is no trace of this story in either Margaret's family history or in John's account of growing up on the farm that he provided for Margaret. Did Carl build up a smaller quarrel into a so-called 'defining moment', the moment when he started to claw his way to freedom?

Even if Rogers did exaggerate the story, there is one powerful piece of evidence in favour of his complaint that the family was controlling and 'gently suppressive'. At the age of 15 Carl developed a duodenal ulcer. It was to trouble him on and off for years. Two of his siblings also developed childhood ulcers. This is a fairly unusual condition, and stress is often an important contributory factor.

I have concentrated more on the family atmosphere than on his school because, while Carl did well at school, he did nothing to suggest remarkable talents. He attended three different high schools and believed these changes also contributed to making him shy. English was his best subject. The curriculum emphasised English writers from Chaucer to Dickens rather than American authors and Carl began to develop the idea that Shakespeare was an over-rated author. He also got good grades in science. His fondest memory of a teacher was of Miss Graham, who was something of a scholar and encouraged original thinking.

The Rogers children were not encouraged to have friends outside the family. For Carl that was frustrating. He was not allowed to meet girls; Rogers reckoned that from the age of 12 he was extremely interested in sex. Books were not much help for once. Nothing he could lay his hands on was specific about the facts of life. By the time he was 17, Rogers had never been out with a girl. So the first time Rogers had to ask a girl out was something of a trauma, even though it wasn't a matter of love.

In 1919, his junior year, Rogers was elected president of his class. Ironically it was his home situation that helped him win. He had few enemies, partly because Julia's rules forced him to go home the moment school was out. The other teenagers got close, quarrelled and split into rival cliques who would not vote for one another. Carl had good grades and no enemies so he became a compromise candidate. As president, he could not miss the big social event of the year, the class dinner, but he had to have a date. There was a girl he wanted to ask but he was scared she would say no. He found it agonising to work up the courage to invite her. He hated his shyness.

Carl graduated from high school in 1920 but his relationship with his parents was not improving. His father thought him the most competitive of the children. Carl, for his part, felt resentful. He was not sure what career to pursue but thought he might try farming. What he really minded was that he had no choice about what college to attend. The University of Wisconsin did have a strong agricultural department. 'This, however, was not my real reason for going to Wisconsin.' It was simply that every member of the family would go to Wisconsin because that was where his parents and brothers had studied.'

Although the Bates & Rogers Construction Company was doing well, his parents expected Carl to work to put himself through college. Their only concession was to give him $50 as a graduation present, but he had to start earning immediately. So his father arranged for him to go to North Dakota to spend the summer working in a chain of lumber-yards owned by three of Carl's uncles.

In June 1920, Carl set off for Kenmore, North Dakota, close to the Canadian border. He took with him a chess set, a journal, and 22 books that he had bought out of the $50. They were a mix of literature and adventure – Carlyle, Victor Hugo, Dickens, Ruskin, Robert Louis Stevenson, Edgar Allan Poe.

Rogers was wise to buy so much reading material. One of his uncles lived by the lumber-yard but Carl was not asked to stay with him. Instead, the young man was given a room in the lumber-yard buildings. He worked from eight in the morning until five in the afternoon, loading and unloading timber. He ate at a boarding house. The foreman at the lumber-yard invited him to dinner twice during the three months. His uncles do not seem to have bothered to spend any time with him. Rogers noted that in Kenmore 'I got lonesome.'

The work was hard and boring but the solitude gave him time to read. He could get through 300 pages in three hours. Reading was still magical. When he was deep in *Les Misérables*, he entered another world where his shyness didn't bother him. 'When at last I reached the apex of the story and laid down the book I could not remember what day it is or what I had been doing.'

Carl also made a note that in Kenmore, away from the family with its rules and routines, he felt he had come to be much closer to God. He went back home just before going to college having made up his mind. Scientific agriculture was right for him. He was going to be a farmer.

## University life

Rogers began university in a very religious frame of mind. He kept a diary which he later found embarrassingly idealistic. Many agriculture students came from a similar religious background and they formed a Sunday morning group led by Professor George Humphrey. In fact, Humphrey left the group very much to its own devices. It made its own decisions, chose what topics to pursue and debated them. Rogers loved it. It was his first experience of groups and, from then on, in many different ways, he sought them out. He discovered he was less shy in this kind of gentle structure.

He started to write to the girl who had been his cycling companion in Oak Park, Helen Elliott. She had come to Wisconsin to study art because she hoped to be a fashion artist. In his first year, Rogers dated her a few times.

In the Christmas vacation in 1920, Rogers attended a conference of a missionary group, the Student Volunteers, in Des Moines, Iowa. Their slogan 'Evangelise the world in our generation' made good sense to him. The conference was inspiring and Rogers realised that he had no real desire to be a farmer. He would go into 'Christian work' instead, so he dropped agriculture and changed to history, intending to specialise in the history of Christianity. He tackled two Protestant heroes in depth, John Wyclif and Martin Luther. As he studied the causes of the Reformation and Luther's motives, what seemed most important to Rogers was Luther's conviction that every human being could pray from the heart directly to God. Priests were not needed as intermediaries. In 1517 when Luther nailed his 95 theses to the door of the cathedral in Wittenberg, Catholic priests were often unspeakably corrupt. For Rogers, Luther's message was crystal clear: every man must trust in his own experience. Rogers also wrote sympathetically of John Wyclif, who was a pacifist, less wily than Luther and who ended up burnt at the stake.

In 1921, Rogers wrote to the YMCA, as he knew a small group would be going to China the following year to take part in the first International Student Federation Christian conference. There were only ten young men and women who would attend. He did not think he had any real hope of being chosen. When he got the letter that told him he was one of the ten who had been picked as delegates, he wept 'with joy and surprise'. It was enormously flattering. It was only many years later that Rogers wondered if he had been picked because his parents were known to be wealthy and the YMCA assumed they would contribute to his expenses.

The prospect of a long absence made Rogers think deeply about Helen. He said he was far too sensible to be falling in love but the more he got to know her, the better he liked her. Finally, just before he was due to leave for China, he proposed. Helen was not sure. She did not feel cut out to marry someone who was going into Christian work. She did not say yes and she did not say no. She said they should write while he was away; then she would decide. Rogers hated the fact that she could make him wait. It felt like rejection and it made him all the more determined to win her over.

In February 1922, Rogers left Wheaton by the Overland Express for San Francisco. The delegation sailed from San Francisco. The sea was extremely rough and 90 per cent of the passengers did not turn up for dinner on the first night. Rogers was one of the exceptions and managed to eat despite the storm. Away from his parents, his ulcer troubles seemed to have disappeared. The boat trip took over three weeks, and Rogers travelled in distinguished company. Other delegates included John Mott, who was head of the whole YMCA, and Kenneth Latourette, a church historian from Yale who was an expert on the Far East. Latourette, in particular, liked Rogers.

The Peking conference was impressive. Though the First World War had left enormous bitterness, the young people tried to over-come the legacy of hostility. Germans and French, Russians and Australians tried to bury the bitterness of the war and plan a fine Christian future. Rogers wrote they all felt 'the world is on the verge of some tremendous changes, that our own generation is going to bring about.' The conference was convinced the present industrial system 'is not simply full of evils but that it is fundamentally wrong. They are beginning to see that a system based primarily on the selfish instinct cannot be made Christian.' After they had reformed industry, the young radicals would reform the military and do their best to see there never was another war.

In an account for the YMCA paper, the *Intercollegian*, Rogers noted that 'In spite of differences of race and nationality, in spite of sore spots in the relations between many countries, never even in the hottest committee discussions, have I seen any of the delegates show anything but the finest spirit.' Discussions were intense and intelligent. The experience forced Rogers to rethink many of his attitudes. 'My intellectual horizon was being stretched all the time,' he wrote.

In his letters from China, Rogers started to explain his new views to his family and to Helen. He knew perfectly well his parents would be upset by his new ideas, which they would see as revolutionary. Bates & Rogers worked for the military; for Walter and Julia, being Christian had nothing to do with socialism. Wealth was proof of being 'separate' and superior. They had to 'keep their standards high' to prove they deserved their status. But the mail went by sea and each letter took a month. However much Walter and Julia disapproved, they were too far away to influence their son. For once isolation helped Rogers. It gave him time and space to grow confident in his new ideas. In his letters to Helen, Rogers told her how much he needed her partly because of those problems with his parents.

So, with the ocean to ease it, 'the rift in outlook was fully established' between Rogers and his parents. Later, Rogers argued that he was far from sure modern communications are a blessing. He wondered if he would have had the courage to break with his parents' views if they had been able to get him constantly on the phone to attack his new-fangled ideas.

Once the Peking conference was over, Kenneth Latourette asked Rogers to accompany him on a tour of South China and the Philippines. Rogers also went to Japan. He was thrilled by climbing Mount Fuji. He felt breathless but he did witness, as he wanted to, the dawn from its summit. Japan made a lasting impression on him.

Rogers might have abandoned capitalism in theory but he had absorbed one lesson from his parents – the value of money. In Peking he had become friendly with a Mrs Taylor, a missionary's wife. She did a little business in Chinese crafts. Rogers bought some stock from her, hoping to sell her trinkets at a profit back in the States.

Even the trip back to San Francisco was intellectually exciting. On the boat Rogers talked to Dr Henry Sharman, a theologian who had made a special study of Jesus. One of the books they discussed was Renan's *Life of Jesus*. One night Rogers was struck by a blasphemous thought. Perhaps Jesus was 'a man like other men – not divine'. Rogers became increasingly convinced and, as the idea 'took root, it became obvious to me that I could never in any emotional sense return home'.

Rogers often suggested that the six months' trip made it relatively easy to move away from the shackles of his family. Being away in China, he did not have to take a stand against his parents. He didn't have to insist defiantly at any point 'This is what I believe' or 'Here I stand, I can do no other.' He did the very opposite of his hero, Luther. He freed himself without any dramatic confrontations. It was so painless, he made it sound like a natural evolution. Yet Rogers would write so much about his troubled relations with his parents that it seems he glossed over some of the pain. There are, however, obvious reasons why Rogers avoided conflict. It could make him physically sick.

Almost as soon as Rogers landed back in America, he started to suffer abdominal pains. They got worse when he got home. The stress of having to justify his new ideas to his parents seems to have provoked the illness. It was not the first time he had had such episodes but previously his parents don't seem to have taken them seriously. When Rogers was finally taken to see a doctor, the diagnosis was not in doubt. Rogers had an ulcer; it had been giving him trouble since the age of 15. The doctor insisted on an operation.

Getting sick had one unexpected bonus. Helen came to see him in the hospital. She had been impressed and moved by his letters and his need. Their friendship became a courtship. On 29 October 1922, she finally said she loved him and they decided to get married. It was wonderful, an evening Rogers would describe for the rest of his life as one of his peak experiences. He needed Helen especially because 'At home, there is continually whether spoken or unspoken the clash of different types of personalities – liberal versus conservative – and it has been a joyous relief to have a lover who is as deeply sympathetic as Helen. I have at times stood in great need of just such a safety valve.'

In a letter soon after this to Helen, Rogers commented that his brother Walter was also complaining about the atmosphere at home. Rogers begged his parents to look at the particular problem his brother raised from Walter's point of view because if they did not 'he would be apt to drift away from them ... And then in order to meet one of mother's pet answers – that she is sorry she hasn't brought us up more as we think we ought to be brought up – I added that nothing I said was any criticism of our bringing up.' Rogers added he was 'a fool' to think such a letter would mend matters. His mother ended her reply by saying, 'Am sorry you feel as you do about your early life and home.' Rogers felt his mother 'couldn't have slapped much harder.' He was an idiot to think he could change things at home or do anything that would make his parents less unhappy. He told Helen he had to talk to somebody about it and signed off, 'It's lots of fun to be a black sheep.' But that was bravado.

After his operation, Rogers could not go back to college at once. Walter and Julia decided then that he had to work, though he was recovering from surgery. The choice of job was also strange; Walter got him a job in a local lumber-yard shifting logs. It is hard to escape the conclusion that Walter and Julia were punishing their son for questioning their beliefs. They seem to have made Rogers feel guilty too, because he took the job though it was exhausting when he was supposed to be convalescing. Perhaps he felt he deserved it for having questioned their faith, but the experience rankled. Loving parents wouldn't have insisted on his working.

There was at least financial reward. Rogers saved all the money he made in the lumber-yard. Together with the profits from the crafts, it allowed him to buy his first car, a model T Ford costing $450.

The tensions and the rules and restrictions irritated Rogers more and more. He wanted to move out and marry. He loved Helen all the more because she was completely on his side against his parents. She liked his radical ideas. He wrote her poems, including one called 'To a Gray Eyed Goddess' who aroused his 'lyric fires'. He compared her to the freshness and beauty of April. Sometimes passion would turn into chattiness. Rogers went to bed one night thinking 'my heart would burst for wanting you' but then was woken up by singing. The university glee club was serenading the Kappa Delta girls across the way with the 'Bedouin Love Song'. Rogers promised Helen they would live as Arabs, always ready to fold up their tents and move on 'to new lands of promise if we feel the urge'. There was no question of the couple sleeping together, of course.

Walter and Julia assumed the couple would wait until Rogers had a secure job before getting married, but he had no intention of waiting. One reason almost certainly was desire. Rogers, all the evidence suggests, was highly sexed and wanted to have sex with Helen as soon as possible.

Early in 1923, Rogers decided to go to New York to do graduate work. He applied to Union Theological Seminary in New York, the leading liberal seminary in the United States. Given Rogers' radical Christianity, the seminary was the ideal choice, but Walter and Julia were very upset. Union was not fundamentalist. Walter then offered his son something 'which was close to a bribe', as Rogers put it. If only the boy would go to Princeton Seminary, which was decently fundamentalist, Walter would pay all Rogers' expenses and also all of Helen's. The couple could marry without having financial anxieties. Rogers rejected this offer indignantly. He suspected his father was not proud of his offer and its implication – that his son's soul was for sale.

As a result of this row, Rogers decided he could not ask for any financial support from his parents. He took the competitive examinations for Union and won a scholarship. The scholarship did not provide an income on which to marry, and everyone assumed the couple would be sensible and wait. Helen wanted to do that. It would allow her to finish her degree, but Rogers was very persuasive and she didn't want another long separation. So, for the first of many times, she gave in to Rogers' wishes and the needs of his career.

Rogers had a number of plans for topping up his scholarship

money. The Chinese crafts he had brought in from Peking had sold well, so he had started ordering goods regularly from Mrs Taylor. He took a gamble before Christmas and placed an order of $400, a large sum. Rogers waited desperately for the goods to arrive. When they did, he dropped all academic work and turned himself into a trader; he became a successful one. The Christian revolutionary and entrepreneur banked between $100 and $400 a day, making a healthy profit. Rogers kept his Bank of Wisconsin book from this period among his papers for the rest of his life. It was a symbol of a battle he had won – against his rich and dominating parents.

On 28 August 1924 Helen Elliott and Carl Rogers were married. The reception took place at neither of their parents' homes but at Helen's sister's. Then the couple climbed into Rogers' model T Ford and set off for a honeymoon on their way to New York. After his bribe that failed, Walter realised he had to do something substantial or he might lose his son's respect for ever. So the new Mr and Mrs Rogers left for New York with a very generous wedding present from Walter and Julia – a cheque for $2500. At the time, the average salary for the male American worker was around $800 a year. Rogers did not ponder the irony that he was going to train for the Christian ministry with a small fortune in his pocket. The money did not make Rogers respect his parents more. It was a generous gift but it was also a very blatant way of apologising for having insulted him.

HAROLD BRIDGES LIBRARY
S. MARTIN'S COLLEGE
LANCASTER

2
___

# From the Divine to the Delinquent, 1924–1928

Before they got married, Rogers had given Helen a book about sex, which he later joked was 'a mark of how avant garde I was in my thinking.' It has proved impossible to find out which manual it was, though Marie Stopes' *Married Love* (1918) is probable. When he was older, Rogers often wrote about his marriage and the problems that sometimes existed between Helen and him, many involving sex. Many great psychologists would have kept quiet about such difficulties but Rogers felt it was important to share his sexual evolution and even his sexual frustrations.

The honeymoon went well, which Rogers later attributed to the fact he and Helen were both sexually very naive. They reached New York very much in love. They knew they had to be careful about money as the $2500 and the considerable profits of the Chinese knick-knack business had to last the three years of Rogers' studies, but they could go to shows, eat out and have a good time. To keep within their budget, the couple took what Rogers called the smallest apartment in New York.

In some ways the marriage was contemporary: as the man, Rogers was not supposed to be the dominant partner. They were in it together. Helen attended some classes with Rogers. She also spent time in the art galleries of New York and took Rogers to see exhibitions he never would have visited but for her. He was pleased they had remarkably similar tastes. The first year of the marriage he described as very romantic. Despite their modern ideas, Helen did not pursue a separate career. She did not look for work as a fashion artist even though she had been trained for that and there was demand for those skills with the growth of advertising in the mid-1920s.

Union Theological Seminary was not just liberal, it also had an excellent academic reputation. The director was Arthur Cushman McGiffert. His teaching style impressed Rogers, as every week, when McGiffert expounded the views of Luther or Hume or Kant, all the students were convinced this was the thinker McGiffert identified with. The following week, however, McGiffert would be as eloquent on a new thinker and a new philosophy. No one knew what McGiffert believed, so it's perhaps fitting that he is best remembered for his two-volume *History of Christian Thought*, which never favours one school or hero. Rogers felt he had never been taught as well as in McGiffert's course 'Protestant Thought before Kant.' Like his high school teacher, Miss Graham, McGiffert left Rogers feeling there was something admirable about the scholarly temperament.

The seminary attracted some very distinguished teachers as well as McGiffert. One was Henry Emerson Fosdick, who was the pastor of the First Presbyterian Church in New York. As early as 1923 he started to explore what pastors could learn from psychology. Fosdick published *On Being a Real Person* (1943), which argued that individuals had to accept themselves for what they really were and not be pushed to aspire to impossible ideals. One of Fosdick's themes was that rigid morals, apparently Christian morals, could cripple human beings. Rogers liked him very much.

Christian work appealed to the idealist in Rogers but there wasn't much science in it to appeal to the reader of Morison. In New York, Rogers found he could marry 'Christian work' and a scientific approach. Fosdick was catching a real mood of interest in psychology. The behaviourist John B. Watson joked that the world had gone psychology mad. Every day he was being rung up by the press, the *St Louis Blade*, the *San Francisco Scoop*, the *Nashville News* and others to give expert comment. Was it scientific to hug babies? Would Freudian ideas emasculate the American male? Rogers himself would be writing for the *Journal of Home Economics* before long at $30 a piece. Many progressive religious groups were eager to learn from the new 'science' of psychology. McGiffert knew his students would have to deal with birth, marriage, despair and death and realised the modern pastor had better be able to quote Freud as well the Gospels. So the seminary introduced courses in psychology from 1921.

Rogers had done a little psychology at Wisconsin. He wrote one paper on William James and another on whether dogs could think. One of the first courses Rogers signed up for at Union was 'Working with Individuals'. It was run by Goodwin Watson, a psychologist who was only a few years older than Rogers and who was to become something of a mentor. The course concentrated on human psychology and on psychological tests; Goodwin Watson also invited a variety of psychiatrists and social workers to discuss how they handled real people in real crises.

Rogers found the discussion sessions the most interesting. In structuring these, Goodwin Watson was influenced by John B. Watson. John B. Watson had left academic psychology to work for the advertising agency, J. Walter Thompson. He knew more than any other psychologist about how consumers behaved. His namesake Goodwin Watson was interested in the psychology of market research and heard John B. Watson speak at evening lectures at Columbia and the Cooper Institute. John B. Watson made all his students fill in a 'balance sheet of the self', a questionnaire that examined their strengths and weaknesses. He argued that the psychologist had to know himself or herself before daring to advise anyone else on how to sort out their lives. So Goodwin Watson made his 'practicals' centre not on social or intellectual problems but on the students' own difficulties. Many students were living away from home for the first time and were under stress. In the 1920s, privacy was respected, pain kept decently buttoned up.

The students did not reveal intimate difficulties but the groups did allow open discussions by the standards of the time. Rogers realised that psychology had a lot to offer in preparing for pastoral work. Moreover, psychology was something of a science or, at least, it was a serious academic area that could be a 'professional enterprise' (Rogers 1965, p. 354).

Rogers did not want to rely on making the $2500 gift last so he looked for part-time work. Through the seminary, he got a job which he described as being the director of religious education at the First Congregational Church in Mount Vernon. The grand title meant he organised Sunday school classes and discussion groups.

Mount Vernon was a middle-class and well-educated congregation. Rogers found the services for young people rather dull and was pleased no one objected when he decided to pep them up. He introduced processionals, organ music, robes for the choir and got the religious education classes to report on their projects to the whole congregation. He did a lot of reading on the nature of worship. There was a debate among theological progressives. Some were wary of making services more theatrical and emotional. Robes, processions, better music might whip up the emotions and please the congregation, but was that the purpose of being a serious, sober Christian? The purists argued that services should not rely on such effects. Others believed the Church should take the lead in social action. Rogers had his doubts about that and stressed 'action' more than 'social'. He was attracted by the philosopher John Dewey's belief that children should learn through doing and that education must be as much a matter of experience as of book learning. That went for worship too. Services should not be a matter of parroting prayers: they had to enrich those who took part. Rogers felt parishioners had to be free to bring their problems to the community; he said 'if their real problem is one of sex adjustment, we cannot turn them toward some problem about God because that is "religious"'. (Kirschenbaum 1979).

Rogers also offered what seemed a very modern argument. Discussions about religious issues would encourage 'a scientific facing of such problems'. They would make it possible to examine contemporary standards of morality, belief in God and in religion simply as 'mere hypotheses'. In the 1920s many young academics hoped to use science to prove the truths of religion. With more advanced methods in physics, chemistry and biology, surely one could demonstrate God's existence. God would be not just a matter of faith but a matter of fact. J. B. Rhine, who would become a famous parapsychologist, studied telepathy and clairvoyance. If he could show there were non-material forces, that would suggest God did exist. In Britain, a young biologist who would become a Fellow of the Royal Society, Alister Hardy, commissioned a press agency to cut out every reference to religion in the newspapers. Hardy hoped to map the distribution of religious experiences in a more scientific way than William James had done in *The Varieties of Religious Experience* (1902). Rogers, hoping to use science to bolster faith, was in good company.

In the summer of 1925, Rogers seems to have had no doubts about his future. The first year of graduate school ended well. He passed the end-of-year exams with honours. The long summer vacation did not mean a holiday, however. The seminary offered its students the chance of running a congregation as an acting minister. Rogers wanted the experience and the money, so in July 1925, he and Helen set off in the model T Ford for the small town of East Dorset in Vermont. The congregation was too poor to afford a full-time minister. For the summer, Rogers would be their pastor. For a young man of 23, it was both exciting and a little terrifying.

Rogers gave 11 sermons while he was in East Dorset. He tackled modern subjects such as the Scropes trial on whether Genesis told the whole truth about creation and the question of how many creation stories in fact were mingled in Genesis. Rogers suggested there were two stories and argued they should be prepared to accept Darwin's theory of evolution as a possible third story. Somehow, Rogers crammed this complex argument into less than 20 minutes as he made it a rule that no sermons should last longer.

The pastoral side of the work introduced Rogers to disturbed people for the first time. He was fascinated to meet individuals such as the 'confirmed alcoholic' Helen and he lived near. This man brought lots of different women back home. Up the road there was a woman Rogers described as psychotic. These were the kinds of people Oak Park had done its best to exclude. East Dorset made Rogers acutely aware of his youth. Then a member of the congregation died from cancer. When Rogers visited the family, the son was laughing hysterically and dancing round the room. Rogers had seen nothing like this before. He had no idea how he could comfort the family and dreaded handling the funeral. Fortunately, one of the neighbouring ministers realised there was a problem, came to East Dorset and took over the funeral. Rogers was very relieved.

In September, Rogers and Helen went back to New York. By now she was pregnant with their first child. There is nothing to suggest that by the time Rogers left East Dorset in September 1925 he was beginning to have doubts about his future. It was in the following months, as he started his second year of studies, that he began to ask himself if he really did have a vocation for Christian work.

Rogers explained in his contribution to *A History of Psychology in Autobiography* and in Kirschenbaum's *On Becoming Carl Rogers* only a little of what made him drop the ministry. Rogers makes the decision sound very much an intellectual one. His doubts surfaced through a series of group discussions. (In his contribution to *A History of Psychology in Autobiography*, Rogers said he was not sure if these discussions took place in his first or second year at the seminary but, given how positive he felt about East Dorset, it seems likely these discussions took place some time after he and Helen came back from the summer there.)

At the start of the second year, Rogers was one of a group of students who complained ideas were being fed to them and they were not being given the chance to discuss significant religious and philosophical issues. A delegation of students that included Theodore Newcomb, later one of the most influential social psychologists of his generation, went to see McGiffert. McGiffert listened. He knew his students were bright. They wanted to organise their own discussion group. They also asked that everyone who attended should get a credit towards their degree, even though no member of staff could be present. Faculty members inhibited them. The proposal seemed very radical but McGiffert agreed, with one proviso. The group had to have one faculty member sitting in, even though this person wouldn't speak unless the students first asked him to.

The groups were unstructured but Rogers liked that. He remembered they discussed many profound issues. Why were they going into the ministry? Were they trying to fulfil some kind of ideal in becoming pastors? Was this ideal a true reflection of their personalities or were they just doing what was expected of them? Rogers later wrote that, through the group, most of these would-be ministers talked themselves out of working for the Church.

It was not just group discussions, however, that provided the intellectual impetus for change. Union Theological Seminary had links with Teachers College, which was part of Columbia University. Rogers applied to take a number of courses in education there. One of the star professors at Teachers College was William H. Kilpatrick who had been a pupil of John Dewey.

Union and Columbia had different atmospheres. McGiffert, analysing Kant and Descartes, was looking to the past. Radicals debated whether religion had a future at all. It was now that Rogers first became seriously interested in psychology. Psychology seemed the very essence of the modern world. Glamorous, scientific, practical, its experimental wizards could read the entrails of the soul, predict the behaviour of rats and offer serious answers to serious social problems. Psychologists knew more than ever before about how to influence behaviour. The American Army had used psychological testing to recruit GIs in the 1914–18 war. The Psychological Corporation had been set up in 1921 to devise tests that industry could use to improve recruiting methods and motivation. Textbooks taught the laws of learning, memory and thinking. One insight into how seductive psychology was comes from the long secret correspondence between Sigmund Freud and William Bullitt, who was President Woodrow Wilson's ambassador in Paris during the negotiations for the Treaty of Versailles. Bullitt wrote to Freud with details of the President's dreams and anxieties; Freud replied with advice so that Wilson could deal better with the tensions during the negotiations for the Treaty. Freud, who was prone to messianic feelings, loved being at the very centre of history in the making. Debates such as that between the behaviourist John B. Watson and William MacDougall, who believed that conditioning was less important than the existence of over 35 human 'instincts', were seen as important intellectual jousts. People flocked to listen to these titans; there was none of today's cynicism about really being able to change people. It's hardly surprising Rogers was seduced by this intellectual excitement. He threw himself wholeheartedly into trying to cope with courses at the two very different colleges.

As well as this crowded programme of studies, Rogers was also running Sunday school classes. Helen saw less of him, and the marriage started to run into difficulties. Neither of them found it easy to talk about their problems. The first thing Rogers seems to have noticed was that all too often Helen would discourage him when he wanted to make love. She would say she was too tired or that she really didn't feel like it tonight. Rogers felt upset and frustrated, but he said nothing. It was to be expected that men wanted sex more than women and he did not stumble on the dreadful truth for a while.

One day, at Teachers, Rogers discovered that a psychologist, G. V. Hamilton, was researching sexual behaviour. Hamilton needed more young couples to complete his sample and was happy to pay people for taking part in his research. Rogers went to talk to him and Hamilton explained he wanted to produce a survey of students' sexual experiences. Hamilton asked Rogers about his sexual development, his sexual experiences and the 'marital adjustment'. Rogers realised he had always assumed that sex was as good for Helen as it was for him. He suddenly saw he did not know how Helen felt or whether she ever had an orgasm. She seemed to enjoy sex with him but perhaps she was only pretending. Perhaps that was why she was too tired or always ready to put it off till the next night.

Rogers seems to have been one of the first American men to face the traumatic possibility that his wife might be faking orgasms and that, far from being a magician in the sack, he was an erotic failure. Even more humbling, he might be an erotic failure who didn't even know he was failing.

Rogers went back to Helen and began what he called 'the frightening process' of talking, really talking. Every question, every answer made each of them vulnerable. He could be criticised; he could be rejected or, perhaps, worst of all, he could be teased. Rogers left very detailed notes about one of their later marital crises but not about this one, unfortunately. The talking did the trick, apparently. They loved each other and they were young enough to change. They used the crisis to explore 'the other's desires, taboos, satisfactions and dissatisfactions'. Talking it out made them feel more tender. As crucial probably, given Rogers' not inconsiderable male ego, Helen started to have unmistakable orgasms.

The evidence suggests Rogers was an intensely sexual man. He had faced the question which, Hamilton told him, most men never face – that of whether they are good enough lovers for their wives. He had faced the issue, talked it through and the relationship had improved. The new pleasure in his marriage and the exciting intellectual atmosphere made Rogers more confident and brave enough to think of telling his parents that Christian work was not for him. He knew they would be disappointed and he was afraid they would make him feel small. First, he had wanted to be a farmer; then he wanted to be a minister. What did he want to be now? Brother Lester was a shining, steady light by comparison. He had stuck to engineering and gone from Wisconsin to work for Bates & Rogers. But Carl was 23 years old and didn't know what he wanted to do. It was typical of Professor Moony.

As Rogers imagined the tense conversations he would have with Walter and Julia, his ulcer started troubling him again. For Helen it was very worrying. She was about to give birth and on 17 March 1926 she bore their first child, David. The celebrations were spoilt, however, because Rogers was ill; his ulcer had flared up badly. Finally, Rogers wrote to his parents to explain that he would be leaving the seminary and would not go into Christian work. He expected disapproval but he was not prepared for his parents' complete rejection of him and their new grandson.


## Moving to Columbia

When the ulcer flared up, the logical place to have it treated was New York. Instead, Rogers, Helen and their baby travelled 2000 miles to the Mayo Clinic in Minnesota. Rogers had been treated there before, but it hardly explains the journey. Helen had to rent a room in a city she didn't know and cope with the demands of her sick husband and her baby. Knowing his parents were upset, Rogers tried to make them see he wanted a reconciliation. Minnesota is less than a day's drive from Chicago, where they lived. Rogers had been big enough to travel closer to them even while he was ill. He wanted their love and attention – and made that touchingly obvious.

Neither Walter nor Julia came to see him. They seemed to be unable to forgive him for even thinking of leaving the seminary. So they left their sick son to wait and stew. Fifty years later Rogers was still angry enough to point out that his family gave them absolutely no help in the crisis. Walter and Julia even seem to have banned Lester, Ross or Margaret from visiting. Lester, who often reproached Rogers for criticising their parents, never queried his brother's version of this episode.

Rogers was shocked by his parents' attitude. Their rejection, ignoring him when he was sick, ignoring their grandchild, showed how high their Christian standards really were.

Rogers had not wholly recovered from the ulcer operation by August. After a very difficult year, he wanted a holiday but money was tight. So he and Helen went to run a workshop on sex and marriage at a YMCA camp in Colorado. They left their baby son with Helen's parents. As part of the workshop they passed out a questionnaire based on Hamilton's work. One of the backers of the YMCA was outraged that such smutty questions should have been asked at the camp. Rogers took it as yet more proof that organised religion was too rigid.

When he got back to New York, Rogers told McGiffert he would not be coming back to the seminary and that he wanted to transfer full-time to Teachers College. McGiffert did not make it difficult because he had no wish to force someone into the ministry. Rogers described leaving the seminary as if it were very casual. He just walked across the road to Columbia. It wasn't casual at all, in fact. He had returned from Peking certain that he would be a pastor and help 'evangelise the world'. In abandoning Christian work, Rogers broke not just with his parents but with much of his own youthful idealism.

At Teachers College, Rogers did a mixture of psychology and education courses. He attended the courses of E. L. Thorndike, one of the pioneers of psychometric testing. Unfortunately, the course was on the testing of mathematical aptitude, which Rogers found boring. Teachers College saw itself as committed to a scientific psychology. Freud was an unscientific charlatan. Jung was obscure. Tests were the real future. Everything psychological could be quantified; they were in love with the magic of measurement.

As a graduate student Rogers did not have to take the elementary psychology courses. He picked those that interested him. This lack of grounding in some basics of psychology would bother him later on and Rogers did sometimes wonder if he was a psychologist at all. He studied little perception, problem-solving and learning. He followed his interests, instead, attending all of Kilpatrick's courses on the philosophy of education and he also started to go to the courses in clinical psychology given by Leta Hollingworth. She ran practicals that allowed students to meet disturbed children. It was through her that Rogers first talked to a 'client'. He found that despite his shyness he could master his nerves and both play and talk to the children.

Then Rogers faced a new crisis. As tests were so popular, the exam at the end of the first year included a paper on statistics. Rogers had missed a large number of classes. Suddenly, he realised he was not well prepared for the exam. He was not used to failing; he had enjoyed one academic triumph after another. Rogers refused to accept either that he had been lazy or that he couldn't handle the material. His IQ test scores showed he was one of the very brightest of all Teachers' clever students. Confronted by exam questions he thought he couldn't answer, he first became depressed, and then angry. He went on the offensive and added to his answers a tirade accusing the instructor of being 'too abstruse' and his methods of teaching of being 'far from the best' (Rogers 1965, p. 356).

Rogers was never sure if he passed the statistics exam because of or despite his outburst. He felt, however, that the whole experience had given him a valuable insight into the panic tests could provoke. Was this the only yardstick by which to measure educational success?

Dropping out of the seminary made for financial problems. The $2500 was disappearing. There was a baby to feed and it would be humiliating to ask Walter and Julia for help. Moreover, Rogers could hardly carry on as director of religious education at Mount Vernon. Luckily his friend Goodwin Watson had just won a contract for some market research on American attitudes to the Orient for the Institute of the Pacific. Despite his shaky grasp of statistics, Rogers was put in charge of part of the project. He had to organise research assistants and he liked it. It was Goodwin Watson who now also pushed Rogers towards his new career.

## Delinquent studies

The first juvenile court was established in America in 1909 as part of a progressive policy. Children who got into trouble should be treated rather than punished. The new science of psychology would surely manage to discover the formula for turning delinquents into model citizens. In 1919 the White House convened a conference on children that helped create what one could call a child-welfare industry. Many of the services we are now familiar with – juvenile courts, probation, psychiatric and psychological assessments – date back to then.

In 1917, a pioneering psychiatrist called William Healy started work on delinquent children. Healy was deeply influenced by Freud and came to the conclusion that sexual problems led to crime. Too much masturbation, too few orgasms or too many orgasms were all causes of violence. The phrase 'sexual adjustment' was popular. Healy helped set up the Judge Baker Foundation, which became a key institution in developing the child-welfare industry. Pioneers such as the husband and wife team, the Gluecks, and Sophie Theis studied the fostering of difficult and disturbed children for over 20 years.

The Institute for Child Guidance in New York was established to provide training for professionals who would staff clinics for children all over the country. Goodwin Watson and Leta Hollingworth both suggested Rogers should apply for a fellowship there. Their recommendations put him in a very strong position.

Rogers was awarded a fellowship but it led to the first of many disputes over money. Rogers had been told his salary would be $2500. Just before he took up the post, he got an embarrassed letter from the head of the selection committee. Psychiatrists would get $2500 but psychologists would get only $1200. 'It was the financial rather than the professional insult which raised my dander,' he remembered (Rogers 1965, p. 356). He responded by writing a forceful letter saying he had made all the plans for himself

CARL ROGERS

and his family on the basis of what he understood to be a salary of $2500. He was a father. He couldn't now be asked to revise all those plans. The letter revealed how tough Rogers could be in negotiations, and it worked. It does not seem to have bothered him that he would be getting paid twice as much as the other psychology graduates at the Institute. He also doesn't seem to have realised that in making such an issue of it, he would make enemies. His fellowship would only last for one year.

## 'Considerably perplexed over sex questions'

Rogers found the approach of the Institute totally different from that of Teachers College. The Institute was basically Freudian though it gave a platform to other psychoanalytic views. Alfred Adler, who split from both Freud and Jung, came to lecture. David Levy, who developed the use of the Rorschach Test (where subjects have to say what an inkblot looks like to them), was one of Rogers' mentors. Levy was trying to use the Rorschach with children and he encouraged Rogers to do the research on which his PhD would eventually be based. On 14 October 1927, Rogers presented an outline of his dissertation to a committee that included Goodwin Watson and Leta Hollingworth. He wrote up a preliminary investigation into the use of tests with children. The PhD proposal was 'to develop tests which would be diagnostic, which would reveal particular emotional difficulties.'

Rogers was, it seems, the first researcher to look at the use of Jung's word-association tests with children aged under seven. Jung argued that both the length of time before someone responded and the kind of associations evoked were revealing. Did this hold for children? Rogers made up two lists of words. The first consisted of 20 words such as 'mamma' and 'naughty', which might have emotional content. The second list was made up of 48 words and its aim was 'to tap definite areas of child life'. Rogers realised it was important to make sure children understood what they were asked to do and that they knew what associations were. He finally hit on the following form of words to introduce the test:

'I have a game that we can play, a game that we play with

54

words. If I say dog, then you tell me some word that it makes you think of like "cat" or "run". If I say "big" you might say "little". Do you see? Just any word that it makes you think of.'

The first words used were 'pencil', 'shoe' and 'horse' to see if the children really understood. Rogers showed that very young children could grasp the instructions. He didn't realise this was in itself an interesting finding, particularly as in Geneva Jean Piaget was claiming that children under the age of seven were egocentric and often became confused when they were asked to do tests. Trying to analyse the data Rogers found frustrating. There did not seem to be a scientific way of interpreting the results. Different judges would offer different, rather subjective interpretations of what the children's responses meant. One judge looked at Betty's responses and concluded the girl was 'considerably perplexed over sex questions'. Another judge thought her associations quite normal. One child called Lillian was very badly 'adjusted and very abnormal' but one would never guess that from her associations, which were quick and predictable. There was a lack of fit between the clinical judgements of the children and their responses. Something more scientific was required.

Rogers turned to the research of Whateley Smith on the measurement of the emotions. Using a galvanometer, Whateley Smith measured the physiological response particular words and associations evoked. It was a little like an early lie detector. High responses were emotional. Smith had developed an elaborate theory to go with the gadget, dividing associations into the outer and the inner. Outer associations were a matter of fact – table, chair. Inner associations were personal and idiosyncratic. For example, man–donkey, brother–twins, friend–his, Smith considered 'inner' because they were a product of that subject's particular history. He subdivided inner association into three classes.

Smith's breakdown seems unnecessarily complicated and a little confusing, but Rogers was very keen to find some scientific base; so he worked out two complex mathematical ratios to find some score, any score, that correlated with the clinical judgements made about the children. None of these baroque calculations worked and the most interesting observation was haphazard. Rogers realised that one test, the picture test where children had to talk about a particular drawing, helped put the youngsters at ease. As they looked at the pictures, the children started to speak about their families and their fantasies without being prompted. Rogers made some telling discoveries about his young subjects. Harold S. admitted longing to be a cowboy. Lillian gave a highly coloured account of a sailor boyfriend. Ernest L. was very imaginative and could spin stories about each picture and make up spontaneous poetry. Foti revealed his desire to be strong and hard, which he manifestly wasn't. Rogers had found a way of establishing rapport with the children but he did not follow up a useful technique. It did not promise scientific correlations.

By the middle of 1928, Rogers had completed most of the pilot work for his dissertation. He wanted to stay on at the Institute but he had annoyed the administration by his insistence on being paid $2500. There was no way they could afford to keep him on for another year at that salary. He had not done so brilliantly that they felt obliged to extend his fellowship. Rogers was rather depressed by this rejection. Helen was pregnant again. He dreaded having to ask his father for help. And yet he might have to. There were few jobs in psychology, and Rogers didn't have the qualifications most university departments wanted. He knew little about experimental psychology, the staple of most undergraduate courses. The future, which had seemed so golden, suddenly looked much bleaker.

The first job Rogers applied for shows how desperate he was. There was an opening at Culver Military Academy and he applied. In Peking, Rogers had argued that 'the second institution that this new student Christianity is going to hit and hit hard, is the institution of international war.' He had written passionately about John Wyclif's pacifism. Now he was looking to the army for work. His family, who had failed to come to visit him in Minnesota, would laugh. They would tease him mercilessly if they ever found out.

3

---

# Learning to Be a Therapist,

# 1928–1937

Getting work was not going to be easy. Even psychologists with PhDs were struggling. The hundred graduates who got their doctorates in 1931 had to compete for just 43 jobs, and Rogers was still far from that stage. But he was lucky. After he had written to Culver, he heard of an opening in the Child Study section of the Rochester Society for the Prevention of Cruelty to Children.

Rochester is far from New York City, at the very northern end of New York State on the Canadian border. Today, it's Twin Peaks country. At the end of the 1920s, it was a small industrial city. Rogers drove up there with Helen. His first impressions were depressing. The Children's Shelter, used to house young people in emergencies, was drab and dingy. The interview at the Society's offices, however, went well. The board were impressed. Rogers had relevant experience and had studied at fine institutions. Again, there were problems over money as Rogers was not impressed with the salary, $2900, and tried to get a better offer. He had other good reasons for hesitating. Rochester was very isolated. Its university was small and not very distinguished. Professionally it felt like 'a dead end street'.

The American Psychological Association had been started by experimental psychologists. Though such men as W. B. Pillsbury, a pioneer of industrial psychology, and John B. Watson always argued that psychology had to be practical, the academics who dominated psychology did not value non-experimental work.

57

Theories of how animals learned were of more empirical interest than trying to understand, and cope with, the messy traumas of everyday life.

In 1928, 68 per cent of psychologists who worked in clinics were women. John Morgan of Northwestern University sniped that 'it was not work for a man'. Henry Goddard, one of the fathers of clinical psychology, lamented 'clinical psychology has so far proved of interest to only a very small number of students . . . and very few take it seriously.' One article asked whether clinicians should continue 'to train psychologists for second-string jobs.' The Society did not improve its offer of $2900. Nevertheless Rogers accepted. He was settling for a 'second-string job' in a second-string city. The employment situation meant he had little choice. Later on, Rogers breezily claimed he had always been sure Rochester would turn out fine; it was, as he had promised Helen when they first got engaged, a question of moving tents like the Bedouin. The truth, however, was that he went to Rochester only because he had no other offers.

While Rogers was talking to the board of the Society, Helen wandered round Rochester. She called at a few estate agents to see what apartments were available but found nothing she liked. However, one of the estate agents showed her a Dutch colonial-style house in the process of being built. It cost $8500. When Rogers had finished his interview, he met Helen. She took him to see the house and, there and then, they paid a deposit and committed themselves to a large mortgage. When Rogers told his parents what they had done, Walter and Julia were appalled they had taken on such a large debt so impulsively.

Three weeks later, Helen and Rogers packed up their apartment in New York. With the two-year-old David in the back, they drove the 300 miles upstate. Helen was not delighted to be swapping the glamour and culture of New York for a small town close to the Canadian border.

Rogers was to work in Rochester for the next 12 years. He portrayed his time there as an experimental period, preparation for the ideas that would make his name. This was a little rewriting of history. For his first seven years in Rochester, he concentrated on devising more scientific means of assessing children so that lawyers, psychiatrists, psychologists and social workers would have a more intelligent approach to handling delinquents. Rogers did treat children and talk to their parents but most of his work was perfecting methods of assessment, not giving therapy. Even in the clinics run by William Healy, the pioneer of 'deeper' therapies, only about 30 per cent of children were ever seen for interview. In Rochester a mere fifth got the 'interview treatment'. It would be years before Rogers focused on parents and why they were failing to bring up their children well.

The Rochester Society for the Prevention of Cruelty to Children was one of many local child-care agencies but its name is misleading. Its main aim was not to prevent cruelty but to reform delinquents. The Intake Department took referrals from schools and the police; the Medical Department examined children; the Protective Department had the power to recommend children be removed from their homes, but that power was used rarely. The Child Study Department was the smallest department; its role was to assess the intellectual and emotional problems of children. Every year, the Society dealt with about 600 children referred by the courts, the police or the schools, a mix of the very delinquent, the very disturbed and the very disabled. After assessing the children and their families, the Society's experts made 'recommendations' for treatment. Basically, there were three options – sending children to an institution, putting them out to foster parents or offering somewhat primitive counselling while they stayed at home with their parents. The counselling usually consisted of lecturing inadequate parents or those 'with foreign family habits' on how to bring up junior so that he or she would fit into America.

Rogers soon realised there was little scientific basis to these recommendations. They relied on hunch, tradition, intuition and, often, on what the Society could get the local courts to accept. The courts had their eccentricities. One judge declared he had never had a Boy Scout up before him for any crime. Rogers commented the judge didn't know that the Scouts refused to accept certain kinds of children – particularly those with 'foreign family habits'.

From the start Rogers understood the need to make good local contacts. He wrote a memo to a Mr Allen in 1929 suggesting improved co-operation with other city agencies. After only a year, Rogers was made head of the Child Study Department. He realized the need to research how successful the Rochester welfare agencies were. Did problem children cease to be problematic? Over the next six years Rogers organised much useful work into fostering, orphanages and what happened if the local juvenile court was so misguided as to go against the decisions of experts. Rogers did not publish many of his findings and there is a surprising number of unpublished papers in his archives at the Library of Congress. These include studies of juvenile justice decisions in the Rochester courts and an intriguing study of children who bragged. The first paper might have caused some offence to the local court but the bragging paper was pure psychology; Rogers either did not think it good enough to publish or failed to get it accepted.

Rogers often wrote about his 'learnings'. There was one dramatic example. Soon after he had started to work at the Society, Rogers led a discussion on how to interview. To prepare himself, he looked in the files and he found an account of an interview with a parent which seemed a good model to follow. The caseworker was shrewd and offered intelligent interpretations which went to the heart of the problem. In the best Freudian tradition, she was digging up the truth that the patient was unqualified to discover. 'I was happy to use it as an illustration of good interviewing technique,' Rogers said, a blueprint for the future.

The professional climate in which Rogers worked was moralistic but, ironically, that morality did little to protect children. Today organisations such as the National Society for the Prevention of Cruelty to Children in the UK and similar societies in the United States focus on preventing physical, sexual and emotional abuse. Social workers have learned the importance of listening to children. In the 1930s, however, children were not often seen as victims but as monsters. Agencies saw their job as making 'bad' children conform and adjust to society. Rogers was no exception; children were the fundamental problem for him, too, but he had an open mind and a sharp eye. It soon led him to develop a slightly more liberal approach to one particular aspect of policy. He suspected many delinquents loved the glamour of being taken to the police station and treated as juvenile mobsters. Better, Rogers thought, for the police to take a softer line, involve parents and not handle 'bad' children as if they already had a record. This did not change the basic attitudes. The Society's caseworkers were part of a team whose task was to turn the problem child into the junior model citizen, who did not defy authority, did not have temper tantrums, did not lie and was not 'mischievous or annoying'. Only slowly did Rogers start to see that even the hard cases were individuals with individual problems.

One of the first boys to make an impression on him was a seven-year-old boy called John. John presented as a very sexually aggressive child. He had molested two little girls and introduced a number of boys to 'sex perversion'. The reports never got more specific but little John was clearly obsessed by sex. One of the first questions he asked Rogers was whether Rogers slept with his wife. Rogers was flabbergasted by the child but did not ask how John had reached this state.

Another child called Dick was the son of a promiscuous mother and a violent father. Provoked by his wife, the husband beat her. Dick boasted his father was 'Satan'. Dick loved knives and, when he could get his hands on them, he tortured animals. Despite his home background Dick was not seen as a victim but as a child who was guilty of cruelty.

These profiles did not lead Rogers to see children as victims. A sheet in the papers at the Library of Congress illustrates professional perceptions at the start of the 1930s. On the sheet Rogers ticked off how many children suffered from different problems. There are 20 ticks against adolescent restlessness, 28 against poor habit training, 28 against poor companions, but only one tick against a case where Rogers suspected parents might have corrupted a child's morals. Even incest was often seen as being the child's fault. In only two cases was a parent or step-parent 'abusive' and the description of abuse suggests 'abusive' meant yelling and neglecting a child's needs rather than sexual or physical violence. Rogers listed nine potential reasons for removal from the home, but no child seems to have been taken away as a result of abusive treatment or corruption of morals.

Given the development of child-welfare services, this failure to uncover any physical or sexual abuse is surprising. Rogers should not be pilloried, for all other child workers at the time were blind to it. Historically, the blindness is telling. Freud, who treated only a few children, such as Little Hans, had raised the possibility that many of his women patients had been seduced by their parents. Masson (1984) has bitterly attacked Freud for reneging on his ideas and arguing later that any memories of abuse were fantasies. The child wanted to be seduced. This is not the place to enter into that argument. Unlike Freud, however, Rogers was seeing disturbed children every week, as were hundreds of other American psychologists and social workers. Rogers had also read August Aichhorn (1878–1949), a teacher gifted at dealing with delinquent boys. He set up a treatment centre in Oberhollabrun and a second one in St Andra, Austria. Aichhorn argued that children who misbehaved seriously had usually been emotionally and sometimes physically brutalised by their parents. Yet Rogers never seems to have wondered why he and hundreds of other professionals didn't see much abuse or question whether their moral emphasis, blaming the child, was fair. Rogers in all his writings never returned to this. (When, 30 years later, 'child abuse' was 'discovered' as paediatricians in Denver came across badly bruised children and realised these weren't cases of accidental injury but of parental violence, Rogers apparently made no comment on the earlier collective blindness.)

## The Component Factor Method

In 1931, Rogers published *Character and Personality*, a series of tests for children. It was the final result of the work he had started under Levy. The tests reveal a consistent theme of the next 35 years – the desire to quantify feelings and personality changes that are hard to measure. Rogers noted the tests are 'largely made up of questions which any psychologist or psychiatrist skilled in children's behaviour might use in an interview.' But the tests were superior, less subjective than interviews and produced measures and scores, the stuff of science.

Many of the tests were imaginative. One explored children's wishes. Rogers divided wishes into three kinds; wishing to be better looking or smarter, wishing for happier relationships at home and wishing for more friends, better social contacts. Another test asked which individuals a child would like to spend more time with. 'The serious cases are the children who gnaw at their pencils for several minutes and then make choices such as a Pet Lion or S, a worker with whom the child had had an hour's contact. Those are the children who live in true isolation,' Rogers noted. The fourth test consisted of a hundred questions that got children to describe what they thought of themselves and their parents. Statistically, it was sophisticated asking children to tick one of seven possible boxes.

Rogers wanted to establish the reliability of the tests – reliability means the extent to which the same subjects tick the same answers and get the same scores when they take the test at different times. Reliability at 0.719 would be good. The only way of judging the validity of the tests – whether they were accurate by comparison with 'real life' – was to compare what individual children scored with clinical judgements of their mental well-being. His experiences in New York had shown him that might be very hard, so Rogers also wrote up detailed case histories. Some were revelatory.

For example, Horace was ten and of average intelligence. He did not score peculiarly except in terms of family relationships. When Horace imagined himself on a desert island, he took his mother and two sisters with him but not his father. Horace also didn't want to go to the circus with his father. He liked his mother best and his father least. When social workers inquired, they found that Horace was an unwanted child who had been abused with 'incredible meanness' by his father. 'I would live any place rather than be at home where my father doesn't like me,' Horace pleaded. But it wasn't the test that yielded those insights but talking to Horace.

This test yielded four scores. One for personal inferiority; one for social maladjustment; one for family maladjustment and one for daydreaming. The correlations between the judgements made by clinicians and scores on the test were not high: only 0.43 for social maladjustment and 0.38 for family maladjustment.

This was the second time Rogers had failed to get scores on tests to correlate meaningfully with clinicians' judgements. It pushed him to develop his own scientific method for assessing children. He called this the Component Factor Method. It claimed to be more thorough than previous systems. There were seven factors the assessment needed to consider. All the factors were rated on a seven-point scale; children who scored poorly on a factor would be given a rating of minus 3 and those who scored well one of plus 3.

The first factor was heredity. Did the child come from a healthy family? What kind of diseases were in the family? A child scored minus 3, the lowest score, if both parents were feeble-minded; a child scored 0 if both parents had normal intelligence but had a few neurotic traits and plus 3 if both parents were college graduates.

The second factor was physical. A child with severe problems, such as a history of convulsions, would score minus 3; a healthy, athletic child would score plus 3. The third factor was that of intelligence, based on the Stanford Binet IQ test. The fourth factor was that of family influence. The caseworkers were told to consider 'the family circle', the emotional atmosphere and the kind of family frictions that existed. Often there was bitterness if a child was illegitimate. Though it was less easy to rate this psychological factor, Rogers insisted on the same seven-point scale. A child whose mother was 'openly immoral' and whose father was 'openly drunk' would rate minus 3.

Fifth were the economic, cultural and social factors, which again were not easy to rate. Rogers saw there could be real dilemmas. For example, a boy who was leader of a gang might seem to merit a minus 3 rating – leading a gang is very anti-social – but controlling a gang of tough kids also required sharp social skills. Gang leaders were often liked and admired. Should they get a minus for being bad or a plus for being leaders? Rogers never resolved this problem.

The sixth factor was education and training. Children who did well at school would get a plus 3 while those who were failing and had discipline problems would get a minus 3. The final factor was Self Insight. A girl who blamed others for all her problems and would not admit she contributed to them would score minus 3; a boy who realised his parents spoilt him but who was not a good judge of his strengths and weaknesses would score 0.

Rogers produced charts such as the following which identified the most hopeful areas for treatment and made it possible to track progress.

## CASE OF PAUL
### TREATMENT POSSIBILITIES

| Factor | −3 | −2 | −1 | 0 | 1 | 2 | 3 |
|---|---|---|---|---|---|---|---|
| Hereditary | | x | | | | | |
| Physical | | | x→ | | | | |
| Mentality | | x | | | | | |
| Family | | | x———→? | | | | |
| Economic-Cultural | | | | x | | | |
| Social | | x———→ | | | | | |
| Education-Training | | | x———→ | | | | |
| Self-Insight | | x———→ | | | | | |

Rogers had come to Rochester still deeply influenced by the psychodynamic approach of the New York Institute. Doctor knew best. The wise therapist, armed with insight and tests, could discover the psychological infection, the germs of the neurosis. The patient was sick and ignorant. He looked up to St Therapist, who would work out the cause of the 'psychological' disease and then explain it to the grateful patient. The Component Factor Method quantified this approach. Its scoring system pinpointed areas of possible progress. Rogers highlighted one case where the Method made it clear what was needed by way of treatment.

Philip was Polish, 14 years old and large for his age. He came to the attention of the authorities when he broke into the house of a neighbour and tried to assault her 18-year-old daughter with a lead pipe.

Philip turned out to be a well-behaved, intelligent boy whose problem the Component Factor Method revealed to be simple: he was desperately curious about sex. His father had died; his mother was prim. Philip 'mulled over the perplexities of sex' and started to watch the 18-year-old girl who lived opposite. He fantasised taking her clothes off; he wanted to see what she looked like naked. Rogers suggested the boy didn't need analysis of his Oedipal conflicts but simple information about the facts of life, information he should have got from his father. In some ways Rogers seems very naive, believing Philip would be satisfied if he could confirm the girl had breasts and different genitalia to a boy's. But at least after learning about the facts of life, Philip did not get into more trouble, though it may be that one of the facts of life he learned was that the police arrest you if you break into girls' bedrooms.

Despite his irritation with religion, Rogers did not sever all his links with the YMCA. From 1929 to 1932, he spent part of each summer at YMCA camps. The camps offered a chance to do some scientific psychology. They could also be fun, but regimented fun.

## The experience of camp

By the late 1920s, camp was already something of an American institution. Middle-class parents saw it as a constructive holiday and social reformers saw it as a useful tool, a reward for deprived children. The most comprehensive study of American delinquents, a study of 1000 children who had been seen by the Judge Baker Foundation, concluded that well over 20 per cent of them would have benefited from a recreational activity like going to camp. There was a magazine devoted entirely to camp activities.

Rogers used his connections with the YMCA to get the Rochester Society to send a number of children to Camp Cory in Pennsylvania. Rogers was under no illusion that camps were a panacea. Poor and disturbed children often found the experience hard. Rogers had seen boys teased mercilessly because they arrived with their belongings in a bundle rather than a suitcase. He had seen them teased because they arrived wearing trousers rather than shorts. He had seen children who had no spending money reduced to tears by children who did.

Rogers tried to introduce into Camp Cory some form of precise analysis. He started by asking parents and schools to provide brief reports that outlined the children's problems, interests and abilities. That way, they could tailor programmes to individual needs; they could be prepared for flashpoints and they could eventually judge the success of the 'camp treatment'.

In 1929, the first year Camp Cory tried to mix middle-class children with 'agency' children, the agency children were made fun of. One boy was so upset he packed his bags twice and asked to be allowed to go home. Rogers put the boy in the tent with other foster-home boys and he stayed on without too much trouble. With his own memories of being teased, Rogers wanted to find a way to help so, in 1930, he put all the agency children together in tents of their own. The middle-class kids couldn't bully or mock them so easily.

There were situations in which Rogers had remarkable success. He dealt with a clever 11-year-old boy, an only child whose mother spoiled him but whose father was inconsistent. The boy never knew what would get him punished at home. In camp, he stole, was vindictive and uncontrolled until someone noticed he was very interested in nature study. He was encouraged to start a nature study group and given a special hut for the project. The boy started to behave much better. Such miracles were rare, however. The bed-wetting saga was more usual.

At Camp Wawokiyeye two boys wet their beds every night and that made them a laughing stock. One boy in particular, Jim, was nastily expert at making Walt and Bill feel terrible. At a tense tent meeting the counsellors insisted that any member of the tent who referred in public to Walt's and Bill's bed-wetting would be punished. They would get no dessert at the next meal. The boys agreed. The honour of the tent was at stake but Jim couldn't help himself. Walt and Bill had to be teased. When he started to make fun of Walt in front of a group of other boys, Jim was told to stop. If he didn't stop, there would be no dessert. Jim didn't stop and didn't take his punishment like a man: at lunch, he ate another boy's dessert. Jim did not apologise even when he was confronted by one of the counsellors. He didn't care. The counsellor summoned all the boys. They were told none of them would get their dessert that evening – and it was ice-cream – unless Jim promised to behave.

Faced by such group pressure, Jim agreed to forgo his ice-cream. But Jim ran out of the tent 'in a perfect rage, foaming at the mouth' and started to chase one of the bed-wetters with a club. Eventually, one of the counsellors took him away to discuss his temper problems. There was no happy ending in this case, Rogers noted, no easy solutions.

Rogers also initiated IQ tests at Camp Cory. He surveyed 208 boys who attended and found that the average IQ was high – 114. That reflected the middle-class majority. Less than 10 per cent of the boys were 'low average'; 40 per cent were superior. Below-average boys often got into difficulties. Rogers had much sympathy for boys such as Henry who was 15, lean, gangling and dull. 'His name became a byword for describing any stupidity,' Rogers said. Henry was teased and, sometimes, even encouraged the boys to make fun of him. At least he was the centre of attention then but occasionally he couldn't stand it. The other boys would call him 'pig face' or 'pig eye' or 'dish rag' and Henry would try to turn on his tormentors.

Henry had a low IQ of only 74 and would have fared even worse if he hadn't been verbally quite sharp. But he was too ambitious, hoping to become a missionary in Africa. Henry stayed in camp for eight weeks and the longer he stayed, the better he coped. The next year Henry returned and was teased less because he knew the ropes. The 'camp treatment' did give him more confidence but it couldn't transform him.

The children were cruel, Rogers noticed, with one remarkable exception; they did not mock those who were physically disabled. Lame, overweight, epileptic children were all accepted by their peers, he claimed. When I first read this observation, I confess I was amazed as it flies in the face of much research on attitudes to disability. It is also hard to believe that fat, short-sighted boys were not teased. Rogers maintained this was true and again it does raise the question of whether professionals in the 1930s missed a great deal.

Despite failures, Rogers concluded that camp could be of great benefit for children who met three conditions. First, they had to have 'adequate mentality' (*The Clinical Treatment of the Problem Child*, p. 265). Second, their parents had to have enough money to send them with the right clothes and kit, and with some spending money. Third, the parents must not panic or insist on the child coming home if there were initial traumas. Camp Cory took boys who had been found guilty of stealing, boys who had been expelled from school, boys who were out of control. As long as the three conditions were met, however, camp could bring about 'definite improvements'.

In writing about children at the camps, Rogers was compassionate but also realistic. There were successes and failures. It was not so easy to admit such mixed results in dealing with the children the Rochester Society treated regularly. Rochester expected solutions. Rogers' compassion fits his image as a liberal thinker. It is possible to see some connection between the idealistic youth who went to Peking and the wise guru who preached a mixture of freedom and responsibility to hippies in San Francisco in the 1960s. It is because of this apparent consistency that I want to draw attention to a paper Rogers co-wrote in 1931. It shows him in a very different light.

## 'I am most crazy'

'We Pay for the Smiths', written with Mitchell Rappoport, is a mix of social and psychological analysis and snide reporting of the history of a particular named family, the Smiths. The *Survey Graphic* piece opened dramatically with two letters – and no punctuation at all. (The authors deliberately kept all the spelling errors.)

> Dear miss Clansy, you haven't got any rubber there that will fit the childrn . . . Miss Clansy, you dont have enny ladys clothes so I am going to tell you I haven't a thing only what I have on i am to go to Hospital to morning I can't go i have nothing to wear no underwear or petcoats I am so discariage I don't know what to do the shape I am in I have to worrie all the time the poor little baby haven't got a dress or enithing to wear Mr Smith hasnt got enny work I am most crazy.

It was a nice line to end ... 'I am most crazy'.

Rogers and Rappoport then reproduced a second letter where Mrs Smith asked for five cents to buy some soap. The authors calculated that, since 1914, the community had spent huge sums on the family. The father was Raymond Smith, a shiftless painter, who met Daisy Schuyler, 'the frowsy heroine of this tale'. By 1922, there were nine small children in the home. Gladys, who was Raymond Smith's daughter by a previous liaison, was 16 and already pregnant. 'The older children were known for rowdy behaviour, stealing and general lawlessness.' One of their escapades was to throw watermelon rind at the baby next door. Did their mother try to discipline them? Hell, no, the irresponsible Daisy Schuyler laughed, along with her no-good kids. Daisy was immoral, too. Once she left home for four days – almost certainly with another man. Raymond Smith called the newspapers which carried 'sob stories' about a man left with nine little ones to care for. Daisy returned, however. In 1923, all but one of the children were removed from the home. The Smiths managed a little better and Raymond got work. The couple even finally got married. But 'an optimistic investigator' now recommended two of the children should be sent back home. Within a few weeks, Mrs Smith was writing ungrammatical begging letters again to Miss Clansy. And she didn't even use capital letters. The piece quoted her plea that 'we will not be able to get milk for the baby after today as soon as he goes to work will let you know.'

The Society had tried in 1927 to offer intensive help but the ungrateful Mr Smith complained about 'a bunch of old maids snooping around interfering in his business.' He and his wife didn't even take seriously an incident when seven-year-old Clarence (who Rogers clearly believed was a hit-man in the making) pushed a small boy over a 100-foot cliff. Curiously, the victim didn't just survive, but had no injuries. Violence to minors was just part of the catalogue of sins, crimes and outrages that Rogers had listed in notes for preparing the article. The Smith children also engaged in bed-wetting, theft of an auto, excessive sex activity and tampering with mail boxes. They were seen as little anti-social 'hellions'. The 'worst' child was 12-year-old Alice whose unlovely character included 'suspected perversion, masturbation, bed-wetting, somnambulism, bad toilet habits and being selfish, sly, untruthful, sulky and aggressive'.

Rogers and Rappoport worked out that this family had cost the taxpayer already the 'stupendous', and precisely calculated, sum of $28,312. In his unpublished notes for the article, Rogers worked out that only two of the children – Herbert, who was in Navy, and Vivian, who was only nine – seemed normal. The family was likely to cost the State a further $19,550 before all the children reached 16.

Rogers and Rappoport drew harsh lessons. They concluded: 'the community has no effective social policy in operation which will curb the formation of further Smith families.' They considered whether laws permitting the State to sterilise parents might work. But the Smiths were neither insane nor defective, just feckless spongers. Birth control would have helped. The article ended by calling for 'bold, far sighted policies of social planning and social control.'

'We Pay for the Smiths' was a powerful piece of writing but its ideology was far from liberal. Rogers continued to keep an eye on the Smiths and their offspring. The results were not encouraging. The piece was Rogers' most polished publication to date and though it does not reflect a liberal view, he never disowned it.

As the piece was published, Rogers and Helen found a site to build a holiday home at Seneca on a lake near the Canadian border. But the only way they could afford it was to pool resources with friends. Rogers persuaded Bill Seaman, who was a psychologist at the Institute in New York, and the social psychologist Theodore Newcomb, his old classmate from Union, to join in. Over the next six months, acting for this 'syndicate', Rogers haggled over the price for the land with a local farmer. In March 1932, the land was finally purchased for $850 and a few weeks later, Rogers started to build a cabin. It would stay in the family for over 30 years. Rogers loved the place. Seneca gave him peace and the chance to wander, and dream, in the woods as he had as a boy. Isolation made him think creatively, he believed.

Rogers came back to Rochester in the autumn of 1932, determined to start a new research project and he had an experience which he argued was important in the development of his ideas.

He saw one child who was a pyromaniac. Rogers interviewed him in the detention home day after day and, gradually, traced the problem back to the boy's masturbation. According to Healy, with this insight the child should have been cured. 'Eureka, the case was solved,' Rogers wrote. He recommended the boy should be put on probation. Unfortunately, Healy's formula did not work. The boy soon started more fires. For Rogers it was 'a jolt'. But it was also exciting as he felt he was learning something that Healy had missed.

As Rogers started to see more children and to interview some of them, he realised there was a gap in the psychotherapy literature. There were no verbatim accounts of precisely what went on during therapy. Freud had written up case histories in detail but Freud wrote them out in his own words, with his own slant. Rogers took a scientific view. How could one improve therapy if one did not know exactly what happened during the process? He was in no position to do anything about this yet.

In 1932, Rogers analysed the decisions made about 108 children. Of these, 30 had been recommended to stay at home under supervision; 23 had been sent for fostering. The other 55 had been sent to institutions. Of these children 22 were mentally defective and, in those cases, there had been no conflict between Rogers and the courts. But in 19 cases, the courts had imposed a decision – usually to send a child to an institution – against his recommendation. The fate of these 19 intrigued Rogers and he kept an eye on them. It was not that he objected to institutions, but the appropriate children had to be sent there. Rogers could see no alternative in about a fifth of the cases. In others he had his doubts.

Rogers published the findings on the 108 but he also circulated a more critical private paper where he called for more decisions to be made in conferences rather than in juvenile courts. He was now well respected locally but he realised that the more he knew about the ingredients of good fostering, the more chance he would have of influencing the policy of the local courts and of the city administration.

## Choosing good foster homes

By 1930, about 100,000 children were being fostered in America. They were placed either by private agencies such as the Jewish Home Finding Society or by such organisations as the Rochester Society. Rogers hoped the Component Factor Method would make it easier for fostering to succeed by weeding out children who were too damaged or too disruptive. It was also important to find out the characteristics of good foster parents.

Gradually, Rogers found there were four qualities to a good foster parent. He published his findings in *Mental Hygiene* in 1933 (January issue, pp. 31–2). Foster parents had to be intelligent and understanding. Good ones could see the behaviour of a child as a natural result of his or her heredity and experience rather than a breach of moral rules. To do that, they needed imagination. Secondly, foster parents had to be consistent about discipline. The child had to feel sure about their rules. Third, good foster parents had to have what Rogers called 'interested affection'. They should neither smother the child with endless love nor be too harsh. Rogers praised a certain Mrs Thompson who got the balance right and so became Rochester's star foster parent. She was given a boy called William who had reduced a number of foster homes to complete chaos and despair. Within a few days of being placed at the Thompsons, William started to misbehave badly. He slapped his chest and boasted, 'I'm tough.'

'Are you?' asked the unflappable Mrs Thompson. She added, 'I'm tough, too.'

William looked surprised and in a rather less aggressive tone, he inquired, 'How tough are you?'

'I'm tough like you,' said the foster mother.

There was a pause Rogers described as 'thoughtful' and then William piped up in a subdued voice, 'Well, maybe I'm not so tough.' (The dialogue has a whiff of the B movie to it, it must be said.)

Mrs Thompson liked the boys but she was never too affectionate. She was imaginative and used simple objects – hammers, nails

– to create projects to keep her charges busy. If they behaved, she took them on outings, picnics and trips to the movies. Her husband helped. Mr Thompson was a painter who was often out of work. He had used some of the money paid by the agency to build a small workshop in his basement. He supervised baths, doled out cod liver oil and gave the rare spanking when it was needed. Rogers often used the Thompsons with particularly difficult children.

Fourth, good foster parents had to show interest if the children did well and reward them with attention.

With many children, however, Rogers saw that, for all the efforts the Society and other agencies put in, there was still no success. Donald's mother developed schizophrenia when he was three. By the time he was seven years old, he had been through seven foster homes. He still wet his bed persistently and masturbated. When Rogers first assessed him, Donald had an average IQ score but he was desperate for emotional security. He was placed with the Thompsons but, for once, they could not work a miracle. The boy continued to be withdrawn and to do poorly at school. He often behaved as if he were being picked on and remained very defensive. At nine, he still wet his bed. Experts and foster parents tried everything – charts, rewards if he was dry, making him wash his bedclothes, restricting the intake of fluids at night. Doctors even tried giving him an injection of sterile water and telling him it was the latest medical cure. Nothing worked. At 17, Donald was not much better. Rogers noted sadly that 15 years of foster care had just left the child 'apathetic'. He had made only a 'very passive adjustment'.

By 1933, there were ten studies of how successful (or otherwise) placements in foster homes had been and one study that looked at the relationship of IQ to fostering success. Six of these had been carried out by the indefatigable William Healy, and Rogers was now determined to work up his own results into a paper. The findings seemed to be clear-cut. Children with an IQ of under 80 did poorly when they were fostered. Only in 26 per cent of cases was the outcome successful. Children whose IQ was between 80 and 110 did well, with over 71 per cent of cases successful.

The literature had few surprises. The less severe the behaviour problems, the more likely fostering was to succeed. The most successful programme was that of the Jewish Home Finding Society which reported 100 per cent success with 19 children but these children were orphans and they did not have special behavioural problems. Children who had not offended or had been caught just once also had a better chance of success. With persistent offenders and with 'girls who are sex delinquents', the success rate fell to between 61 and 64 per cent. Today that would be considered a triumph but, in those days, expectations were high, and 64 per cent success seemed more like failure.

In 1933, Ross, Rogers' brother, died suddenly. The death brought him closer to his family again, though he also had the first of many political quarrels with Lester. They quarrelled about a workman who complained he had been badly treated by his foreman. Lester took the side of the foreman; Rogers of the worker. Lester saw their different attitudes as quite significant and accused his brother of not being interested in hearing both sides of the story.

After six years in Rochester, Rogers was more confident but also more realistic. He saw how often the Society's interventions failed. Two particular experiences stayed with him. First, Rogers had to lead a discussion on interviewing techniques. He remembered the verbatim interview he had praised in 1929 and reread it. Now, he was appalled. The caseworker had behaved more like a prosecutor than a therapist; she had been pedantic and her clever questioning 'convicted this parent of her unconscious motives and wrung from her an admission of her guilt'. Rogers could now see this kind of approach wouldn't work. The caseworker didn't try to understand the mother's point of view at all.

The second key experience was with an intelligent mother whose child was 'something of a hellion'. To Rogers it was clear that the problems stemmed from the mother's rejection of her son. Rogers drew her out, asked her to think about what she had told him and tried to get her to see 'the pattern'. She rejects, son rebels. Rogers tried saying it nicely and saying it harshly but he got nowhere. It was all lies. She was a good mother with a bad son. Finally Rogers gave up. They agreed they had both tried and they got up and shook hands. The woman walked to the door of his office. Then she turned around and asked if they ever took adults for counselling. He said yes and, rather to his surprise, she said that she would like some help.

What followed was dramatic. The woman headed back for the chair she had just left. She sat down and began to pour out a tale of misery and despair. Her marriage was wretched. She felt confused and a total failure. When she had been talking about her son, everything the woman had said had been 'sterile and intellectual'. Now Rogers was seeing the real woman in all her pain. He was bearing witness, to put it in Christian language he knew so well, to her suffering. Rogers was transfixed. He often wrote of this interview as a turning-point, as the moment when he started to realise 'that it is the client who knows what hurts, what directions to go, what problems are crucial, what experiences have been deeply buried' (Rogers 1965, p. 359). This was a revelation for Rogers, but it may have been a revelation he was ready for. Rogers had been reading two therapists who were criticising Freudian orthodoxy, offering a new approach. He had started to read Jessie Taft and Frederick Allen attentively partly because he had been invited to give some courses at Teachers back in New York. He had to be aware of the latest controversies. In 1933, Jessie Taft had published *The Dynamics of Therapy*. One of her allies was Frederick Allen, who published an influential account of a case in the January 1934 edition of the *American Journal of Orthopsychiatry*. They emphasised that effective therapy with children required the 'undirected flow' of the child's interests and that attention should be paid to the nature of the relationship between the child and the therapist. Allen wrote graphically in the first person, 'I am providing an opportunity for this child to experience himself in a new and present relation, and in terms of the present, not in the past. I am in a position to deal with the feeling the child expresses towards me. I can understand his struggle to control without giving in. I can understand his need to dislike me without threatening him with my own dislike.'

Allen went on to say, 'I can help him experience these feelings as his own with less anxiety and enable him to resume growth with less anxiety and denial.'

Rogers was not quite prepared to accept all this and he stayed cool. He argued a little pompously that Allen was relying on a psychological phenomenon known as 'transfer of training'. If a child learned Latin, he would find it easier to learn French. In therapy, the child learned skills and responses he or she would be able to use in 'real' relationships with parents, friends and teachers. Unlike child psychoanalysis with its heavy baggage of interpretation, Taft and Allen stressed the need to look at the present. Rogers wrote, 'There is none of the theoretical assumption so frequent in the psychoanalytic literature that an individual may gain complete insight, be permanently integrated and solve all his problems.' Taft and Allen did not try to remodel the child to fit society. Rogers approved of that but he still believed their approach was a little idealistic and could be used only with a limited number of children.

The end of 1935 and the beginning of 1936 seem to mark a turning-point in Rogers' ambitions. The child welfare system depended on professionals collaborating. Rogers had got enough local support to help make the juvenile justice system in Rochester less punitive. He had discovered that his classes at Teachers had been well received and that students saw him as one of the best lecturers. His ties with his family were getting closer. His father had suddenly given him an unexpected present of a parcel of land near Wheaton. His brother Walter set up as a doctor in Rochester. The two families saw a lot of each other. Then, the Governor of New York State nominated Rogers to be his representative at next year's National Social Work Conference. Rogers kept the gold medal that went with the position and it is among his papers in the Library of Congress. With all this, Rogers felt he could reveal what was something of a master plan.

On 20 and 21 May, at a meeting of the staff of the Society, Rogers explained what he saw as the way ahead. He wanted to unite the various agencies offering services for children and to create a psychological clinic in the city. The public would feel that going there was 'like going to the chemist'. A single clinic would cater for all their needs. The staff meeting approved the plan and Rogers started to lobby for what he felt from the start was his clinic. Unfortunately, not everyone would share his view that he was the perfect, indeed the only, choice for the job.

# 4

## From Children to Therapy, 1937–1942

The five years from 1937 to 1942 marked a decisive break in Rogers' career. He stopped working with children. He wove the ideas of Taft and Allen into a distinctive therapy for adults. Howard Kirschenbaum, despite being often uncritical, is a little ungenerous in suggesting client-centred therapy merely systematised and took to extremes many ideas then current among therapists. Rogers didn't just offer a synthesis of other therapies but a particular personal flavour of his own.

Rogers had left behind his youthful Christian ideals. Oddly, though, a key element of client-centred therapy seems quite Christian. Giving a client unconditional positive regard, that combination of total attention and total acceptance, is not unlike bearing witness in the religious sense. It could be argued, perhaps a little melodramatically, that Rogers was willing to be there with his clients, in their suffering, in the counselling room instead of at the foot of the Cross.

By 1937, Rogers had helped set up a relatively progressive system for dealing with disturbed and delinquent children in Rochester. Children who were picked up by the police were 'not clapped in jail or in a detention home.' The routine was for the police to take the child home so that the arrest did not become 'a first step towards glorification as a criminal'. Parents were expected to make sure the child did not reoffend. 'Use old-fashioned police methods ... place the youngster behind bars and he will respond like a

criminal, be profane, defiant, delinquent in outlook and determined to run away. Treat him as an individual, give him the feeling
that he is understood . . . and he will respond like what he is –
a confused unhappy child,' Rogers noted. Many children were
prosecuted, but to have helped persuade Rochester's judges to
think of attacking the underlying causes of delinquency was no
mean achievement. Ironically, however, just as Rogers could con-
gratulate himself on such improvements, he himself created an
unexpected crisis among the social agencies in the city.

When he wrote his contribution to *A History of Psychology in
Autobiography* in 1965, Rogers said he had 'stubbornly followed
his own course' in going to Rochester, believing it would turn out
well. As a world-famous therapist in the sixties Rogers either for-
got, or glossed over, the insecurities he felt both in 1928 and in
1937, when he had to fight hard for power and position.

By 1937, Rogers was campaigning for setting up the new Guidance Centre. He chaired the social-work division of a committee
set up by the Council of Social Agencies to consider the problems
of Rochester's 55,000 teenagers. Young people needed more information about jobs available in local industry, and Rogers complained of 'the serious lack of case work resources for the
maladjusted young person . . . the proposals in this regard warrant
immediate consideration' (letter to Mr Swan). The solution was
simple. Set up the Guidance Centre. One man in town was ideally
placed to do that. Rogers drafted a report for the board of the
Society to send to the Community Chest; it stated, 'we favour
the establishment of the Child Study Department as a separate
independent agency to be a child guidance centre.' The Guidance
Centre would offer more than the Society could. It would treat
children up to 18, not 16. It would counsel adults who were
plagued with marital troubles, depressions and anxieties about
parenting. The Chest would be worried about the cost but many
families would pay for counselling, Rogers was sure.

The Centre had to be in a special setting: not in an office building
– too austere; not in a hospital – too medical. The ideal place was
a spacious residential house. Rogers was in a hurry, adding in his
submission, 'if the Chest were to make a slight additional allow-
ance', they could get started immediately. Clients could get services

sooner and the move would 'dramatise the fact that the recommendations were being followed'.

The paper worked out the staffing in detail. From the start Rogers assumed the job of director was his by rights as the Centre was so much his idea. He would have to employ a psychiatrist but he had no intention of being supervised by one; rather, the psychiatrist would work to him. The Centre would also need five psychologists, a social worker and administrative staff. He budgeted the first year at $37,700, an increase of $13,117.19 on the annual cost of the Child Study section but the community would get value for money.

Rogers framed the proposal carefully. It would be a psychological clinic, so its director did not need to be a doctor. His crafty drafting, however, did not persuade local doctors who insisted that only a psychiatrist could run such a facility. The medical lobby was strong. One of Rogers' friends, Dr Samuel Hartwell, told him that he should go back to college and qualify as a doctor. Then he could be director. Rogers was 35, had a family to support and was distinctly not amused. As late as 1973, he still wrote bitterly about this struggle for the Guidance Clinic as one of the major professional battles of his life.

At the start of the controversy, Rogers still felt insecure and that he had something to prove. His brother Lester was helping to run Bates & Rogers; his brother Walter had gone through medical school and was a successful paediatrician. Rogers had too many assessments to do and reports to write to establish any reputation outside Rochester. The Society was seeing 20 children a day. The summer break at Seneca provided the only opportunity to develop ideas and to write, so he had published surprisingly little, and what he had published often appeared in undistinguished periodicals. His three-page piece on IQ and the camps appeared in a small magazine devoted to 'camp' activities. Rogers had also written a short article on social workers and the law and co-authored 'We Pay for the Smiths'. The only paper to have appeared in a major academic journal was the study of the characteristics of good foster parents (January 1933; *Mental Hygiene*).

This poor record exposed Rogers to a snub. After his classes at Teachers College, Rogers had suggested to the University of

Rochester that he teach some psychology courses; but its psychologists sniped he was not doing psychology and declined his kind offer. When the American Association for Applied Psychology was set up in 1937, he was just an ordinary member. He was not asked to serve on any committees. When the *Journal of Consulting Psychology* was set up in 1938, he was not on its editorial board.

Rogers decided his best strategy to secure the directorship was to continue to lobby locally and also to publish something significant – a book. But just what would he write about? Unfortunately, there were well over 50 specialist books on various aspects of 'problem children'. As well as Taft's and Allen's, there were such sociological books as Clifford Shaw's *Delinquency Areas* (1936), Henry Thurston's *The Dependent Child* (1930) and Harry Baker and Virginia Traphagen's *The Diagnosis and Treatment of the Problem Child* (1935). There were more personal books, too, such as *Low Company* by Mark Benney (1936). This was a graphic memoir in which a 26-year-old Londoner described his life as a child thief and his progress through industrial school, borstal and prison. George Orwell and H. G. Wells praised its talented author who wrote so vividly from personal experience.

What could Rogers offer that might be new? The Component Factor Method had not been recognised as a major contribution. Nevertheless, in 1937 Rogers approached the publishers Houghton Mifflin. He suggested a book that provided an up-to-date analysis of the latest trends and techniques in dealing with delinquent children. He pointed out he knew all the latest research, all the latest trends and had been working nine years in the field. Their initial reaction was cool. They weren't sure the market needed another book on this topic, but Rogers was determined to press ahead with it.

Rogers found this determination at a time when counselling was under attack for the first time. The humorist James Thurber published some deliciously wicked satires in the *New Yorker*, scoffing at various brands of therapy. Could any sane American believe that being too fat, being in a car accident, forgetting to fix the roof or even – one of Thurber's pet topics – bicycle riding were the result of sexual problems? Thurber was describing the idiocies of psychobabble before the phrase was invented. He poked fun at therapies that guaranteed a life of complete happiness or your money back. Thurber had one consistent theme. Experts, Freudian, Jungian, oral, anal, banal, behaviouristic, sadistic, nihilistic or any other 'istic' didn't hesitate to lecture folks how to live their lives. And folks didn't need it. Thurber gathered his pieces into a book, *Let My Mind Alone* (1936). A scientific approach to dealing with disturbed children would put Thurber's satires in their place.

Rogers was still not sure if he really was a psychologist. When he went to American Psychological Association conventions, he complained, he found most papers explored the details of learning theory and rat perception. It was psychiatric social workers who 'seemed to be talking my language' – not the rat-obsessed, lab-based researchers. But the psychiatric social workers were seen as second-string people. Rogers was torn. He argued that it was wrong for the status of psychologists to depend on their experiments and their research results (Rogers 1939). But the academic reality was that this was precisely how psychologists *were* judged. He felt he belonged with those who had the least status in his profession.

When Rogers, Helen and the children went on holiday to Seneca in the summer of 1937, he started to draft the first chapters of the book. Houghton Mifflin had promised to consider it sympathetically but no more. Rogers let it be known in Rochester he was writing a book. He swallowed his irritation at his psychiatrist friend, Samuel Hartwell, and discussed some of the chapters with him. It was a sensible approach.

Rogers' first book was very different from all his other books. He wrote in the third person in an academic style, referring to himself as 'the author' or to 'the author's experience as a counsellor'. The tone was dry and detached, a scientist trying to find a way through a maze of complex problems.

For the book, Rogers wrote up both published and some of the unpublished research he had carried out since 1928. He argued that when courts followed the recommendations of experts such as himself, children thrived, but arrogant judges who ignored the advice of psychologists imperilled children and society. In 13 of the 19 cases where the courts had rejected the advice of the Society as to treatment, the result was complete failure. The local judges were among those who were insisting the new Guidance Centre should be headed by a psychiatrist, so Rogers took some pleasure in exposing their errors.

*The Clinical Treatment of the Problem Child* offers a comprehensive guide to the critical child-care issues of the 1930s. One of its strengths is that it is written by someone who is steeped in the field. It is only two-thirds of the way through the text, however, that Rogers deals with the main dilemma of when the State is justified in removing children from home. The book first introduced the technique Rogers had tried so hard to develop, the Component Factor Method of assessing children; he argued it offered the best basis for treatment. Rogers stressed the importance of dealing with problem children young for 'the child who today exhibits personality problems and behaviour deviations is the delinquent, the criminal or the neurotic of tomorrow.' These unhappy children damaged their families, their society and themselves. Despite the cynicism of 'We Pay for the Smiths', Rogers still believed psychology could offer solutions but 'only as treatment of such problems can be placed on a scientific basis can we hope to deal significantly with the social ills which they bring upon society,' (p. 15). It was vital to find 'rational means of treating childhood symptoms.'

Rogers argued one had to study 'all the aspects of the life situation'. Assessments shouldn't be based on the ideas of one school of psychology. Freud, Jung, Adler, behaviourism, all had their limitations. The book constantly reiterates the need for proper research to get at 'significant cause and effect relationships'. Just what aspect of parenting would lead a child to become a thief? Just what treatment was best for particular children?

First, the book considered 'changes of environment' – fostering and institutions. Building on the 1933 paper in *Mental Hygiene*, Rogers offered a sophisticated analysis of what made for good fostering. Psychologists and social workers had to match the child's personality and that of the foster parents, particularly the foster mother. Children who had the best prospects had either average or high IQ, were not very attached to their birth family,

83

were under nine when first placed and had not yet taken to regular delinquency. Older children or those who had organic brain damage were less good bets.

Foster care was much better than institutional care in most cases but Rogers did not object on principle to children being sent to institutions. These were often the best solution for the mentally retarded and could offer 'a healthy degree of restraint and control over the child who has for too long been the egotistical centre of his universe' (p. 144). The negative tone, insisting on the selfish child, was typical of the professionals of this period.

Institutions, Rogers pointed out, had many drawbacks, however. They were too regimented and too slow to change. The first American facility for young criminals was the House of Refuge on Randall Island in New York which had opened in 1825. It had to be closed in 1935, Rogers said in one of the few ironies he allowed himself, because it had hardly changed in over a century.

Disturbed and disruptive children needed individual attention, which institutions found hard to provide. Rogers had visited many such places all over the country. Often children were put in uniforms. They had to sleep in crowded dormitories. There was no social worker they could trust. Sometimes, there were bizarre rules about not speaking during meals. Rogers admitted there were some progressive institutions such as Whittier in California but even these offered 'an artificial and unreal environment for the child' (p. 131). To show how artificial they could be, Rogers singled out absurd policies on smoking. In 1937, few had argued that smoking was bad for one's health. Cigarettes were meant to soothe the nerves. Instead of recognising that inmates used tobacco, nearly every youth institution banned smoking, usually on moral grounds. The ban encouraged all kinds of cunning and deceit, Rogers noted. There was often a black market in cigarettes. In *Low Company*, Benney recalled that in borstals older boys would use cigarettes to buy sex from younger boys. Rogers did not reveal anything so shocking but the smoking ban led to boys 'snitching' on each other to win privileges. A study at Whittier found smoking was a prime cause of children being put in the quaintly named 'Lost Privilege Cottage'. Rogers thundered that smoking, which 'is not a delinquent or immoral act, which has no relation to successful after-adjustment is raised to a problem of prime importance simply by the artificialities of institutional life.'

Finally, Rogers came to the key question of the book. In what circumstances was it right to remove children from home? I have argued that it is remarkable the 1930s child-welfare industry failed to recognise the existence of either physical or sexual abuse. Only one situation that Rogers described resembles the thousands of cases of physical and sexual child abuse social workers routinely see now. Rogers outlined the case of an intelligent nine-year-old girl, Dorothy, whose father had incestuous relations with her while her stepmother was pregnant. Dorothy was fostered out. Rogers talked of protecting children from parents who committed 'gross moral lapses' (p. 157) but gross moral lapses tended to mean parents who were 'selling liquor and drugs'. In one case parents were also 'conducting a house of ill fame'. But Rogers did not ask, for example, if their child was being forced into prostitution.

Rogers was sharp, however, about the practical dilemmas of child care. He wrote,

How can we know whether Mrs Bolton will ever be able to show any real affection for Jimmy? Can Arthur's parents modify their ambition for him and expect C's and D's on the report card instead of A's? Could George's mother change her over-indulgent ways and give the boy a healthy degree of discipline? (pp. 162–3)

Instead of asking what we would consider obvious questions about whether parents or relatives were abusing the children, Rogers emphasised the child's anti-social behaviour. He called one child a 'hellion'. The more anti-social the child, the more reason for removing the child from his parents. The longer the child had been acting anti-socially, the less hope of sorting out problems at home or of finding a foster home that could cope. Even the dreadful Smiths were accused more of abusing the taxpayer than of abusing their children.

Yet Rogers had many insights. He saw how children who were neglected still often loved their parents. The children it was simplest to remove from home were not those whose parents did not love them but those who did not love their parents. Rogers had seen many cases where badly treated children still adored their parents. He had hit upon a crucial paradox but it still didn't help him understand how hard it was for children to reveal the truth about being abused or to see that conventional 'interview techniques' only scratched the surface.

Rogers did devote some sections to the way parents should be treated and included a long account of a couple called Perris whose marriage was under great stress because the father believed the mother was unfaithful. Here again, however, many questions were not raised. In most cases, Rogers concluded, parents mainly needed more education, education about sex, education about how to reward and discipline children and, sometimes, lessons in reality. The mother of a 'mongol' (Down's Syndrome) child, for example, simply had to learn that her child would never get better and would never be 'normal' at school.

All this shows that, in 1937–8, Rogers was still quite conservative. A useful comparison is with Jessie Taft. In *The Dynamics of Therapy* she stated that the goal of therapy was not 'socially desirable behaviour' but, rather, that it was an 'individual affair and can be measured only in terms of its meaning to the person, child or adult; of its value, not for happiness, not for virtue, not for social adjustment but for growth and development in terms of a purely individual norm.' For Rogers in 1937 and 1938, his work was part of the juvenile justice system that had to impose the disciplines of society. He wrote, 'Our work cannot be measured ... save in the degree to which it allows the individual to fit normally into the group. It will have been noted that every study of results, whether of environmental treatment or interview therapy, is a research in social outcomes.'

Rogers ended his book with a survey of the different kinds of organisations that could provide help and by pleading for collaboration between different agencies. It was a moderate end to a moderate book. There is no reason to think that it did not reflect his real views but he also knew, as the struggle for control of the Guidance Centre continued, it would be unwise to outrage local opinion and the powerful Community Chest by being too radical.

Rogers cannily used a book review in *Mental Hygiene* to describe the kind of atmosphere of a well-run Guidance Centre, implicitly the kind he would run if given the chance. The book looked at the Institute of Juvenile Research in New York. There, everyone had to fit in with the Institute's procedures. Rogers sniped that a child was put through an inflexible round of interviews with psychiatrists, psychologists, teachers and recreation workers, and added, 'one feels it would be very disturbing to the Institute if the child' broke the unspoken rules, and instead of talking about his educational problems to the educational expert, and about his psychological problems to the psychologist, 'took a liking to [one] worker and started to pour his troubles out to them.' Rogers' Guidance Centre wouldn't organise therapy for the convenience of therapists.

The publication of *The Clinical Treatment of the Problem Child* was a modest success and it finally gave Rogers academic respectability. The writing of the book also gave him considerable ammunition in his battle for the Guidance Centre. Late in 1938, after many rows at the Chest, Rogers was appointed as its director. In public Rogers was extremely gracious. In private, he resented having to struggle so hard to get 'his' job.

The Centre opened in 1939. Ironically, Rogers would spend less than a year there. In *A History of Psychology in Autobiography* and in *On Becoming Carl Rogers*, Rogers made it seem as if he left Rochester almost as a result of an accident. He was offered a good job and he took it. Biographies can sometimes overcomplicate but Rogers did more than leave Rochester. He was about to leave behind 14 years work with children and start on a new tack. This requires some explanation and he never gave it.

Rogers had shown how competitive he was in his battles to get the Centre established. Why did he not now run it and prove he could deliver a useful service? Many research studies from Rochester that Rogers reported in *The Clinical Treatment of the Problem Child* indicate a high degree of success. He reported (p. 373) a study of 58 consecutive children admitted in January 1934: 13 of them had been placed in institutions. Of the other 45, only 3 failed to make a significant improvement in adjustment. In the study of 108 other children, he claimed that in 88 out of 89 cases where the courts had followed his recommendations for treatment, there had been success after 15 months. Psychologists today would glory at such statistics and secretly fret that the computer had gone mad or that some overkeen assistant had massaged or faked the data.

In the 1930s, despite Thurber's barbs, professionals were more optimistic about what interventions could achieve. Nevertheless, I want to suggest that Rogers had started to realise the statistics were not telling the whole truth. The correlations might look impressive but did they reflect reality?

Analysing the book closely reveals many more pessimistic outcomes. For example, one study of 163 children who were assessed found that only 91 were fostered. Over half of them (52 per cent) had to be removed from the foster homes because the placement was not working; this was rather bleaker than getting it right for 88 out of 89 children. The study of these 163 children is referred to less often in the book, however. It seems that Rogers, like many other child-welfare workers, was under pressure to produce positive results. He was wounded by the failures, by children such as Donald where to claim success was not a blatant lie but nothing like the truth either. Donald did not get into trouble with the police again but he achieved, at best, a sort of apathetic, passive survival.

In the book, Rogers reported on 26 individual cases in considerable detail. These were cases where he gave the child's background, described the assessment, explained why a particular option was chosen and then looked at the child's subsequent history. Four were in the summer camps and two had just been given sessions of play therapy. The data on the 20 other children were never put together, but looking at them as a group makes it plausible to argue that Rogers knew that many cases had less rosy outcomes than the statistics suggested. I briefly summarise and list 24 of these cases and their 'results'. (I have excluded the two play therapy cases, as the children were young and the therapist was not Rogers.)

Jim, no cure for his malicious behaviour towards the bed wetters, Walt and Bill.

Henry, camp did provide some confidence building.

Walt and Bill, no improvement through the camp.

Paul (p. 56) eight-year-old boy, stealing, no real change.

William, no final data but Mrs Thompson stood up to his tough behaviour.

Donald, a sour child, 'unsuccessful adjustment'.

Arthur, dull 12-year-old boy badly placed with intelligent foster parents, failure.

Franklin, ten-year-old with general delinquency problems, some success.

Elwyn, boy born to Flora, who was herself a product of the welfare system, conflicts with stepfather, removed from home. No real improvement noted.

George, 14-year-old, no real change in his 'adjustment'.

Kurt, 14-year-old, threatened his stepmother with murder, no final data, though Rogers noted that after a year of fostering, Kurt was starting to be on friendly terms with her again.

Floyd, oversexualised seven-year-old, successful 'adjustment'.

Unnamed 'Mongolian [Down's Syndrome] child', data provided only on how giving information about the disability to the mother was of some help. The child here was not helped but the mother taught not to have unrealistic expectations.

Arthur, ten-year-old, mother advised to change the way she punished him. A case of some success.

Perris family, Rogers described a complex set of problems and found that good progress had been made by the parents and three children, through the 'relationship therapy' approach. But it was the adults who were helped; Rogers said little about the three children.

Nye family, son still in despair because parents favoured his sister, no sign of success.

Unnamed father of 15-year-old child. Father continued to be dictatorial and aggressive, to vent the frustrations of his dull job, which was taken to indicate there was no real improvement.

Dorothy, nine-year-old girl, victim of incest, successful fostering and re-establishment of contact with father.

Philip, 14-year-old Polish lad ignorant of sex, moderate success at least in that he did not reoffend though he remained rather remote.

John, 14-year-old, very childish, relationship with parents much
    improved.

Robert, 17-year-old sex offender, in and out of treatment, failure
    as he reoffended.

There were five cases out of 24 in which the child was really
helped; in two cases, the parents were helped. In four other cases
Rogers described only a small improvement; in another instance,
Rogers focused on the parents. Eight out of 24 children showed
progress. The other cases were either total failures or, at best, a
containment of the situation, as with Philip. This was hardly rous-
ing success. Rogers was also a little disappointed that the
Component Factor Method had been taken up by at most 5 per
cent of child guidance clinics, a figure that hardly suggested his
scientific approach was making large numbers of converts.

The first study of the psychology of psychologists is that by
Anne Roe in 1953. Phenomena we now recognise – principally
that of 'burn out' – were not recognised in 1937, but that does
not mean they did not exist. Rogers had to face the fact he had been
over-optimistic; he had not managed to devise precise scientific
methods for treating disturbed and delinquent children. As director of the Guidance Centre, he was going to have great power
and responsibility over Rochester's problem children. What if the
wretched youths didn't improve any more than before? The question is – was he disappointed? He never admitted it, but Rogers
was never inclined to admit therapeutic failure. And when the
offer of a new job came, he was surprisingly receptive to it.

## Ohio and the Minnesota Mangle

The publication of *The Clinical Treatment of the Problem Child*
brought Rogers to the attention of the University of Ohio. Henry
Goddard, one of the pioneers of American clinical psychology,
had retired and the university wanted someone to replace him.
Ohio wanted a person who had experience of dealing with students
and their problems. Rogers did not quite fit the picture, but the
book had given him some stature. He was offered a job as a full
professor at a salary of just under $5000.

In his essay for *A History of Psychology in Autobiography*, Rogers said he was reluctant to leave Rochester but that Helen reminded him how badly he wanted an academic job. He wrote as if she persuaded him to take it. One can either accept his explanation at face value or, as I would suggest, wonder why Rogers, who always took such key career decisions himself, should now let himself be so influenced by Helen. It seems likelier that he was in any case ready to leave.

After his departure, Rogers wrote one paper that supports the view that he had doubts about how well the Guidance Centre would perform. Co-authored with Chester Bennett, the paper was a follow-up of 200 children, aged three to eighteen, who had been through the hands of the Society and the Guidance Centre. The follow-up was very negative, given the grand claims made in the mid-1930s. It showed clinicians were quite good at helping families to improve 'family emotional tone', but getting children to change was tougher. Rogers and Bennett admitted, 'we were most consistent in being overly hopeful in this area. Perhaps this reflects a true error in our thinking, a tendency to magnify the child's resiliency in shedding years of tension and conflicted loyalties especially if he enters a new and congenial family group.' Disturbed children did not mend their ways and therapy did not mend their minds but the children did learn to mind their words. They developed more 'self insight'. How did the therapists know? The children said appropriate things. From our post-modern perspective, it looks as if the children had learned to speak therapy, to discuss their problems in a language the therapists had taught them and which proved the 'young thugs' had insight.

Bennett and Rogers found there were many cases still where the courts did not follow the recommendations of the clinicians and that resulted in 'far less progress'. It was a pretty sombre follow-up. Rogers liked to say that the facts were always friendly but, in this case, after 11 years, they were also depressing (*American Journal of Orthopsychiatry*, 11, 1941, pp. 210–21).

Perhaps it was symbolic that Rogers and his family drove to Columbus, Ohio, in a blizzard. It was not hard for Rogers to see the break with Rochester as a triumph for himself, however, especially given the spectacular promotion to professor. He was entering the academic world at the top and would be spared the common-room politics young researchers had to manoeuvre through.

In Ohio, Rogers was dealing with adults and, often, with very privileged adults. He had to supervise the counselling services on the campus. The only link with his past was that he also was responsible for counselling in local schools. To illustrate the contrast with Rochester, it's worth recalling that the case study that made Rogers' name in Ohio – the case of Herbert Bryan – was one of a young neurotic would-be novelist. Bryan was articulate and went into therapy full of theoretical knowledge about rival therapies. He described one of his problems as having 'an axe crushing his libido' – an image that makes it clear he had read Freud. This was very far from the Smiths' 'I am most crazy' and the young toughs of Rochester with their 'foreign family habits'.

The middle-class students and 'patients' or clients were disturbed, unhappy, sometimes even suicidal but they managed to cope. They lived on campus and attended classes. They were rarely in trouble with the law or in danger of being committed to an asylum. One of the earliest portraits of an Ohio client is a long account by William Snyder, one of Rogers' first graduate students. The 'counsellee' was a neurotic insurance salesman who turned out to have intellectual ambitions. He asked for a reading list of 'decent psychology books'. He told Snyder he intended to abandon insurance and become a therapist himself as soon as he had cured his complexes (Snyder 1945).

The move to Ohio meant another change. Rogers' contract specifically stated he would have to teach for three-quarters of the year. As he started to map out his courses, he realised he had to put his ideas about treating adults into shape. He taught a course by the antiquated name of Mental Hygiene and another called Techniques of Psychotherapy. Rogers was determined to give his students a full review of what different schools of therapy offered.

By 1940, there was an enormous literature on psychotherapy in the United States. The arrival of many psychologists and psychiatrists from Nazi Germany had sparked even more debate. The ideas of Taft and Allen were causing controversy. Historically, psychoanalysis assumed the analyst had the knowledge to unlock the secrets of the psyche. The patient was ignorant. All he or she could do was report on childhood memories, dreams and associations; the therapist was the expert who would diagnose the patient's sickness. But did psychoanalysis work? Many critics thought not. Taft and Allen wanted therapy to help people find their true personality. Whether they conformed or not was irrelevant. In the question-and-answer sessions that followed his lectures at Ohio, Rogers was constantly being asked exactly where he stood on these controversies. It must have reminded him of his student days when he wanted to know where McGiffert stood on Kant. The students obliged Rogers, in fact, to refine his views. Unlike McGiffert, Rogers quickly made his ideas known and set out a position that he would refine further but never really change. He said sometimes he was a man who had had one big idea. It was in 1940 that he came to understand what it was.

In *On Becoming Carl Rogers*, Rogers suggested that client-centred therapy was born on 11 December 1940 when he gave a talk at the University of Minnesota. The place was chosen deliberately. Minnesota had a school of therapists such as E. G. Williamson and John Darley who believed therapists could persuade clients how to reshape their lives. Thorne (1992) claims Rogers showed great courage in taking his message about non-directive therapy to Minnesota, the capital of 'directive' counselling. Williamson, however, did not see himself as holding extreme views and came to resent the blunt distinction Rogers made between directive and non-directive therapy. Williamson denied he just told his patients what to do to solve their problems.

Psychologists are as good as anyone else at rewriting their careers. An examination of his publications and speeches of 1939 and 1940 suggests Rogers was wrong in making Minnesota the birthplace of non-directive therapy. By the time he gave his speech there, he had already outlined many of its key ideas in print. Williamson was not going to be surprised as he was well aware of Rogers' views. They had been published in a short piece, 'The Process of Therapy', Rogers wrote for the September 1940 edition of the *Journal of Consulting Psychology*.

In the *Journal*, Rogers addressed an audience familiar with the debates within psychotherapy and he described what he saw as good practice rather than as his own exclusive theory. He wrote, 'The time is perhaps ripe for various workers to formulate and describe the fundamental aspects of this process in order that such descriptions may serve as hypotheses to be tested by research.' As ever, Rogers wanted proof.

Rogers pointed out that before any therapy is possible the client – this seems one of the first uses of the phrase – 'should feel some dissatisfaction . . . some fundamental need of help.' Rogers added that if there were too many 'adverse social factors' – exactly the situation of many families in Rochester – then however well motivated a person might be, therapy was not likely to work since what they really needed was a radical change of circumstances, a new job rather than a new therapy. Confidently, Rogers then announced the main aim was to 'release and strengthen the individual rather than to intervene in his life.'

Rogers wrote of six crucial steps in therapy. I want to consider each in turn because they all point the way to Rogers' later thinking.

## The six steps

The first vital step in therapy was to establish rapport between counsellor and client. Rogers argued this was the heart of the therapeutic relationship and insisted the rapport had to be real. It was not a matter of 'tricks' of interviewing. The counsellor had to be genuinely interested in the client's problems and there must be 'a warmth of relationship'. Rogers looked briefly at the perils of counter-transference. Where Freud worried the therapist might be blinded by his or her feelings for the patient, Rogers accepted that the degree to which a therapist identified with the patient needed to be 'to some extent controlled' but he refused to over-agonise about it. One had to balance 'identification and objectivity' but the crucial thing was to build up trust and a 'personal bond'. These bonds had to be slowly destroyed at the end of the therapy but that was not so hard. Therapists should not be frightened of being warm towards their clients. The warmth, the rapport allowed the client to take the vital step in dealing with problems – to seek help for himself.

The second step Rogers insisted on was 'free expression on the part of the client'. Therapists had recently found new ways of encouraging catharsis and the release of feelings. In analysis, the patient lay on the couch and did not look at the therapist, the idea being to get the patient to associate freely. In fact, the situation emphasised the power relationship as the 'invisible' therapist looked down at the patient. The patient lay as if on an operating table. In the new therapy, the client and therapist sat face to face as equals, Rogers stressed. He also argued that interviewing techniques had improved so 'we tend to avoid that blocking of free expression which is so characteristic of our older case records.' The paper went on to break decisively with Freud and Jung; Rogers maintained that these blocks to free expression are not necessarily the result of repression of past traumas. Nothing proves it is always more therapeutic to deal with old material. Exploring the here and now can lead to as much progress as unravelling childhood terrors and frustrations. 'There seems to be no evidence that one is more therapeutic than the other since, in an important sense, all roads lead to Rome,' Rogers said.

Rogers defined the ultimate goal of therapy simply. It was – and this was his third step – the 'recognition and acceptance by the client of his spontaneous self.' The spontaneous self was often buried in fears and covered in masks. The therapist was no magician; he or she could not dissolve the fears and remove the masks. The best the humble therapist could do was to make the client feel accepted enough to recognise the root of the trouble, the fears and façades that crippled. Rogers said, 'in the rapport situation where he is accepted rather than criticised', the client should feel free to see himself 'without defensiveness'. The absence of defensiveness made it possible to acknowledge the real self with all its childishness, pain, aggressive feelings and ambivalences. It was not the wise therapist who achieved this breakthrough but the client. The therapist was the minor player whose 'only contribution' was 'to verbalise the feelings that are expressed in words or behaviour or play activities.'

The fourth step was for therapy to lead to the client's making responsible choices. 'Perhaps the sharpest difference between present day psychotherapy and earlier practice is the degree to which responsibility for the client's life is left in his own hands. The therapist at his best does not suggest, advise or persuade.' The therapist encourages the individual to take responsibility and often, hesitantly, the client starts to do so. For Rogers this was the beginning of real progress. The helpless client stops blaming his past, stops blaming others and 'finds that he can successfully take responsibility for himself and can direct his energies towards new, self chosen goals.' Rogers argued it was 'something exciting and dramatic' to see a client make such positive choices. It also made sense in terms of psychological theory. Clients were learning through doing, as the philosopher John Dewey recommended. 'Intellectual insight,' Rogers said, did not really change behaviour but feelings could transform lives. In this paper, there is the first mention I can find of 'growth', for Rogers talks of 'growth towards independence'.

The fifth step was 'the gaining of insight through assimilated interpretation'. Rogers sniped that therapists often made great play of their insights, but 'such interpretations, largely explanations of motives for behaviour, serve no useful purpose and may retard progress.' The 1940 issues of the *Journal of Abnormal and Social Psychology* carried a number of case histories that proved these profound interpretations 'may leave the individual wiser but little better to cope with his situation'.

Sixth, the final point of any therapeutic experience is education or re-education. Clients might need information and support from therapists because it wasn't easy to make new choices but if 'the initial aspects of therapy have been successful, this final period comes to a close quite naturally'. Both the therapist and the client would feel a sense of loss, but the client would now have the confidence to handle the separation. Perpetual therapy was not a good thing.

Last, Rogers insisted there had to be research using the latest recording techniques. If psychology were to help find 'answers to the problems of human relationships which are so urgently needed in a distraught world', it would have to allow scientific research in the consulting room. Analysts would have to permit their inter-actions to be recorded and studied, something they had always resisted.

This September 1940 paper may even have led to the invitation to Minnesota. The September issue was published at the beginning of the month. Theodore Sarbin, the chairman of the Minnesota programme, wrote to Rogers on 19 September saying 'at the present time much discussion centres upon therapy and the clinical psychologist's role in therapy . . . it seems that you have thought this problem through. We would like to have you address on this topic or a related topic.' Rogers was flattered by the invitation. The Minnesota meetings were distinguished. On 23 October Ernest Hilgard gave a critical résumé of Hull's theory of learning; on 19 February the speaker would be the famous therapist Charlotte Buhler. Many of the Minnesota audience on 11 December had read Rogers' paper to have some idea of their guest's position. He faced an informed audience.

Rogers made some small new points and offered one provocative case history. He insisted much more forcefully than in his September paper that it was wrong for therapists to give advice to patients. He told the history of a student who hated mathematics and who was told by his counsellor that he had to change his attitude. The intervention worked; the guilty student reformed. But was this the man's only or his real problem? Rogers criticised this form of 'therapy'. The audience did not know, as some of those on the platform did, that E. G. Williamson was the mathematician's counsellor. Williamson had discussed this case with Rogers privately. It was extremely aggressive of Rogers to use confidential information as part of his critique. Rogers did not name the client or the counsellor, of course, but Williamson was angry. However, Rogers was hardly Daniel in the lions' den. The audience wanted to hear what he had to say.

'The aim of the newer therapy is not to solve one particular problem,' Rogers declared, but rather to make it possible for the client to grow. By December that word, 'grow', was part of his routine vocabulary. Having outlined the ideas in his September paper, he went on to stress that therapy would allow clients to come to terms with their real selves. Then they would grow. The therapist had to create the climate, the rapport that allowed the client to find his or her voice.

As Rogers noted, some of the Minnesota audience were very much in favour, but this was the first time he saw an idea that was 'shiny and glowing with potential' provoke hostile reactions. To Williamson and to John Darley, this new emphasis on listening represented 'a great threat', he said.

Letters in Rogers' own papers suggest this was perhaps a little melodramatic. The President of the Chapter wrote him a fulsome letter, saying 'the viewpoint which you ably expressed has been in need of more emphasis with us' (letter of 16 December). Charles Bird, the professor of psychology in Minnesota, was also affirmative. 'The need for an approach to personality problems such as yours is extremely great in this university. Your emphasis should start some of these counsellors thinking and I hope the outcome will be less dependence upon the emotional glow as an index of useful work' (letter of 12 December).

Even John Darley, Williamson's colleague, was not that hostile. In a review of *Counselling and Psychotherapy* in 1943, Darley merely claimed that the value of direct therapy had at least been tested. He added, 'by over-characterising the outcomes of bad directive interview he [i.e. Rogers] does not prove the superiority of a good non-directive interview.' This was more a call for caution than a vicious attack.

It seems, in retrospect, that Rogers exaggerated the hostility his new ideas provoked. He was neither the first nor the last psychologist to do so. McClelland (1977) has argued that psychologists – especially of his and Rogers' generation – had an enormous hunger for power. They liked to represent small victories as massive achievements against overwhelming odds. Rogers' account of the birth of non-directive therapy in Minnesota is a nice illustration of that theory. Rogers' next step was much more likely to provoke resistance.

## Research

Rogers was determined to establish a programme of research into the process and outcome of therapy. He would spend much time over the next 25 years trying to prove that non-directive therapy works. He did not enter this area of study as a neutral but there is no suggestion that he ever faked his results. Getting therapists to agree to being researched meant overcoming some well-established resistances, however.

Even today there are many psychotherapists who are nervous of recording sessions of therapy; they argue it interferes with the process of therapy and is a breach of confidentiality. These concerns were present in the 1940s. In a footnote to one of the early published accounts of non-directive therapy (Snyder 1945), William Snyder, one of Rogers' first graduate students, noted his client had insisted on checking whether or not anyone would get to hear of his revelations. Snyder assured him everything he said was private and confidential, and then went on to publish a detailed account of the sessions. Snyder justified himself by saying he had so changed details of the identity of the client that no one could possibly recognise him. Rogers felt it was more important to establish the validity of his approach than to preserve confidentiality, for he never criticised Snyder. As long as the names and a few details were changed, clients could hardly complain.

Critics of therapy have always argued that the real reason for evading research into therapy is that therapists suspect their methods do not work and have never wanted to face the unpalatable truth. There may be two other reasons. The first is also unflattering. Once a transcript of a session of therapy is produced, the position of the therapist changes. He becomes a performer. One can judge his moves just as one can judge the moves of a chess player. The therapist is as exposed as the patient. The second reason is more honourable. I believe that its roots lie in Freud's early career. In 1885–6 Freud spent a year studying in Paris at the Salpêtrière Hospital under the great Jean Martin Charcot. Charcot had opened up the Salpêtrière. On his wards, patients were photographed, filmed and recorded. In the process, these patients often became objects of research. Freud had vivid memories of presentations such as that of Louis Vivet (for a good account of these see Ian Hacking's *Rewriting the Soul*, 1995) and may well have felt that these procedures robbed patients of their dignity.

Given Freud's influence, the importance he attached to confidentiality, and general defensiveness about just what psychoanalysis does achieve, it is not surprising there was so much resistance to objective research. In 1935, the Yale Institute of Human Relations had managed to persuade an analyst to have a stenographer present to transcribe an analysis. As soon as he arrived at Ohio, Rogers got hold of these transcripts and determined to press forward with his own programme. One graduate student in Ohio, Bernard Covner, was a radio ham who also had considerable experience in electronics. Rogers persuaded the university to put up $200 to purchase the equipment Covner needed. A series of 78-rpm discs was set up with two channels. Covner described the apparatus in detail in *Journal of Consulting Psychology* (Covner 1942).

The recordings would allow Rogers to study himself as a therapist and to improve his technique. They also would reveal the differences between non-directive therapy and other more traditional forms.

Rogers got a graduate student, E. M. Porter, to study 19 different therapists using the recordings Covner made. Porter was able to note a few significant differences. Of these 19 therapists, ten were described as directive and nine as non-directive. Porter was able to analyse the dialogues in detail and to describe the different techniques. The directive therapists were much more likely to ask very specific questions which required either a 'yes', a 'no' or some clear information by way of answer.

The statistics were telling:

|  | directive therapists | non-directive |
|---|---|---|
| questions eliciting yes/no answers | 34.1% of interventions | 4.6% of interventions |
| therapists explaining, giving information, telling clients what was wrong | 20.3% of interventions | 3.9% of interventions |

The non-directive therapists were more likely, however, to recognise a feeling the client had just expressed and 'to interpret or recognise' feelings or attitudes. Rogers became more hostile to interpretation only gradually; at first, it was still a routine procedure.

The directive therapists talked far more. Porter counted the number of words the counsellor spoke and the number of words the client spoke. The ratio of words spoken by the counsellor and the client ranged from 0.15 to 4.02. So, in the most directive case, the client said one word for every four the counsellor spoke. Some clients almost had problems getting a word in edgeways! On average the ratio of counsellor words to client words was 2.77 for the directive interviews and 0.47 for the non-directive interviews – a staggering difference.

Porter's research confirmed there really were two styles of therapy. Rogers pointed out that the different word counts 'make graphic the fact that in non-directive counselling the client comes "to talk out his problems". In a directive contact, the counsellor talks to the client.' In directive therapy, the client was even sometimes bullied to take a particular course of action, as the reluctant mathematician had been.

Rogers' new ideas attracted new students. Many were bored with the laboratory work and wanted their psychology to relate to real human problems. They flocked to Rogers' seminars. He was asked to supervise many doctoral students and did not realise that made many more senior faculty members jealous.

As well as the recordings, Rogers initiated sessions where, under supervision, students gave therapy. He claimed this 'practicum' was the first instance of such training in a university. He boasted, 'neither Freud nor any other therapist had ever managed to make supervised experience in the therapeutic relationship a part of academic training'. They would discuss in class the exchanges between clients and students and use them to refine their approach.

Rogers used some of the material from the Yale Institute research to point up the difference between his approach and the traditional one in the 1944 paper 'The Development of Insight in a Counselling Relationship'. His analysis was a factor in turning him against interpretation. In one exchange, the Yale analyst asks a patient what eating candy makes him think of. The reply is 'home'. 'And what does home make you think of?' The patient's answer was his mother. And his mother made him think of babies.

Analyst: Yes. And as you think of babies, what comes into your mind?

Patient: Girls, I guess. Barbara Royce.

Analyst: Barbara Royce?

Patient: Yes. (Very long pause)

Analyst: You see you have guilt about Barbara Royce. You undoubtedly have sex feelings about her and something within you has been trying to convince you that this is wrong. That same part of your personality is making you feel guilty about eating, about going down to the cafeteria, about asking for a second course, about eating candy. You see, it connects right up with the thoughts that come, that somehow you – one part of you is trying to make you believe that all of that is wrong. Well, we know it isn't. (Pause) Why shouldn't you feel that way towards girls?

Patient: Well, I don't see any reason why I shouldn't. That's just ... well it's all right.

Rogers argued all the symbols and hidden meanings were in the mind of the therapist who imposed his interpretation; the patient's role was passively to accept the expert's wisdom. How could that motivate the client?

As he was finding his voice, Rogers was also getting public recognition. In 1940, he became a member executive of the clinical section of the American Psychological Association and in 1941 he became an associate editor of the *Journal of Consulting Psychology*. All this must have been very gratifying, especially as it allowed him and Helen to attend his parents' 50th wedding celebrations in some style. At last he was as successful as his brothers. The golden wedding celebrations took place on 1 July 1941 at Warwood. Walter and Julia had invited 200 guests. Rogers and Lester talked a good deal, though they skirted around what Lester at least saw as their ideological differences.

Despite the focus on adults, at first Rogers maintained some interest in children and their problems. The university asked him to help with a survey of mental health in local schools. Rogers got a number of his graduate students to take questionnaires into schools. The results led to pessimistic predictions. Two per cent of children would spend long spells in prison; five per cent in psychiatric hospitals. On the basis of the responses, Rogers concluded that between 30 and 50 out of every hundred children 'will be maladjusted individuals failing to reach maximum efficiency or happiness'. These would be the Smiths of the future, emotionally unstable, petty criminals, a drain on the State. Rogers made a series of predictable recommendations – more counselling, more remedial work, more psychological testing and a helping teacher with specialist skills in coping with problem children.

This straightforward survey for the Columbus authorities (Rogers 1942) seems to have been Rogers' last formal study of children. He was now set on developing his vision of a new therapy.

## Counselling and Psychotherapy

Rogers had difficulty in getting *Counselling and Psychotherapy* published by Houghton Mifflin. Given the low status of clinical psychology, they were not clear what kind of students would use the book. Rogers' track-record as an author was not brilliant. *The Clinical Treatment of the Problem Child* had not sold particularly well. Annoyed, Rogers pointed out that his students at Ohio needed a book on counselling and threatened to take the manuscript to another publisher. Only then did Houghton Mifflin agree to go ahead but they printed only 2000 copies (1942).

The book shows the extent to which Rogers was becoming an

original thinker and an effective writer. He was beginning to bring case histories to life, and a critical part of the book was the story of Herbert Bryan. Rogers recorded eight sessions of therapy and in all about 600 different 'speeches' made by the counsellor and the client. His method in the book was to comment on the interventions and through that to expound his new ideas. Though I have argued that both Taft and Allen influenced his approach (and did so perhaps more than he was willing to say in his contribution to *A History of Psychology in Autobiography*), Rogers now branched out more radically.

Rogers first tried to clarify why Herbert was coming into therapy. Was it because of pressures that were being put upon him? Like many clients, Herbert tried at first to suggest he did not need or want help.

'Your purpose is to satisfy Miss G?'

'That's right. No, it isn't. It's for my own improvement.'

It was vital for Herbert to accept he was there of his own free will. Another early exchange stressed that Rogers' role was not to offer answers but to create a climate in which Herbert would have the freedom to find – or not to find – his own solutions.

'It's up to you.'

'It's up to me?' The client lingered on the 'me', Rogers noted. Until then Herbert had imagined he would be badgered into doing things against his will. Rogers pointed out the contrast with psychoanalysis and other traditional therapies.

Rogers also used the case history to emphasise how vital it was to encourage the client to say what was troubling him or her. Clients often wanted to make a good impression on therapists and to conquer their sense of shame and failure. The therapist had to make them see they were not being judged. Rapport was crucial to that. So was calm acceptance. At one point, Herbert said he would rather be dead than alive. This dramatic declaration did not panic Rogers. He did not try to cheer his client up or agree with him. Gently, he batted the question back. 'You'd rather be dead than alive. Can you tell me a little bit more about that?'

These first steps would encourage 'release' and, until there had been release, it was unlikely that the patient would make any progress.

The case history of Herbert Bryan still makes compelling reading and it contributed greatly to the success of the book. As he examined the transcripts, Rogers saw ways of improving his own therapeutic practice. The book got a very respectable reception, though some reviewers felt Rogers overstated the case for non-directive therapy. Many of his colleagues, however, saw the technique as immensely useful.

By the end of 1942, Helen Sargent of Northwestern University claimed that non-directive therapy was helpful even if one was limited to just one interview. She described her treatment of Mr A, who was a janitor. His daughter Betty was very withdrawn in school and the school doctor wondered if she was showing early signs of schizophrenia. Mr A and his wife were both worried and defensive. Only Mr A came to the interview. He said his daughter was 'awful pokey. You just can't get her going.' Sargent described how non-directive methods made Mr A much less antagonistic and how he started to volunteer information about their family life.

The move to Ohio changed Rogers' career. By the end of 1943, *Counselling and Psychotherapy* had sold nearly 10,000 copies. He had shown Houghton Mifflin, his parents, his colleagues, and himself, that there was a national audience for his ideas.

## Conflict

In Chapter 1 I pointed out that a number of psychologists of Rogers' generation reacted against their very religious upbringing. Rogers' rebellion was amongst the most extreme, it could be argued. His parents had believed not just in discipline but in being respectable, God-fearing citizens. Rogers was now embarked on a different journey. In Rochester, his task had been to make children reform and conform. Now the purpose was to allow people the freedom to find themselves. Only if they discovered who they were and who they wanted to be, could they be happy – and responsible. Rogers no longer needed his parents' approval. The young man seemed finally to have fulfilled his early promise.

Five months after Walter and Julia Rogers celebrated their 50th wedding anniversary, the United States went to war. It is an indication of how well known he had become since 1937 that Rogers was soon approached by the Air Force to counsel airmen. In 1928, looking for work at Culver Military Academy had been a sign of desperation. Fourteen years on, it was the military who came to Rogers to ask for help. He was only just beginning to realise the extent of his success. Rogers was determined that he would contribute to the war effort and, in doing so, make clinical psychologists 'second-string men' no more.

# The War and the End of Ohio, 1942–1945

Psychologists had played a large part in the American war effort in the 1914–18 war. Robert Yerkes, who is best known for his work on monkeys, had promoted the use of psychometric tests including the Stanford-Binet versions of IQ tests in order to select GIs. John B. Watson had been hired to design an effective programme of education so that young American soldiers who went to France would be 'continent' and avoid the seductions of Parisian floozies who were sure to have VD. American psychology had helped keep American boys pure – or pretty much so. Watson reported that many soldiers felt the military's educational materials were a bit exaggerated. There had been many other projects in 1914–18 that had shown the potential value of psychology.

The status of psychologists had fallen, however, during the Depression. A study in 1935 showed that nearly 200 psychologists – or 10 per cent of the 2000-strong membership of the American Psychological Association – were out of work and, more damning, the President of the APA felt some of them were unemployable. After Pearl Harbour, psychologists waited desperately for the call from the White House, but as D. S. Napoli has suggested in *The Architects of Adjustment* (1979), the government did not think they had much to offer and so it was the American Psychological Association that started to call the military and the administration to offer its expertise. The politics of psychology and conflicts between the rival professional organisations helped to weaken the discipline: by 1941, there were eight organisations claiming to speak for psychology, including the American Association for Applied Psychology (of which Rogers was a member) and the Association for Experimental Psychology. Members of the AAAP did not want the war effort taken over by experimentalists.

It was not clear what psychology had to offer. The main 'discovery' of the 1914–18 war had been 'shell shock'. In 1923, a British army report argued that many men who suffered from shell shock had not been recognised as having a genuine psychiatric condition. Strict commanders had court-martialled thousands, suspecting them of malingering; over 600 were shot for 'cowardice'. British psychiatrists went into the 1939 war determined that no man would be shot for cowardice if there was the slightest possibility he was ill. The American military had been briefed on this development by the British. Though the conditions were different in the Second World War, it soon became obvious that many soldiers and airmen were not coping well. Morale was poor. Rogers was running a counselling service at a major university and his family had good connections with the military because Bates & Rogers worked for the army. Early in 1942, Rogers was approached informally by the commander of a local air base. Too many of his pilot cadets never made it through training. The commander wanted help.

Rogers never made much of the work he did for the military for a number of reasons. He did not want to draw attention to the fact that in the 1950s he had been one of many psychologists whose work had sometimes been financed by the CIA. That hardly fitted his liberal image – especially as some of the projects were extremely controversial. Second, one of the best cases was never published. In the Library of Congress the typescript is marked 'for private circulation only'. Moreover, the largest project Rogers worked on was never published in its entirety because it might bring comfort to enemies – first the Germans and then the Soviets. These omissions mean that few have realised the extent to which Rogers' war work helped crystallise some of his ideas about therapy and taught him to communicate to non-psychologists: the commanders who read his reports were military men.

The first job Rogers was asked to do was to look at why many pilots failed training. Churchill's doctor, Lord Moran, had pointed out that pilots were likely to be the elite in a new war. They would be well educated, brave, competent at dealing with the latest technology and highly motivated. They were modern equivalents of medieval knights.

The Air Force took great care in selecting its men. Yet the number of aviators who were 'washed out' during pilot training remained high. The recruits were intelligent and well motivated, so if they failed to learn to fly, it must be either poor teaching or due to 'emotional patterns and reactions which block learning and performance . . . These emotional reactions may be in the form of anxieties, fears or unconscious desires to fail.' Rogers argued that the usual statistics did not show up these kinds of failure 'because they are concealed in more superficial categories,' concealed because these were embarrassing failures when young pilots were meant to be heroes in the making.

Rogers suggested counselling had much to offer because the pilots were capable young men with no psychiatric histories. Many had just finished college or interrupted their studies to go and fight. They were not mental cases. His 'counselling procedures' were 'applicable in dealing with most of the emotional blockings'.

The first trainee on the local air base whom Rogers was asked to help was a cadet he called J. L. Rogers seized the chance to show what counselling could achieve. It seems likely that J. L. came to the university for the sessions: these were recorded and the equipment would not have been easy to move from Rogers' 'lab'.

Cadet J. L. badly wanted to fly. He was highly intelligent. He had done well in the first weeks of training but he had started to have problems when he had gone up in an aircraft with an instructor. Suddenly J. L. could not cope so he was never allowed to fly solo. He was on the verge of being thrown out of the training programme because he was 'washed out'.

Rogers found J. L. to be an engaging young man of 21 who was bitterly disappointed, and rather mystified, by his failure. Learning new skills was not usually a problem. In the first two sessions, J. L. went over his family history which he initially described as very ordinary. In the third session, J. L. started to talk about problems he had with 'Dad' and hinted his father had 'whipped him' a lot. In the next session, J. L. explained his father had once told him to build a cabin and then 'whipped him again' because he did not like the way J. L. had constructed it. His father was always criticising him, always telling him how to do things. This was a problem Rogers could understand very well.

Fifteen sessions were recorded. In their case history Rogers and a graduate student, G. A. Muench, made much use of direct quotes from the counselling sessions. Some of these exchanges reveal how Rogers' technique had evolved. In the seventh session J. L. had started to think about how his relationship with his father, and his hatred of him, had affected areas of his life. J. L. had gone into the counselling sessions aware of his resentments but ashamed of them. He felt free to reveal his feelings but Rogers at no point offered an interpretation. He did not suggest there might be any connection between J. L.'s anger and hatred of 'Dad' and his performance as a pilot. It was J. L. himself who eventually brought the possibility up in the eighth session. J. L. said, 'Could it be that I still hated my father and it acted up in my flying?'

The essence of non-directive therapy is calm. The counsellor did not leap up and say 'Eureka, you finally got it.' This was a crucial insight but the procedure was to listen, wait and then feed it back to the client.

R: You wonder if perhaps your hatred for your father is tied up with your flying difficulty.

J. L.: Perhaps the instructor's role, showing me what to do – laying down the laws, his attitude, may have struck that note somehow because I hated him.

R: You hated the instructor.

J. L.: That's right and thinking it was my father. Here he was giving me something that had to be done. Oh yes, and another thing. When I was young I was always bawled out for something I didn't do. The instructor said on our last flight, 'Why didn't you do it?' I gave the same answer I always gave my father: 'I don't know.'

Rogers pointed out it was only towards the close of the ninth session that J. L. started to accept that his hatred of his father might be the block. J. L. went on to admit 'it seems logical but I was hoping someone else would point it out to me and then I could dismiss it immediately.'

Rogers did not comment that J. L. was obviously trying hard to reject the influence his father had had on him and looking to the therapist to solve the problem. The non-directive therapist believes the insight will come, in time, from the client. In the tenth interview J. L. finally found the courage to face what his insight meant. In the air, J. L. particularly objected when his instructor asked him to do gliding turns. J. L. admitted he was 'deliberately disobeying' and that he never gave the instructor a rational excuse. He simply would not do the gliding turns. Rogers did not look for the deeper meaning of gliding turns but encouraged J. L. to say more by a very simple prompt.

R: You didn't follow his instructions up in the air even when he was telling you.

J. L.: It seems that way. If you could apply that to other manoeuvres it might be ... I really want to fly though. Maybe that's why I haven't done so well – a dislike to follow directions. Gee, that's pretty well tangled up. Let me try and draw a parallel there. My instructor is to my father as my instructor's directions are to my father's directions. Even though I thought I wanted to, I really didn't want to.

R: You feel there's a parallel to your father's and the instructor's directions.

J. L.: I wanted to fly badly. That may be the block. That's probably the answer to the question. I guess I didn't have it formulated before today but I sure do now.

R: You feel that may be at the centre of your problem.

J. L.: That's right. Flying is grand. By George, why did I have to get an instructor that reminded me of my father?

J. L. added wryly that if he had not been handicapped by an instructor who reminded him of his father, he could have been the best pilot in his group.

Rogers emphasised that it was J. L. who came to see the instructor symbolised his father and that this identification made him fail even though he badly wanted to fly. 'It appears very clearly that the discovery of the significant relationships, the development of what we call insight, is an achievement of the client, not the counsellor.' Rogers added the counsellor's responses are 'particularly weak' but this did not seem to hinder progress. That only 'serves to emphasise the extent to which the client is the creative centre of the counselling situation' (p. 11).

In the 12th session, J. L. was asked to describe the block in more detail.

J. L.: Well, since I consciously felt that my father was in the cockpit and his tone would imply that it had to be done – that's the most important part and that's why I didn't like to do it. It makes me laugh but that seems the block that kept me from flying even though I did want to do it so much . . . If that's what it is, then instantly, in my next flight, all this I should be conscious of. I should know why I didn't carry out the instructions. Then the next flight it will all disappear and I'll be able to fly solo really well.

J. L. added that he had read of such cases but he never imagined he would be one of them. Rogers was now moving to the conclusion of therapy.

R: And you feel that you have everything straightened out now.

J. L.: I feel confident now. We seemed to go at the problem in a roundabout way but it's certain in my mind now and I'm hoping and expecting that this won't take even a little bit of time to clear up in my flying.

R: You feel certain of the solution to your problem now.

J. L.: It's all solved. I think it is. (Short pause) I know it is.

R: Then perhaps you feel that you won't need any more contacts.

J. L.: Well I'm going to prove to them that I can fly. I'm confident now more than anything and I'll do it.

There had been nothing wrong with J. L. He had been pitchforked into an intense learning situation which evoked destructive aspects of his past. Rogers' success in this case led to a more substantial project.

Rogers was invited to go to Buckingham army air field at Fort Myers in Florida to look at the psychological condition of gunners. There were rumours in the Air Force that the stress of flying bombing missions was so great that most gunners wanted to leave the service. Rogers' eventual 90-page report, 'A Study of Returned

Combat Gunners and Their Utilisation in the Flexible Gunnery Training Programme', remained a classified document for 20 years. In some ways that is not surprising because Rogers confirmed the high stress levels among the gunners at Fort Myers. Once the Cold War started, such a finding could boost Soviet morale.

Rogers interviewed gunners when they returned from missions in Europe. Two-thirds of the men resented their assignments and 60 per cent were found to be 'seriously malassigned', which led to poor morale. In addition, 74 per cent showed either a moderate or severe degree of 'combat stress'. A significant number had no idea why they were fighting the war, though Rogers did not give precise figures even in this top-secret document. Fort Myers was not a happy ship.

Rogers studied a hundred combat gunners at length. Psychological tests showed they were a stable and intelligent group when they entered the service. In combat, however, 24 per cent were so stressed they did not perform well as gunners. On their return from active service, 12 per cent were still so distressed they were not really efficient while 46 per cent showed what we would now recognise as symptoms of post-traumatic stress; they were restless, had nightmares and could hardly ever sleep through a night. Rogers profiled a number of the men in some detail. One was S/Sgt George Macintosh.

Macintosh was not one of the worst cases. He was 24 years old and had spent eight months in the Mediterranean as the lower turret gunner on a B17. He had flown over 50 missions in Sicily and Italy. Macintosh came from a small town in Pennsylvania, from 'a family characterised by satisfactory relationships'. He spent a lot of time at the local YMCA but his family didn't stop him going to dances. He had started to date girls when he was 17.

In 1937, Macintosh got work as a machine operator in a plant that made defence equipment but he didn't like it much. In the summer, he worked for a small company which made, and hung, awnings. It was only temporary but he enjoyed it. The third summer, the owner of the awning business had to go away and he put Macintosh in charge. He handled the responsibility well. Macintosh enlisted soon after Pearl Harbour and was sent to train as a gunner. Seven weeks before being sent off to the Mediterranean, he married.

Macintosh was sensible and had experienced enough missions to have useful insights. He said 'flak is the thing that bothers gunners the most. You can shoot at the fighters but there's not a damn thing you can do about flak.' He could cope with the tension when they were airborne but 'the hardest part is sitting on the ground waiting for a mission'. Combat had its effects. He now tended to get angry and emotional for no reason. 'I cry at the movies where I would never have done before.' At the YMCA, Macintosh had loved being part of a gang, and being part of an air crew was similar. He suggested that in his unit more officers than enlisted men had cracked up partly because the officers did not form a gang and 'were less social, more melancholy and did more daydreaming'. These particular officers were not sticklers for discipline. Macintosh contrasted the fairly relaxed atmosphere in his squadron with another one where a 'strict Army man' was in charge and 'that strict formality kept the fellows on edge. They had 80 per cent casualties and I think their "edginess" was part of the reason.'

Macintosh had not been specially religious until he started flying. 'I found one thing – a fellow gets a lot of religion over there. Fellows who have not been to church for ten years begin to do so. When you come through a tough mission, you feel that somebody is up there beside yourself.' Macintosh was thoughtful, independent and mature. Rogers suggested he would make an excellent gunnery instructor. But even Macintosh had been disturbed by his experiences. He was quite angry about civilian attitudes because in the States civilians 'don't know there's a war on. If they had seen the people over there – they think they do without things in this country but if they had seen the people over there! They just don't know how swell it is over here.' Macintosh did not want to go back on combat duty 'when there are so many fellows sitting around here and not doing a damn thing.' One of his main complaints was that he had been sent from one posting to another when he had returned from the Mediterranean. He had spent two days in one fort, some time in a tent, some time at another base. It was confusing and unnecessary.

Rogers found Macintosh's fury to be typical; there was much resentment against civilians. One gunner who returned home went to a football game and said that 'all that life and gaiety and luxury – it makes you so mad.' Another gunner was so exasperated with a man who had not been drafted that he knocked him down. In the paper, Rogers quoted Macintosh saying he wanted to bomb at least six American towns because 'these people don't know there's a war on'.

These men were not isolated malcontents. Two-thirds of the gunners resented military discipline; 40 per cent felt hostile towards civilians. Rogers added that uncomfortable as these attitudes might make people, they had to be faced by society. He recommended the same techniques he used with his clients. Military personnel had to be given the chance to express their anger freely; there could not be any taboos in the counselling room even if the country was at war.

Rogers recorded 16 findings and made 14 recommendations in his restricted report. Many related to how the Air Force should improve assigning personnel to particular jobs. He continued to be firm about the need for research. His study led to a hypothesis, 'that men who do not show excessive combat strain' are those with good family relationships, higher IQ, religious faith and who can draw strength from their group. Rogers suggested that only 31 per cent of those who came back ought to be considered for posts as gunnery instructors. He drew up a list of qualities instructors should have. They should have emotional stability, at least a high-school education and no visible wounds. They should have flown ten combat missions and have an AGCT Score of 110. The AGCT was a test that combined items taken from the IQ tests with special questions relating to gunnery.

Rogers recommended that the military listen to what the gunners had to say, though he phrased it more tactfully. Returning gunners should not be allowed to remain idle for six months while the administration discovered what it wanted to do with them. He also suggested officers should use techniques of leadership that 'will utilise the informal "team loyalty" attitudes developed when the men were fighting'.

Rogers carefully screened out the confidential material and got permission to publish some findings in 1944. In 'The Psychological Adjustments of Discharged Service Personnel', he also complained of 'the indiscriminate labelling of men as psychoneurotic and the like' (p. 691). One officer had to endure hearing his psychiatrist reveal that he suffered obsessive compulsive neurosis and that he was in danger of living in a world of his own. The officer was terrified this meant he was likely to go mad.

Rogers was spending a lot of time away from Ohio, which caused him some problems with his colleagues. They felt he was neglecting his main job. That got worse when Rogers was asked by the United Services Organisation to help train counsellors. The USO was a welfare organisation that used volunteers to advise servicemen and their wives. It was based in New York and arranged tours all over the country. Rogers was enthusiastic. He liked travelling and he would have a large audience for his ideas. The exercise would also teach him to think about how to put his message across to a lay audience.

In the workshops, Rogers outlined the problems servicemen and their families would face. These would always be individual. One wife would be shocked the first time she saw her husband coming home disabled. Another woman would be frantic because she and her husband quarrelled when he was on leave. Was divorce the only solution? USO volunteers often counselled desperate wives who had not heard from their husbands and didn't know if they were dead. For some that meant total despair; for others, maybe, guiltily, new life.

The travelling led to one unpleasant situation. In the 1940s, the colour bar operated in most southern States. One of the workshops took place at a hotel in a southern city. When Rogers got to his hotel he found that it refused to serve blacks – and some of those the USO had sent for him to train were black. Rogers had a fight with the hotel, pointing out that if black men were good enough to die for their country, they were good enough to be served in their wretched hotel. The ban was lifted. It was one of his first 'political' acts.

One of the pamphlets Rogers wrote for USO volunteers shows he had learned to be much more direct in his writing. In it Rogers advised volunteers to use self-restraint as 'that is an important part of the art of healing'. Good counsellors did 'not try to play the role of God.' He then gave a list of what to avoid. It's worth quoting: 'Don't give advice. Just help the man to talk out his problems more clearly and think them through more adequately. When we are tempted to say "Now if I were you" we should remember that we have already expressed the fallacy which undermines all advice. You are not this other person.'

Rogers went on to list other 'don'ts' including:

Don't reason with him. People are not argued into behaving in different ways.

Don't judge him. The purpose was to help, not to pass judgement.

Don't pity him. Pity only helped the worker. The best thing to offer the client was acceptance.

Don't identify with him. 'We do not help people by wading into the same emotional puddle in which they find themselves,' Rogers noted pithily.

Don't moralise.

Don't talk too much. The evidence from recordings of therapy showed that the most helpful counsellors let clients talk for three-quarters of the session. 'Let it be the client's hour, not yours.'

In these snappy phrases, Rogers gave an excellent description of the basics of non-directive therapy – and one which the volunteers found easy to understand.

Almost from the start of American involvement in the war, psychologists began to worry about how to integrate people back into civilian life after the war ended. It was, Rogers learned quickly, a real issue. Many of the airmen were very anxious about returning home; many felt they would lose a great deal as soon as they got out of the service. The military had given them status and purpose. Air Force colonels and majors would return to 'Civvy Street' with 'sharply reduced pay and prestige'. One man told him he would stay in the military because that way he would be guaranteed his three square meals a day. For others 'normal' life would be very boring. They would return home depressed and unsure what to do with their lives. Psychology ought to be able to help them readjust, Rogers suggested, and he offered USO volunteers some principles to guide their counselling. First, the soldier should be treated as a whole individual. Rogers noted 'no veteran is merely a man without a leg or an AGCT score of 95 . . . or a compulsion neurosis or a personality profile.' It was important to see servicemen not just in terms of their abilities, as in the First World War, but in terms of their 'emotionalised attitudes'. Rogers also emphasised the need to allow servicemen to express their hostility; this was especially true for men who had become disabled. Rogers attacked the trend to treat the disabled casually; 'the handicap' would have caused 'deep emotional disturbances'.

Lastly, Rogers warned against the dangers of allowing returning soldiers to become dependent. He warned that 'one of the deeply frightening things about the future is the growing distrust in the individual's ability to do things for himself.' Healthy individuals had to be independent, not like the dreadful Smiths.

With the publication of *Counselling and Psychotherapy*, Rogers had established a national reputation and he was now recognised as a man with distinct ideas of his own. Jessie Taft and Frederick Allen remained well respected in the profession but it was increasingly Rogers who was seen as the voice of the new therapy. His work for the United Services Organisation was a great success. At the end of 1944, however, his position at Ohio was becoming more and more difficult, partly because of his absences working for USO. When USO offered him a job as director of counselling, Rogers was not sorry to leave the university. Conscious of money as ever, he noted that the salary was good. He and Helen moved back to New York with their children. This time, they did not have to live in the city's smallest apartment to make ends meet.

Unfortunately, Rogers had not realised how boring his new job would be. He found himself moving all over the country repeating exactly the same course, giving the same message time after time. He eventually worked out he had conducted workshops for 655 USO trainers. His research into how therapy worked had to be put on hold. It felt very frustrating.

In the spring of 1945, Rogers was approached by the University of Chicago. They wanted to set up a counselling centre – and they had a proper budget for it. He would be a professor at a major university and he would also have the chance to set up a Guidance Centre again. And his salary would be a princely $8500. He had no hesitation about accepting.

Rogers never suggested the war had given him important opportunities. Yet, the pressing needs of the military made it possible for him to test his new therapeutic techniques on a wide variety of people – most of whom would not have sought psychological help in normal circumstances. The war had also taught Rogers something he would never forget – how to make his ideas clear to people who had no training in psychology.

In returning to Chicago, Rogers was going back to his childhood home. The city would prove to be less lucky for him than he expected.

HAROLD BRIDGES LIBRARY
S. MARTIN'S COLLEGE
LANCASTER

# Chicago, 'losing the self only to find it'
## 1945–1956

In Chicago, Rogers claimed, 'our basic views about the helping relationship came to fruition' (Rogers 1965, p. 364). Soon after arriving, he started to win national recognition as the founder of non-directive therapy and as a spokesman for a so-called 'third force' in psychology. The third force rejected behaviourism as too narrow and psychoanalysis as too esoteric and, frankly, a little unAmerican in its pessimism. With Fritz Perls, founder of Gestalt therapy, and Abraham Maslow, advocate of peak experiences, Rogers was seen as the leader of 'humanistic psychology'.

In 1945 Rogers and Helen took a house at Stony Island Avenue within walking distance of the university. David had gone to Cornell to study medicine and Natalie had also left to study at Stephens College. Rogers often walked home to have lunch with Helen.

The Counselling Centre was given as premises the south and west sides of Lexington Hall. Rogers was still wary of psychiatrists and, though he would be providing mental health services, he recruited no psychiatrists. This annoyed the faculty at the university's well-established school of psychiatry. But Rogers vowed his Counselling Centre would have nothing of the asylum to it: students would come for help voluntarily.

## A democratic centre

The Counselling Centre would cater not only for the students but for the whole local community. Rogers looked for staff who could offer a range of skills, and recruits included Nathaniel Cantor, who would become well known for his work on employee psychology, and Virginia Axline, who already had a reputation as a play therapist.

When his contract was signed, Rogers insisted he would not become the director of the centre but its executive secretary. He argued he did not want to be burdened with making every single decision; the atmosphere would be healthier that way. In Rochester, he had been very insistent on his own position. Seven years later, titles and positions didn't matter so much as he was achieving national recognition. Rogers often said educational institutions were too rigid and hierarchical. He devoted much energy to creating a style of management and leadership where he, as leader, did not always get his own way. Eventually even the receptionists and the maintenance staff had some voice in Counselling Centre decisions.

As soon as the buildings were ready, Rogers made sure all the 12 counsellors lent a hand in redecorating. It was good fun, Rogers claimed, but it was also a way of developing group spirit and making everyone feel they had a stake in the place. The university Chancellor, Lawrence Kimpton, did not query his new professor's 'radical' notions but let him get on with it.

Kimpton was astute in giving Rogers so much latitude. By 1945, as American psychology reorganised itself after the end of the war, it was clear Rogers would have a large role to play. He saw the need to unite its many squabbling professional organisations. Experts in animal perception accused counsellors of being irrelevant anti-scientists; counsellors snarled that experimenters lived in ivory towers, only interested in the minutiae of their narrow research. What was the point of finding out how rats learned to discriminate different coloured triangles? Would that reveal anything about the human condition? So much dissent discouraged government and industry from investing in research.

Even among the counsellors, there were rows and rivalries. A survey of 50 practitioners in Los Angeles, published in 1946 (*American Psychologist*, Vol.1), shows that psychobabble – and psychobicker – were already flourishing in California. The survey found that 18 per cent of therapists practised some form of psycho-analysis, 12 per cent practised Jungian therapy and a further 12 per cent spiritual analysis; 12 per cent also practised non-directive therapy. The remaining 44 per cent offered patients an eclectic mix of diet therapy, 'common horse sense', hypnosis and courses in 'public speaking' – a kind of elocution therapy, it seems.

Rogers was well placed to build bridges between the warring interests. He understood the anxieties of counsellors but he also believed psychology had to be scientific, a view he shared with Robert Yerkes, who had promoted the testing of GIs in the 1914–18 war, and who was probably the most influential person in the discussions about the future shape of the American Psychological Association. He took a liking to Rogers and saw in him a future leader for psychology.

The negotiations about the future of the Association meant many trips to New York and Washington for Rogers. There were more rows, as members of the different specialisms haggled over a new constitution for the APA. In 1946, the *American Psychologist* finally announced agreement had been reached. The APA would be one organisation representing all psychologists. The journal's editorial warned members would have to learn to tolerate one another's foibles.

Rogers got his reward for the hard work. One of the first actions of the new board was to decide who the next set of presidents would be. By 1945, Rogers had published two books – one of which was successful. Many men had better claims to be the next president of the APA, like Yerkes and Clark Hull, one of the most distinguished learning theorists. Carl Rogers would hold the office from September 1946 for a year. Previous presidents of the APA included William James, James McKeen Cattell, E. B. Titchener and William MacDougall. Rogers was joining a very distinguished band.

The presidency involved a good deal of work away from Chicago. The Centre could manage well when Rogers was absent because he had recruited, and encouraged, some very able staff such as Thomas Gordon, who could take responsibility. Rogers was sincere in not clinging to the role of the traditional leader. He had no intention of cutting back on therapy, for he saw the counselling room as his laboratory and said that his seven to ten clients a week gave him most of his new ideas.

## More stress on empathy

In the negotiations before he was appointed, Rogers had asked for the university to provide some backing for research – and help in raising money. The moment he was appointed the Centre's executive secretary, Rogers started to approach such organisations as the Rockefeller and Ford Foundations for support to study the effects of psychotherapy. He realised raising funds would take time and, in the meantime, he did the best he could by scrounging from the university. He was a capable scrounger and got the money to record and transcribe many therapy sessions even though that cost over $250 for every client. Expensive as they were, these transcripts were pure gold, an essential database that made it possible to analyse and re-analyse what went on in the consulting room. One reason so many of Rogers' books remain fascinating is their excellent use of telling quotes from the transcripts.

The transcripts offered more than good quotes, however. They offered a replay of what had happened between the counsellor and the client. Rogers didn't have to rely on his fallible memory. With the recordings he could listen again and again to what had been said – and not said – to clients. He could become his own harshest critic. As non-directive therapy required great self-discipline, this was vital. The technique was subtle. The therapist had to listen for every nuance and suppress the urge to intervene too much, to offer false reassurance. The recordings made it possible to pinpoint moments when the counsellors deviated from these rules.

The transcripts made Rogers aware of his mistakes and, unlike many pioneers, he did not flatter himself he was always the best therapist, the Napoleon of counselling. Rogers was humble enough to believe he could learn from others and he saw one of Axline's sessions in which she was dealing with a client called Gil as a model of how to stay non-directive under stress, and of how not to panic when a client was begging to be told what to do (Rogers 1951).

In the sessions, Gil said she didn't have the courage to kill herself ... 'and if someone else would relieve me of the responsibility or if I would be in an accident I . . . I just don't want to live.'

Axline's response was measured, 'At the present things look so black to you that you can't see much point in living.'

Gil went on to say that she felt totally worthless but that in her dream world, she was a wonderful person. Again, Axline did not panic but reflected back to Gil that she felt 'it was a tough struggle, digging into this like you are.'

The crunch came when Gil asked Axline if the process of therapy wasn't a total waste of time. The temptation would be for the therapist to reassure her frightened client and promise to make her better in time, but Axline said, 'It's up to you, Gil. It isn't wasting my time . . . but it's how you feel about it.' It was up to Gil if she came, if she came more often or less often. Gil panicked again. Was Axline suggesting she come more often? (It is one of the curious features of a number of the cases Rogers records that clients seem to be scared of being asked to come more often.) Axline didn't rise to that either. She just said, 'You say you may be afraid of yourself – and are wondering why I don't seem afraid for you.'

Gil: (short laugh) You have more confidence in me than I have . . . I'll see you next week (again a short laugh) maybe. (Her attitude seemed tense, depressed, bitter, completely beaten. She walked slowly away.)

There are similarities between Gil's despair and the moment when Herbert Bryan said he wanted to kill himself. But Bryan soon retracted. Gil was more on edge and Rogers recognised the situation had been harder for Axline to handle. He said he learned courage from Axline.

As his practice developed, Rogers insisted on the need to accept the client completely as a human being. That mattered more than sticking rigidly to any techniques. To accept the client was an absolute, a moral and personal imperative, but Rogers ignored an inevitable problem. What do you do if you feel ambivalent about a client? How do you cope if they are so demanding, irrational and exasperating you can't be positive or warm? And what if, very unprofessionally, you hate them?

Despite this omission, the Centre in Chicago soon established itself. That secure base gave Rogers the confidence to explore areas beyond therapy, such as personality theory and how society could use psychology now that the war was over.

## Gestalt influences

After 1945 Rogers started to compare his ideas with those of the Gestalt school. The Gestalt psychologists studied perception and claimed the brain tended to look for patterns and to impose them on ambiguous stimuli. One classic Gestalt stimulus is a figure that can be seen as the bottom of a jar, or a candlestick, or two faces peering at each other. Just as 'by active effort' one could see the picture as two faces rather than the bottom of candlestick, Rogers said, so by active effort the counsellor could see the problems clients reveal from different angles.

At times, Rogers also likened his approach to that of the child psychologist Jean Piaget. In the 1940s, American psychologists knew little of Piaget's contemporary work, and publishers were bringing out translations of his early books dating from the 1920s. Piaget argued children's intelligence develops in stages. The most important stage, from Rogers' point of view, was the so-called 'pre-operational stage'. Before seven, the child is egocentric and can't grasp logical operations. He assumes, for example, that the way he is now seeing an object is the only possible way. A four-year-old looking at a toy mountain from the front will not realise the mountain will look different from another angle. Subsequent research has cast doubt on Piaget's findings (Bryant 1972) but, in the late 1940s, he seemed to have proved the essentially egocentric nature of the young child. Piaget argued this was not a failure on the part of the child; the seven-year-old just did not have adult perceptions and the adult's frame of reference. Psychologists shouldn't compare the child's performance with that of the adult. Their task was to get inside the mind of the child, to see things with seven-year-old eyes.

Rogers claimed Piaget's philosophy was useful for therapy. He gave as an example a client who recalled an ideal childhood. The client said, 'I find myself and my thoughts going back to the days when I was a kid and I cry very easily. The dam would break through. I've been in the Army four and half years. I had no problems then.' The client remembered his service in the Philippines when he had been nice to local children, buying them ice-creams, a memory that made him dissolve into tears.

Conventional Freudian technique would lead the therapist to ask himself what Rogers called external questions. What could he do to get the client talking? Is his lethargy 'a type of dependence'? What might make him unable to make a decision? The client is talking of a 'dam bursting', which makes it sound as if there is a great deal of repression. I, the wise Freudian, must dig into those early unhappy childhood experiences to get at the truth.

If, instead, one tried to perceive from inside the client's mind, if one adopted Piaget's view that the child perceives differently, or, to put it in another language, if one changed Gestalts, the comments would be different. Examples, Rogers suggested, would be:

You're wanting to struggle towards normality.

It's really hard for you to get started.

Decision-making just seems impossible to you.

You want marriage but it doesn't seem to you to be much of a possibility.

You feel yourself brimming over with childish feelings.

Being nice to children somehow has meaning for you.

But it has been – and is – a disturbing experience for you.

These interventions were more like prompts than questions. They sympathetically nudged the client to reveal more. In some ways Rogers was anticipating the best ideas of R. D. Laing who, in *The Divided Self* (1961), tried to explain what schizophrenia felt like from the inside. This required imagination and guts. Many dismissed the very notion as idealistic and bizarre.

Rogers went to the Menninger Clinic in Topeka, Kansas, to give a talk on 15 May 1946. Karl Menninger was a psychiatrist who was appalled by the standards in most State asylums and he had pioneered treatments that were radical in their own way. Rogers outlined his ideas on empathy knowing full well he and Menninger had major theoretical differences. Where Rogers was essentially optimistic about the ability of clients to cope, Menninger was pessimistic. He believed patients – and Menninger talked of 'patients' – were sick and needed treatment. There was no point in trying to think or feel the way they did. Empathy was the wrong approach.

Rogers was intrigued by his differences with Menninger because he had considerable respect for him and the work being done in Topeka. Wanting to make a good impression, Rogers prepared meticulously for the meeting.

In his presentation, Rogers returned to the need for research. He wanted to know enough to be able to state the necessary and sufficient conditions required for therapy to work. He told his audience at the Menninger Clinic, 'It may be said that we now know how to initiate a complex and predictable chain of events in dealing with the maladjusted individual, a chain of events which is therapeutic and which operates effectively in problem situations of the most diverse type' (*American Psychologist*, 1946, pp. 415ff). The three stages were catharsis, insight and solutions. Having expressed their feelings (stage one), clients could develop insight (stage two), make positive choices about their lives and so arrive at solutions (stage three). Faith in the client was vital. Rogers argued that far too many therapists ignored the reality that 'within the client reside constructive forces whose strength and uniformity have either been entirely unrecognised or grossly underestimated.'

The debate between Rogers and Menninger continued until both these pioneers were old men. Menninger had one advantage, though. As a psychiatrist, he had seen schizophrenics throughout his professional life; Rogers had worked so far only with clients who could more or less manage in the outside world. He knew little about asylums and the despair they generated.

Rogers adapted the talk he gave at the Menninger Clinic to form part of his presidential address to the APA at the September meeting in 1947 in Philadelphia. Rogers entitled it 'Some Observations on the Organisation of Personality'. The lecture reflected his interest in Gestalt psychology. In therapy the client could reorganise the most important of all perceptions – the perception of self. Rogers outlined the case of Miss Vib. Her behaviour changed, she changed, as her ideas of herself changed. Subjective truth mattered as much as objective truth. The implications were radical, Rogers suggested, and affected every aspect of psychology. Psychometric tests, for example, aimed to be objective, measuring skills and personality, but they ignored the most important reality, the self-perception of the client.

Rogers proved a good choice for president of the APA. Though he was still only 44, he could identify both with counsellors (who felt patronised by the academics) and with the experimenters, who feared the scientifically illiterate, woolly-minded therapists would take over the profession. The 1947 convention was a success.

Almost as soon as Rogers got back to Chicago, he was off for a period to Los Angeles where he was visiting professor at the University of California. It's a measure of how well his radical, democratic management was working at the Counselling Centre that there were no great crises while he was away from Chicago.

The first report of the Centre covered the period from May 1946 to May 1947. The Centre was thriving; it had seen 1059 clients. Two-thirds were students; 819 stayed for counselling. The Centre had a flexible policy on charging. Clients were told a session cost $17.50 but were asked to pay what they could afford; some paid nothing at all. Most clients came once or twice a week. The Centre had five recording machines installed. Rogers continued to hope that proper analysis of therapy sessions would improve practice and prove that therapy worked.

His colleagues Donald Grummon and Thomas Gordon (*American Psychologist*, 1948, pp. 166–71) noted, however, 'the evaluation of psychotherapeutic results has been a very puzzling problem for the Centre as for elsewhere.' They had started by asking counsellors to rate on a scale of 1 to 9 how well they felt the therapy sessions went, but many counsellors did not think these ratings were very meaningful. One good sign, however, was that only about 11 per cent of cases were 'interrupted', with clients dropping out. Grummon and Gordon remained optimistic; there was an ongoing research programme; it would soon provide definite answers on 'evaluation'.

Rogers now managed to pull off one small and one spectacular triumph. First, he published a pamphlet, *Dealing with Social Tensions*, with a small Philadelphia publisher, Hinds, Hayden & Eldridge. It was his first attempt to set out how psychology could save the world. He started with a dramatic statement, 'It is well recognised by all intelligent men and women that the life of civilisation hangs in the balance.' Human beings had to learn to handle 'the tensions, frictions, antagonisms, and fears which divide social and cultural groups into warring camps' much more constructively. Non-directive therapy could be used to resolve social and political conflicts. Part of its process was to make unconscious hostilities conscious, to bring them out in the open. Often conflicts were not what they seemed: too many unacknowledged feelings and prejudices made people irrational. If one could teach politicians to make their unconscious fears conscious, they would handle conflicts more maturely. They would posture less and negotiate better.

In the pamphlet, Rogers outlined the work of his colleague at Chicago, Nathaniel Cantor, who had been studying trade union organisers. Cantor found they sometimes compared the traumas of negotiating with bosses with the traumas of marriage. One man said there were times when he wanted to kill the 'labour relations men' he had to bargain with because they made him so furious. Just as his wife did. And for many of the same reasons, too. The labour relations men would never decide anything without going back to their bosses; his wife would never decide anything without going back to her mother. This homely comparison offered insight into political conflicts, Rogers suggested. It might even help defuse the Cold War. He was succumbing to an old dream shared by Freud, John B. Watson and many other lesser men. They believed their particular brand of psychology could transform international relations. The social psychologist Gardner Murphy wrote in 1938 that psychology could prevent future wars by getting Hitler, Mussolini and other dictators in for treatment. A dash of therapy and they'd be happy and stop slaughtering innocents. Rogers' fantasy seemed to be that if he could only get Truman and Stalin into client-centred therapy, the Cold War would melt into a warm peace.

## The *Journal* issue

Rogers' second triumph was academic – and very spectacular. He was on the editorial board of the *Journal for Consulting Psychology*. At the end of October 1948, he and his colleagues from Chicago offered the *Journal* a set of papers on their research findings. Rogers persuaded the editor to run them all together and devote the June 1949 issue entirely to their work. It was part of Rogers' campaign to prove how well non-directive therapy worked. Modestly but also cannily, Rogers pointed out his introduction to the issue was 'non-objective', and readers needed to be warned of that. He hoped psychotherapy would become more of 'a science applied with art' than an art which 'has made some pretence of being a science.'

But Rogers had more than sharp phrases to offer. The scientist in him could not resist setting out what he called a calculus of therapy. This was a set of equations which claimed that 'if conditions a, b and c are met then a process of therapy is initiated which involves changes y and z in the attitudes and personality of the individual.' As mathematics, this is both simple and totally speculative since it is notoriously hard to measure his y and his z, personality and attitudes. But the June 1949 issue offered many equations, some remarkably complex, which dangled a splendid carrot – the marriage of the human insights of Freud with the precise scientific ones of Einstein.

The 1949 issue was the first of four attempts by Rogers to bring together research data on the outcome of psychotherapy. It deserves to be examined in detail because so many of the methodological problems recurred over the next 18 years. Rogers' inability to solve these problems would eventually push him to seek new ways of doing therapy.

The June issue consisted of eight papers by different authors. Rogers wrote the introduction, contributed to the longest paper and masterminded the enterprise. The papers drew on data from the recordings of therapy and on a sample of 32 cases seen in Chicago from May 1946 onwards. There were three main questions. How had non-directive therapy evolved since the early 1940s? What kind of changes did it produce in clients? Was it effective in curing them?

The first question was the only one that was easy to answer. Julius Seeman compared the utterances of therapists in 115 interviews in 1948 with a similar study of their utterances in 1942 and 1943 (Snyder 1945). Seeman concluded that counsellors were becoming more non-directive. Only 15 per cent of their statements were directive. Interpretations were made in under 3 per cent of sessions, Nathaniel Raskin found. Counsellors stated the problems clients suffered from less and highlighted the need for empathy more. Non-directive therapy was becoming a clearly defined technique, something Rogers had every reason to feel proud of.

The questions of how people changed and whether therapy was working were harder to answer. Establishing a proper basis for such studies is still a conceptual quagmire today. Who decides what constitutes improvement? Rogers had amassed enough transcripts to look in some depth at 32 or 33 cases. The clients were not just given counselling sessions but also asked to take a variety of tests, including the Thematic Apperception Test, the Rorschach Inkblot Test, the Willoughby Emotional Maturity Scale and the new Q-sort technique. The Q-sort was a subjective psychometric; it tapped the inner perspective. Subjects were asked to choose a number of a set of cards. Each card had a statement on it such as 'I am nervous' or 'I like reading books'. By piling up a set of cards one could arrive at an individual profile of personality which conventional tests did not do. But the Q-sort also produced quantifiable results which made it possible to generate statistical comparisons between different individuals and also between the way someone responded before, and after, therapy.

Rogers also thought it useful to ask two friends to rate how each client's behaviour had changed. The professionals might be fooled in the clinic but not people in the client's everyday life. In theory, this was a well-designed set of parallel studies. Six of the papers claimed that non-directive therapy was succeeding. Butler and Gerald Haigh argued that after therapy clients felt their self was closer to their ideal self; Rosalind Dymond argued the studies with the Q-sort showed clients were less anxious and less depressed. Haigh argued that clients became less defensive during the course of therapy.

Rogers and his colleagues presented data from ten of the patients in an elegant series of graphs which confirmed this positive pattern. Individuals who became less defensive did improve on the Q-sort and were rated as having had successful therapy by their counsellors. I want to look at two of the papers in more detail, however, to illustrate the methodological difficulties Rogers was facing.

Defensiveness is precisely the kind of attitude therapy seeks to change. Using common sense, Haigh reckoned clients were defensive when they showed denial, withdrawal, justification, rationalisation and hostility, amongst other less than lovely behaviours. Haigh counted up the instances of these from the transcripts. Miss Vib seemed to have been almost wholly cured of defensiveness. In her first session, Miss Vib notched up 24 instances of defensiveness but she then improved. Over the next eight sessions she scored between two and six defensive episodes per session. In her final session, Vib's score was a perfect zero – no defensiveness at all.

Other clients, however, seemed to get more defensive as therapy progressed, such as Bav, who started out with a score of five in his first session and ended with the impressively neurotic score of 32.

The results were inconsistent. That was perhaps inevitable. But Haigh made things worse by his interpretation of what the scores meant. The most blatant example was his analysis of Mr Que. Mr Que scored zero from the beginning to the end of the therapy. In his transcripts, he never betrayed any hostility, withdrawal or other sign of defensiveness. His perfect 'non-score' did not lead Haigh to wonder if Mr Que might be a therapy-addict who loved to spend two hours a week talking about his problems. Perhaps Mr Que didn't need help. Haigh never considered such alternatives. No, Que's total lack of defensiveness was a ground for suspicion. Haigh argued, 'it seems probable that Mr Que is operating on a high level of defensiveness to the extent that he never communicates any of his vulnerable views or concepts . . .'

In other words, in the case of Miss Vib a score of zero was a sign of cure; in the case of Mr Que it was a sign of disease.

Other clients scored low, just one or two instances of defensiveness a session, but Haigh did not ask himself whether these low scores might not, as in Que's case, mask an appallingly high defensiveness. No, these low scores were proof of cure.

Despite these inconsistencies, when Haigh put all the results together, the conclusion was not satisfactory. Defensiveness did not decline significantly from the start to the end of therapy. He was then driven to compare the five best cases with the five worst cases. Now he was at last able to achieve results with a level of statistical significance that proved something positive was happening. The best clients had indeed become less defensive than the worst patients, but just who were the best and worst patients, and how was that decided? By the counsellors! The only measure Haigh used was their ratings of the therapy sessions. It's hardly surprising that therapists would rate clients who became less withdrawn and less hostile as having improved more than clients who remained withdrawn and hostile. Haigh's findings are circular. But Haigh ignored that and concluded individuals were 28 per cent less defensive by the end of therapy than they had been at the beginning. Rogers did nothing to draw attention to these methodological problems.

Rogers' summary of the results also has its oddities. There seems to be a discrepancy between the number of cases he says he is talking about and the number he lists. It matters because the sample is so small and because there was something of a scandal about the theft of data in a later study by one of his collaborators. Rogers writes of 33 cases but in fact the number of 'names' of patients he lists comes to only 32. Very usefully, Rogers provided the basic raw data for each of the clients; it is only this laudable practice that makes it possible to re-analyse these cases. For each client, Rogers got the following measures – the counsellor's ratings of how well therapy had gone, the client's own ratings, ratings from two friends on how the client had changed and a score of Emotional Maturity.

Rogers reckoned that an outcome score of 7–9 meant that the treatment had been a success; a score of 6 showed moderate success; and a score of 1–5 suggested failure. Clients were rated as soon as they had finished treatment and then asked to return to the Centre for a six-month follow-up. The majority were students on the campus and it should have been easy to get them to come back for the follow-up. In fact, nearly half the sample did not reappear. It is not reasonable to proceed as if those who did not show for follow-up never existed. In fact, Rogers reported scores for only 17 clients at the six-month follow-up. This would have mattered less if ignoring the 15 absent clients did not alter the results so much.

The data Rogers presented of the follow-up were as follows:

*Counsellor ratings at follow-up*

| | |
|---|---|
| 7–9 (highly successful) | 7 cases |
| 6 (moderate success) | 5 cases |
| 1–5 (failure) | 5 cases |

So, Rogers argued, 12 patients out of 17 had benefited from therapy. But when one looks at the raw data Rogers provided, a very different picture emerges. Of his initial group of 32 patients, four had dropped out before the end of therapy. Usually that is counted as failure. Of the remaining 28, the ratings at the end of therapy were as follows:

*Counsellor ratings at end of therapy*

| | |
|---|---|
| 7–9 (highly successful) | 10 cases |
| 6 (moderate success) | 5 cases |
| 1–5 (failure) | 13 cases |

To sum up, at the end of the sessions of therapy, a truer picture is that 15 cases out of 32 seemed to show therapy was successful, just under 50 per cent. Six months later, the results were worse. In three of these 15 successful cases, the clients had relapsed. Only 12 out of 32 could be said to have benefited. The harsh truth is that only a third of the cases were positive. And that was the judgement of the counsellors themselves (not impartial individuals). Looked at this way, the findings hardly point to a major therapeutic triumph.

The raw data reveal other contradictions. The highest score in terms of counsellor ratings was given to 'Bene', but the client himself and one of his friends felt he had actually become less adjusted during the course of therapy.

In public Rogers always had an admirable attitude; his mantra was 'the facts are friendly'. The role of the scientist was to inch towards the truth. Favourite hypotheses might have to be tossed away but that didn't matter. Although very commendably he published the raw data which make it possible to re-analyse his results, Rogers seems, as many psychologists before and after, to have massaged his results consciously or unconsciously to arrive at the conclusion he most wanted. He was, as he had warned, non-objective. The interesting question is the same as at Rochester in 1938. Was Rogers aware that his study pointed to a much more pessimistic conclusion than he was claiming? At Rochester, Rogers was looking back on ten years' practice; with the 32 cases, however, it was work in progress. Admitting that the truth was not the truth he hoped for would be a slow, painful process.

Professionally, the June 1949 issue was a great success. Rogers realised he needed a larger sample and, ideally, a control group. The university was not in a position to fund such a comprehensive research effort but, after the June 1949 paper, Rogers put together a proposal to seek funding from both the Rockefeller and the Ford Foundations. The Rockefeller Foundation was initially more impressed.

In 1949, Rogers signed the contract for the book that would become *Client-Centred Therapy*. The book was to include a further report on the research but Rogers wanted to look at some other issues, too, so he recruited three co-authors. One of them, Elaine Dorfman, was a specialist in play therapy. On 11 March Dorfman told him she could not write the chapter and added that her father had died. Rogers wrote her back a very generous letter, offering to wait till she was ready to finish the chapter – he was more interested in having the book right than having it on time – and also offering to loan her $1000 against future royalties. Dorfman was staggered by his kindness: $1000 was a massive sum. This offer was all the more remarkable because Rogers was in the midst of one of the most serious crises of his life. He thought he was going mad.

## Breakdown

Between October 1948, when the papers were submitted to the *Journal of Consulting Psychology*, and June 1949, when the issue appeared, Rogers went through a desperate personal crisis. In May, just before the appearance of the issue, he fled from Chicago and cut himself off for three months from the university and psychology. Rogers wrote a little about this flight in his chapter for *A History of Psychology in Autobiography*; he also spoke to Kirschenbaum about it; there is one letter in the Library of Congress which offers some useful new insights. Rogers became so desperate he wondered if he had any future in psychology or psychotherapy. Ironically, the immediate cause of his breakdown was his attempt to treat a schizophrenic woman. He seems, surprisingly, to have got out of his depth.

In 1949 a client he had worked with in Ohio moved to Chicago. Rogers believed this woman could be classed as a schizophrenic. Rogers never revealed how, or why, this woman moved to Chicago and renewed her therapeutic contact with him. As we have now become accustomed to revelations of therapists sleeping with clients, the question of whether sex was at the root of this crisis has to be asked. I can't claim to have found an answer. Clearly, Rogers was not calm in dealing with her. He vacillated between being professional and being 'warm' and 'real' – an interesting dichotomy since his technique was based on being warm. The woman became troublesome. She insisted on at least three therapy sessions a week. She would turn up on the doorstep of Rogers' house. 'She said she needed more warmth and more realness from me,' Rogers wrote. But he then added a sentence which suggests he was over-involved. He said, 'I wanted her to like me though I didn't like her.' He certainly didn't manage to conceal his dislike which not only made the woman feel very hostile but also made her feel 'dependence and love' toward him. It wasn't surprising she felt hostile. Her therapist preached unconditional positive regard, care, warmth and the need to accept clients. But he made it plain he didn't like her.

Her behaviour 'completely pierced' Rogers' defences and he started to experience her as 'a real drain on me'. Stubbornly and perhaps a little vainly, he felt that he, the famous therapist, should be able to do something for her. So, he allowed the contacts to continue long after they had ceased to be therapeutic and when, as he put it, 'they involved only suffering for me'.

Rogers began to lose confidence in himself and got to the point where 'I could not separate my "self" from hers.' He said he lost the sense of his own boundaries. His client had a dream which he saw as important; in it, she was a cat who was clawing Rogers' guts out. She did not want to do that but the dream had emotional truth, Rogers felt. She was destroying him.

Rogers turned to his colleagues and warned them he felt he was going insane. In this state he saw a strange film (unfortunately he did not give its title) and he thought that when he was locked up and started to hallucinate, people would imagine all his ravings came from within. He would know better. The film had started the hallucinations. Rogers understood he was in deep trouble but he still continued to treat her because he 'recognised her desperately precarious situation on the brink of a psychosis and I felt I had to be of help.'

In the weeks that followed, Rogers' fear of having a breakdown became intense. He did little to seek help until he was quite desperate. This delay meant that he allowed himself to act in what seems an unforgivable manner. Rogers went to see a young psychiatrist, Louis Cholden, who agreed to take this patient at an hour's notice. Rogers then pulled what he confessed was a 'desperate trick' on her. Cholden came in at a prearranged signal at the start of a session. Rogers said a few words to introduce them and left. He almost ran out of the room. Within a few minutes, the patient had burst into a psychotic state – perhaps not that strange, given the extraordinary way in which Rogers had treated her. The woman claimed Rogers was related to her in some way. Later on, she tried to gain entrance to his home and left a large sign on the front door saying she had called.

Rogers went home and told Helen he had to get away. Within an hour they were on the road. They stopped at a shop and Rogers bought some beer. He felt quite astonished he had been able to do something as simple as that because he felt 'fairly far gone'. He and Helen made for the house by Lake Seneca. He would be safe there. It was the middle of May.

Helen comforted her husband and Rogers felt he owed her a great deal. She kept on telling him he would come out of it and she listened and listened as he started to talk about some of what he had experienced. They walked in the nearby hills and she taught him painting as best she could. Rogers said Helen stood by him for the second time when many wives would have become angry and frightened. A few years earlier – and Rogers was not specific as to the date – he went through a year when he felt 'absolutely no sexual desire – for anyone'. There didn't seem to be any medical cause but Helen simply accepted him, sure that it would get better. Rogers never explained what might have caused either the loss of desire or its return.

After about ten weeks, he felt able to go back to Chicago. He was still far from well. He felt inadequate as a therapist and worthless as a person. One of the staff, Oliver Bown, told him he was still obviously in distress. Bown added he was not afraid of offering Rogers therapy, and Rogers had the sense to see he needed it. The sessions with Bown taught him he was not such a monstrous failure and, Rogers added, he became less frightened of accepting and giving love. He never said what happened to his client, however.

Kirschenbaum (1979) suggests Rogers was still bearing the scars of his childhood and that the true causes of his breakdown had little to do with the schizophrenic woman but were deep in his past. It was his mean Calvinist parents again. Rogers told Kirschenbaum, 'Nobody could love me, even though they might like what I did. I was an unlovable person. I really was inferior but putting up a big front' (p. 193). There was still a lot of the shy, insecure boy in him and he had been wounded so badly he had not yet outgrown his childhood – and childish – self.

This interpretation (which Rogers certainly approved and possibly inspired) is not the only possible one, however. Trying to explain the cause of a breakdown nearly 50 years on is a risky exercise. I think, however, there are two other possibilities. First, there is the telling phrase that the schizophrenic woman had 'pierced' his defences. In some way, she saw through Rogers' façade to a guilty secret. He did not like her. Yet she was a client, she had a right to unconditional positive regard. Rogers didn't even care enough to conceal his dislike. No wonder his unloved client wanted to claw his guts out. No wonder he was frightened by her. She made him see he was breaking one of his sacred rules. The guilt and shame were more than he could bear, so he fled and he had to reject her so brutally to let all his repressed anger out. His client became his victim.

Today, the need for therapists to 'ventilate' is recognised; in the 1940s, therapists were supposed to be powerful and problem-free. 'Acceptance and empathy became the therapist's tools for helping the client ... Little or nothing was said of the therapist's feelings . . .' (Kirschenbaum, 1979, p. 191). Therapists had no way of dealing with their ambivalences towards clients. For all its openness and democracy, the staff meetings in Chicago don't seem to have included sessions in which therapists could talk about the stress caused by listening to their clients. That stress may have contributed to Rogers' breakdown but there is, of course, another possibility.

Was the schizophrenic woman who followed Rogers from Ohio just a client, or is it possible Rogers had an affair with her, rejected her, then felt guilty and frightened (the university would have sacked him if anything of the sort had come out) and that the panic led him into a breakdown? This possibility is hinted at in a letter that his brother Walter wrote to him on 1 June 1949 just after he had escaped with Helen to Lake Seneca. Walter had heard from their mother that Carl had had a 'nervous breakdown'. Walter added, 'I think I can sympathise with your present state to a very considerable degree because I am sure that I've been through the same mill altho probably in a lesser degree.' Walter went on to say that in the years since the end of the war he had spent much time 'in a tremendous blue fog, depressed, discouraged, confused and useless. I twisted and turned every which way trying to escape I know not what but trying to escape I am sure.' Walter went on to add, 'a couple of women may have had something to do with my previous predicament' and that for a period 'life was just too complicated to be worthwhile'. Walter admitted he had often been on the verge of 'packing off to talk to you' and added that perhaps now, Carl, 'you should come on out and talk to me (Strictly non non directive advice).' Rogers didn't take up this offer.

It should be stressed that there is no firmer evidence for suggesting that Rogers had been sexually involved with this client, but Walter clearly thought a woman might have been the cause of his brother's breakdown.

None of this trauma emerged in the 1950 annual report for the Centre where Rogers wrote the Centre was thriving, partly because the democratic style of leadership allowed people to express their feelings, which meant that, at times, 'we have been annoyed with each other.' That was a rare privilege in the buttoned-up America of the early 1950s. Rogers did not say in the report that he believed he emerged from the crisis a better therapist than before. But that came to be his view. The crisis had made him grow.

The reserve that was so much part of Rogers' make-up was also evident in his relationships with his children. They imagined their parents were the perfect married couple. David Rogers was studying medicine at Cornell from 1944 and he became engaged to Cora, known as Corky, Baxter in 1945. Much of the time he was away David wrote to his father, whom he admired enormously, but he was always on the defensive about Corky, first because she had had a traumatic relationship with her mother and, later, because she drank too much.

Natalie made a smoother marriage. In January 1950, she became engaged to Larry Fuchs, a young political scientist. Larry would turn out to be a marvel, for he often read and commented on Rogers' manuscripts. Corky was a burden, however. She was often on the phone for hours as she wrestled with her own inner demons. Helen had a thorny relationship with her and David started to worry about the way his parents saw his wife. He felt they were unjust to her. Being a successful psychologist, Rogers was realising, was no guarantee of having a happy family, and the family would make more and more demands on him.

## Client-Centred Therapy

Rogers' growing reputation was confirmed by the publication of *Client-Centred Therapy* (1951). Rogers wrote only part of the book himself; chapters were contributed by Elaine Dorfman on play therapy, by Nicholas Hobbs on group-centred psychotherapy and by Thomas Gordon on group-centred leadership. In Part One, entitled 'A Current View of Client-Centred Therapy', Rogers reported on the latest results of the research project. In many ways, the book dealt with themes that Rogers had already explored. But there were three interesting developments. Though Rogers was not yet ready to deal with the hostility therapists might feel towards some clients, he did start to think about the therapist's own attitudes.

Empathy was no longer enough; the therapist had to enter into the client's 'phenomenal world' to perceive the world with the client's eyes. Rogers quoted Nathaniel Raskin, who said the counsellor's task was 'to absorb himself completely in the attitudes of the other'. This was hard enough with distressed students, but now Rogers tried to apply non-directive techniques to psychiatric patients at the local hospital, Billings. Recovering from his 'breakdown' had given him the confidence and the ambition to try.

One of the accounts of treatment in *Client-Centred Therapy* is of a depressed male schizophrenic, Mr Vac, at Billings. Vac clearly was given to brooding silences, for the session started with his saying nothing. The therapist said it was fine, Vac did not have to speak but the therapist was there to listen, at hand, available, all empathy. This outburst was followed by a very long silence of 17 minutes.

After that Mr Vac did not become much more verbal. The recordings show that he uttered only the following phrases:

'No, just lousy.'

'No.'

'No. I just ain't no good to nobody, never was, and never will be.'

'Yeah. That's what this guy I went to town with the other day told me.'

'Uh-hum.'

'I don't care though.'

Despite this almost total lack of communication, Rogers felt they were getting somewhere as Vac did collapse into tears at one point.

Entering the client's phenomenal world did not mean accepting everything the client said but it did mean being alert, as 'the client-centred therapist aims to dip from the pool of implicit meanings just at the edge of the client's awareness.' Again, Rogers hardly mentioned the considerable demands that made on the therapist. The chapter on the attitudes and orientation of the therapist has such headings as 'The Basic Struggle of the Counsellor' but it deals only with the moral choice the counsellor has to make, the moral choice of having faith in the client. Rogers was still not ready to face the question of how therapists struggled to handle clients they disliked.

The closest the book comes to dealing with this issue is a long statement by Oliver Bown. Bown suggested it was important for the therapist to acknowledge his own needs in the therapeutic encounter and to recognise his own anxieties and repressions. However, Bown turned this not into an analysis of the ambivalences therapists felt but into a plea for being there with the client and experiencing the marvel of that contact. No client was too demanding, too unlikeable or just too awful. Bown's piece suggests rather that if a therapist dislikes a client, the therapist is incompetent and should feel guilty. So Bown only reinforced the taboo and no one faced the issue that probably contributed to Rogers' distress in 1949 and 1950. Rogers emphasised the upbeat. He said moments of real empathy were wonderful and that 'to enter deeply' with the client 'in his confused struggle for selfhood is perhaps the best implementation we know for indicating the meaning of our basic hypothesis that the individual represents a process which is deeply worthy of respect' (Rogers 1951, p. 45).

It is strange – and in some way rather splendid – that Rogers believed therapists must 'take it like a man' and not admit any pain. Contrast that with the rather neurotic preoccupations of many modern practitioners who fret about their own psyche and worry about the impending threat of burn-out. Yet, it does reflect a curious aspect of Rogers' approach: denial of the bad.

*Client-Centred Therapy* did, however, confront a problem that was fudged in the June 1949 papers – that some patients actually got worse. Rogers admitted (p. 18) that this was a 'sobering finding', for it meant that 'sincere attempts by experienced therapists damaged the personality integration among some schizophrenics.' Rogers returned to this problem in the chapter 'The Process of Therapy' and said only one study examined the reasons why therapy might fail with some patients. It was unrealistic to expect final conclusions with the small samples used so far. Rogers pleaded for time.

In *Client-Centred Therapy*, Rogers tried to develop a theory of personality. He often rhapsodised about feelings. Intellectual insights were much less important, he claimed. Yet his theory of personality draws on a complex mix of influences. He used existentialist philosophy, the ideas of Gestalt psychologists and the work of Jean Piaget to arrive at 19 propositions. Rogers' personality theory was sophisticated and developed a number of interesting angles. The only comparable theory then being developed was that of George Kelly, who devised the Repertory Grid Test, a subjective test that had many of the same aims as the Q-sort.

Rogers stressed the importance of the perceptions an individual has of his or her self. To understand a person, the psychologist should look not at their behaviour but, rather, at their subjective view of themselves. Objective reality was less objective than it appeared. The Gestalt psychologists were among the main influences on Rogers. He built on their ideas to suggest that human beings try not only to make sense of the way they perceive the outside world; they try to make sense of their *inner* perceptions, too.

As experiences occur, they are either perceived and organised in relation to the self or ignored because there is no apparent relation to the structure of the self. Rogers used his knowledge of

Piaget to develop this notion. If experiences do not fit with the structure of the self, they are either not symbolised (which seems to mean their very existence is denied) or else they are symbolised in a distorted manner. This was rather like the Freudian idea of repression. Despite his doubts about Freud (*Client-Centred Therapy*, p. 505), Rogers did not quibble with this concept. Then Rogers argued, psychological maladjustment exists when 'the organism denies awareness to significant sensory and visceral experience. They are not seen or heard and so, consequently, they are not symbolised and organised into the gestalt of the self structure.'

The reviews for *Client-Centred Therapy* were more than respectful, and confirmed Rogers' position as the spokesman for humanistic psychology. The book had just appeared when Hans Eysenck published what remains a seminal paper in the critique of psychotherapy. Eysenck (1952) argued that psychoanalysis and psychotherapy had no curative effect and that most patients who improved did so as a result of spontaneous remission. He listed a plethora of methodological flaws in the research on therapy.

Eysenck's paper was published in the *Journal of Clinical and Consulting Psychology*. Though Rogers had always said that the facts were friendly, the paper annoyed him. At various points in the next few years, Rogers claimed he had refuted Eysenck. Eysenck, for his part, believes still that the paper raised issues that psychotherapists have consistently refused to deal with.

On top of these professional problems, Rogers' family now entered a period of many troubles. Some of the best insights into Rogers come from the letters his children wrote. In 1952, David Rogers was serving as ship's doctor on the USS *Leyte* and was writing to his parents regularly. In one letter, David finally found the confidence to raise matters that had been troubling him for a long time. Corky had a problematic relationship with her own mother and looked up to Helen. But Helen did not return much love. David accused his mother of 'absolutism' and of minding too much that Corky was often disorderly. He also complained his parents were so content in their marriage they had little sense of the struggles facing other couples. 'Perhaps it is so few times that two people find the happiness and satisfactions that you two have and that it glows so that others are bound to feel dazzled and small,' David wrote. They were less tolerant of those 'who were taking somewhat different tracks to get there.' David Rogers' letter is eerie because it shows how little of his father's conflicts and troubles were then known to his family.

As Rogers had become more successful, holidays no longer meant Seneca. From their late forties, Rogers and Helen usually took holidays at the start of the year and went in search of the sun. Rogers liked to swim, snorkel, take photographs, sometimes paint and, most of all, find time to think. He often got up early, at 6 a.m., to write. In 1952 they went to Mexico. In a letter of 15 January, which he sent to his secretary with instructions to copy it to a number of family and friends, Rogers said they had found a dream cottage within six hours of arriving at Taxco for just $100 a month. He admired the look of the white houses in the moonlight and, one morning, when he was supposed to be concentrating 'on a weighty and constructive paper', he decided instead to describe the marvellous fiesta they had attended the evening before. There was romantic music and 'girls with round, smooth faces, men with dust and straw in their hair from sleeping on the ground . . . men with faces like bandits . . . girls in their confirmation dresses . . . it was unforgettable.' The letter is interesting. On the one hand, Rogers was bothering to keep in touch with his children and his family; on the other hand, there was a strange impersonal touch to it. No one deserved a letter all of their own.

The only problem on the holiday was that Helen developed an infected cyst and had to go into hospital. It was irritating to have to worry because Rogers, perhaps a little disappointed by the interminable problems of psychotherapy research, was developing interest in a new field – creativity, which he linked to a concept he called 'openness to experience'.

Three months after they got back, Rogers was invited to the Association of Marriage Guidance Counsellors' annual meeting where he found himself sparring with Albert Ellis, the founder of rational emotive therapy. The subject was psychotic patients. Ellis warned it was idealistic and futile to apply Rogers' methods to them, as they were mad and sick. Rogers ignored Ellis. Rogers did not want to limit his work to neurotic patients and pressed on with plans to offer some long-term patients at Billings a course of non-directive therapy. That took some negotiating with the psychiatrists.

In the summer, Rogers read Kierkegaard, who was a revelation to him, Sartre, A. N. Whitehead and tried to master two physics books because he was interested in keeping up with a different science. He also worked his way through Donald Hebb's *The Organisation of Behaviour* (1949). Rogers was preparing to branch out.

## Constructive creativity

Throughout the summer of 1952 Rogers prepared some rough notes on creativity which he worked up into a paper he gave in Granville, Ohio, at a conference that took place on 5–8 December.

Rogers' starting-point was a critique of contemporary society. The American way of life and of business valued conformity. Creativity was dangerous. Only certain privileged individuals – such as managers – were allowed to aspire to that. The workers had to work like drones. Rogers claimed this ignored a basic human need, the need to self-actualise, to achieve as much of our potential as possible. Every person strove not just to be, but to become. You couldn't be satisfied if you didn't reach your authentic selfhood. (Instead of working to have a better car and a better fridge, you had to work to have a better self.)

Rogers also claimed there was a close link between creativity and what he called openness to experience. Defensiveness and repression, the evils faced in the counselling room, destroyed the possibility of creativity; it was only 'when the individual is open to all of his experience', in the pink of mental health, that 'his behaviour will be creative.'

On the face of it, this theory is bizarre. Long ago, Aristotle noted that genius it usually touched by madness. Many artists have been very disturbed. Those who have needed formal psychiatric care include van Gogh, Nietzsche, the great French comic writer Feydeau, Ezra Pound, the dancer Nijinsky, the American poet Robert Lowell, the composer Robert Schumann. Some who were never committed to asylums suffered from alcoholism and depression, including Edgar Allan Poe, Ernest Hemingway, Dylan Thomas and Tennessee Williams. James Joyce spent some time in analysis. Some theories link creativity and manic-depressive psychosis. Rogers ignored all this cultural history, however. Creative people were psychologically healthy and their 'creativity may be trusted to be essentially constructive'. Rogers cited Socrates as an example. Aristotle, who knew men who had known Socrates, might say genius was touched with madness but, for Rogers, Socrates was 'notably non-defensive and open to experience'. He just frightened the Athenians with his radical educational reforms.

Rogers was himself a good photographer and did some painting and sculpting; his son was an excellent amateur sculptor; Helen had studied art. So this was not a man who knew nothing about art or the history of artists. He had just been reading the incorrigibly gloomy Kierkegaard. Yet his theory of creativity flies in the face of the facts and seems remarkably naive. Like much of Rogers' thinking, it accentuates the positive and avoids the negative.

Rogers did make one attempt to deal with the problem of disturbed artists by suggesting the creative person does not have to be open to all experiences and thus in perfect psychological health. A great painter, for example, could be exceptionally receptive to form and colour so that it would be only in their way of seeing that they are totally open to experience. He wrote, 'This means that instead of perceiving in predetermined categories – trees are green, college education is good, modern art is silly, the individual is aware of this existential moment as it is, thus being alive to many experiences which fall outside the usual categories (this tree is lavender; this college education is damaging; this modern sculpture has a powerful effect on me).'

Unfortunately, Rogers never asked about other areas of the hypothetical great painter's life, areas that might be dark, closed, sick. As I write, the Arts Council of Great Britain has refused to back a biographical film about Francis Bacon, one of the great painters of the last 50 years, because the script is too brutal and honest in outlining his drinking, his violence and his sex life. Bacon was horse-whipped on his father's orders, an ordeal that, his biographer Peppiatt suggests, both maimed him psychologically and nourished his art. Great artists and creative scientists have often been contradictory, obsessive, recluses and even malign. Newton was fearful of women, probably a virgin, and believed in strange occult theories. Milton was blind, bitter and impossibly demanding of his daughters when he wrote *Paradise Lost* and *Samson Agonistes*. Mozart careered from one personal crisis to another. Van Gogh was beset by frightening, fantastic religious ideas and felt overwhelmed by a sense of artistic failure and personal worthlessness. Rogers cannot have been ignorant of such well-known cases.

Eysenck, Rogers' *bête noire*, has found (1995) a number of studies supporting Aristotle's link between artistic genius and madness. More recent evidence includes a study of 200 well-known German artists who do not rate high in the normalcy score. Not only do many have unstable personalities but quite a few have eccentric habits such as sleeping on tables and preferring a diet of beetroots.

Rogers not only flew in the face of Aristotle's ancient truth but he made another oddly innocent suggestion. Creative persons were so strong psychologically they did not care about 'external evaluation', about how people reacted to their works. Critics couldn't hurt them. Artists cared only about whether they had been true to themselves and expressed their thoughts and feelings. Again this was bizarre. Many artists are extremely insecure and worry desperately about the reaction to their work. Rogers blithely ignored the fate of Thomas Chatterton and van Gogh who could not stand their lack of recognition.

The dark side of human nature and the fact that this dark side – call it Freud's Id and some aspects of the superego – often fuelled great art was something Rogers did not want to see.

Rogers was also romantic about the solitude of the artist. The creative person always had the feeling of being alone. 'No one has ever done this before' was a phrase Rogers relished; he felt it applied to him, as he often described himself as 'a frontiersman' carving out new territories in psychology. (Freud saw himself as a conquistador and also identified with Moses; Rogers identified with Freud at times, and, oddly, Freud's conquistador turned into a cowboy opening up the new frontier. Freud believed it was his confidence in his mother's love that made him like that. Rogers certainly didn't share that sentiment but both these identifications support McClelland's 'theory' that psychologists seek power.) Rogers claimed the creative person could cope with thinking 'perhaps I am foolish or wrong or abnormal'. The conforming executive could never do that.

Rogers sent his notes out for commentary. One critique warned that his arguments were circular. If a person is open to experience, his creative acts will be healthful and make his personality all the more open to experience. Creativity could also be 'unhealthy', sparked by insecurity and rejection. The critique pointed to Lenin and the French poet Baudelaire, who was depressed, alcoholic, suicidal and a drug user. But he wrote good verse, including that fine example of constructive creativity, *Les Fleurs du Mal*.

Very occasionally, Rogers seems to have asked himself why he was so incorrigibly positive. In 1953 he again went to the Menninger Clinic. He stayed at the Hotel Jayhawk and, after he had given his talk, 'The Concept of the Fully Functioning Person', he saw Karl Menninger at 11 o'clock. They discussed their differences – Menninger, the pessimist who wanted social reform, and Rogers, the optimist who at this stage of his career was not interested in social issues – without being able to resolve them.

Some months later at the APA conference, Rogers chaired a session on the fundamental purpose of the Chicago Counselling Centre. His paper reflected his new interest in personality theory. It suggested connections between changes in the maturity of behaviour and changes in the concept of the self. As he turned 50, Rogers was showing signs of wanting to move away from the emphasis on counselling and therapy that had driven his work ever since he left Rochester. There is rarely one cause for such complex choices—starting to work in a new area or abandoning an interest—but it seems likely that one reason for Rogers to explore new areas was that, yet again, an ambitious research project was not turning out as he had hoped.

## The results of the research

With the investment of over $172,000 by the Rockefeller Founda-
tion, Rogers had been finally able to start on the large-scale study
of the results of therapy. In 1954, Rogers published *Psychotherapy
and Personality Change* (co-edited with Rosalind Dymond). It
included contributions from nearly everyone who had written for
the 1949 *Journal* issue, and reported on the latest state of the
research. Five years years on, they were still rather far from any
final proofs but that did not stop Rogers presenting it as a major
step forward. The reviewers were much more sceptical. In the
*American Journal of Orthopsychiatry* (vol.25, p. 428), Richard
Jenkins noted that the work of the Chicago school should be
treated with great respect and regretted no other schools were
attempting to provide answers to such fundamental, if difficult,
questions. Yet, Jenkins added, the samples were small, and the
ratings relied on the counsellors, who could hardly be considered
impartial witnesses. Jenkins concluded: 'Many readers have definite reservations about the adequacy of the Rogerian method of
therapy.'

Ruth Tolman in the *Journal of Abnormal Psychology* praised
many aspects of the book but said that in relation to psychology
'one feels a disappointment. Perhaps it is in part because we want
too clean and orderly a body of theory to emerge.' (*Journal of
Abnormal Psychology* 1955, 50, p. 407ff.) *The British Journal of
Medical Psychology* also voiced reservations. While commending
the effort that had gone into the work, M. Desai asked why in a
book of this length there was no space 'for a detailed description'
of the problems of the patients which would have given a 'clearer
picture' of the kind of patient client-centred therapy helped. Desai
doubted that the research allowed any conclusion to be drawn 'in
regard to the efficacy of client-centred therapy in relation to mental
illness.' (*Brit.J Medical Psychology* 1956, vol.28, p. 69)

Perhaps the most cutting assessment though was in the *Journal
of Consulting Psychology* – on whose board Rogers still sat. E. J.
Shoben of Teachers College at Columbia sniped that the approach

seemed rather tired and antique. It had been innovative in its time but Rogers should recognise it seemed stuck. The book had failed to convince outsiders and sceptics. It was no answer to Eysenck's sceptical analysis of the outcome of therapy; it did not prove even to friendly critics that psychotherapy worked. Despite the fact that creative people did not care about 'external evaluation', Rogers was beginning to weary of having to put a positive gloss on less than positive results. So much effort since 1942 had not proved what he hoped it would. The facts were not being friendly.

In 1954 Julia Rogers died in Daytona Beach where she had been living with Margaret. In her will, she left a small amount of money for educational purposes. It took the family some time to settle on what would be an appropriate way of spending the money.

Another sign of Rogers' dissatisfaction was that he started to have semi-public quarrels with the university about money. Members of the faculty at Chicago were on fairly high salaries but they had to hand back to the university their earnings from speeches, consultations and even writing. Chicago didn't want its faculty to spend too much time on outside activities. In 1954 Rogers got into a battle over expenses for a trip Helen had accompanied him on. Rogers claimed for her travel and accommodation, but the university administrator ruled spouses should not go on trips lasting less than 45 days. Rogers asked ironically if he could see the specific rules governing such a situation, which he termed a 'Kinsey report in reverse'. 'Is 45 days the average time that faculty members can go without their wives?' he asked. He kept a long, ironic letter about the issue and always claimed to have won this argument.

As a result of the disappointment of the psychotherapy research project, Rogers now tried a different tack. He had described the three stages of therapy back in 1947. Now he set about listening to great numbers of tapes to understand better what was really going on during the counselling sessions. This led to one of his most interesting papers on the process of psychotherapy (Rogers 1958). It placed the concept of openness to experience at the very centre of the therapeutic process. This paper shows again one of Rogers' great talents – that of choosing brilliantly apt quotes from the recorded interviews to illustrate his ideas. Rogers argued there were seven stages to therapy and that the client moved from a stage of 'fixity and remoteness of experiencing'. In fixity, the client is unwilling to communicate; he, or she, does not recognise feelings or own them; close relationships are seen as dangerous; there is no wish to change and the client denies there are serious problems.

By the third stage, clients become acutely uncomfortable as they circle round significant feelings and memories. One client tensed up and then cried saying, 'I have been getting a little too close to something I want to talk about.' Almost against her will, something had 'seeped in', as Rogers put it, to her awareness.

As therapy developed, clients were able to discuss their conflicts. One man told Rogers, 'My conscious mind tells me I'm worthy. But someplace inside I don't believe it. I think I'm a rat – a no good. I've no faith in my ability to do anything.'

Another client told Rogers, 'Something in me is saying "What more do I have to give up? You've taken so much from me already." This is me talking to me – the me way back in there who talks to the me who runs the show.'

By the sixth stage, the client is able to tolerate contradictions and discoveries. Rogers quoted one client who put his hands up as if in prayer and, when Rogers pointed out what he was doing, responded fiercely, 'Who me beg? That's an emotion I've never felt clearly at all – something I've never been ... I've got such confusing feelings. One is it's such a wondrous feeling to have these new things come out of me ... It amazes me.'

Rogers became almost poetic at the end of this paper describing 'the flowing peak moment of therapy in which all these threads become inseparably woven together ... as this process reaches this point, the person becomes a unity of flow, of motion.' Students of Rogers (Thorne 1992) rightly see this as an important paper, but it was wholly based on the assumption that psychotherapy was producing positive results.

In September 1955, Rogers went to the American Psychological Association convention. One of those giving a paper was the physicist Robert Oppenheimer. Oppenheimer said that as psychology became more sophisticated, it would have the means to control people, so its perils were even greater than those of atomic physics. Rogers was impressed and started to work on 'Implications of

Recent Advances in the Prediction and Control of Behaviour'. Bringing all the data together certainly suggested psychologists needed watching. They knew how to get people to buy certain goods. Rogers cited Solomon Asch and R. Crutchfield's work on social influence, which showed that, if everyone in a group says B is larger than A, most individuals will agree, even if the evidence of their eyes proves the opposite (Asch 1953 and Crutchfield 1955). The research at McGill on sensory deprivation showed psychology could produce 'vivid hallucinations and other abnormal reactions'. Normal people could be unbalanced, disturbed, destabilised. 'We know how to influence psychological moods, attitudes and behaviours through drugs,' Rogers said. Psychologists could predict the conditions that would turn a child into a criminal.

The next generation of psychologists had to be taught to be wise so they could handle their awesome power to control minds and personalities. In his paper on control, Rogers talked about the sensory deprivation studies but he did not reveal something he knew quite well. These studies were being backed by the CIA as part of a large secret programme, the aim of which was to brainwash the Communists before they could brainwash the West.


## The CIA

In late 1955 and early 1956, Rogers was approached by Harold Wolff of Cornell Medical School to do work on what Rogers called a Department of Defense matter. This was a coy way of saying that he had been approached by the Society for the Investigation of Human Ecology, which is now known to have been an organisation that fronted research for the CIA. The Society was heavily involved in quite unethical sensory deprivation experiments that were taking place at McGill under Donald Cameron. The experiments included subjecting patients and student volunteers to sensory deprivation, sleep deprivation and other manipulations; the aim was to see in what circumstances people could be first softened up and then brainwashed. Some results were reported in learned journals but some results were for CIA eyes only. The

McGill experiments have been criticised as being cruel, and a number of subjects have sued for compensation. A good history of this is Thomas' (1988). Rogers was not directly involved in running them but he was well aware of their true purpose. The CIA hoped to find ways of mentally toughening agents and soldiers so that, if captured, they could resist brainwashing. They also hoped to find ways of brainwashing the Russians.

Rogers did not hesitate to accept the assignment despite his history of preaching the need for East and West to understand each other. He was flattered to be considered 'one of the five leading mental health men in the country' and so threw himself wholeheartedly into the programme. The secrecy was, of course, rather at odds with his public liberal position, but Rogers argued he was working for the good of the country.

# 7

## California, Here I Come . . . ,
## 1956–1969

In the next 13 years, Rogers' career and interests changed dramatically. He became less interested in individual therapy and more interested in groups. Together with a few other professors such as Herbert Marcuse, Rogers would become a hero of the counterculture, an unlikely fate for a man who constantly moaned he had no idea how to have fun. But, as he and Helen celebrated the start of 1956, he seemed settled in Chicago and about to enjoy one of the 'peak experiences' of his working life.

Today, there is cynicism about what psychology can achieve. High hopes have not been fulfilled; offenders and drug users haven't been rehabilitated; inattentive students haven't been transformed; unhappiness hasn't been eradicated. Forty years ago, however, in 1956, hope reigned – even among professionals. Despite his inconclusive results, Rogers was sure research would soon lead to foolproof therapy. He claimed psychologists were like the Wright brothers back in 1903. No one believed they could fly, but once they did, their feat quickly changed the world. Like aviation in 1904, psychology in 1956 was on the verge of important advances, Rogers declared. Only no one realised it yet.

Rogers' comparison illustrates the way psychologists in the 1950s exaggerated their achievements and likely future. The comparison with flying isn't entirely accurate. Just ten years after the Wright brothers flew, the skies were full of reliable planes. Fighters and bombers changed the course of the First World War. But in 1956 Rogers wasn't one of a band of psychology enthusiasts tinkering away on experiments in sheds at the bottom of the garden. Psychology was already quite old; it actually predated aviation. The first psychology labs had been set up in Harvard by William James and in Leipzig by Wilhelm Wundt in 1879. Seventy-five years of research and millions of dollars of effort had revealed few truths about 'human nature'. The best-established laws of psychology applied to small, specific topics such as animal perception, how rats learned (mainly to run in mazes), how people learned and memorised lists of syllables and the effect of social influences on some actions. The English psychologist Donald Broadbent pointed out that ambitious claims about psychology tended to be false (Broadbent 1958).

Like most of his colleagues, however, Rogers had faith in the power of his discipline but he also believed in the need for ethical control. That would bring him into confrontation with the behaviourist Burrhus F. Skinner of Harvard, who argued that human beings were machines with no free will and that we should rejoice in the fact. Skinner's achievements were massive and, at times, amusing. Using conditioning techniques, Skinner had taught pigeons to play ping-pong and had even tried to persuade the Pentagon that the birds could be used to guide missiles!

## The Skinner debate

Skinner's books *Science and Behaviour* (1953) and the utopian novel *Walden Two* (1948) exemplified the scientific approach to psychology. In *Walden Two*, Skinner described a stable, creative and conflict-free community; all its children had been conditioned to be happy and productive. Skinner saw *Walden Two* as ethical, but Skinner himself gave rise to many dark rumours. He was said to have brought up his children in a Skinner box, an apparatus he first designed to dole out rewards at various times to laboratory rats. In an interview for *Psychologists on Psychology* (Cohen 1977) Skinner adamantly denied such rumours but they helped create an image of him as a psychologist with a sinister taste for social engineering, the very embodiment of all those tendencies Rogers distrusted.

On 27 December 1955, Skinner wrote to Rogers enclosing a copy of the *American Scholar*. Skinner assumed Rogers would be 'in strong disagreement' with the article he had written for the journal and he suggested that 'an airing of our points of view . . . might be profitable and timely' (letter of Skinner from Harvard to Rogers). Skinner put forward the idea of a special session at the 1956 American Psychological Association convention. They might invite a third person 'to avoid misrepresenting the session as a personal contest between us', though the simplest format would be for the two of them to debate their different positions.

Skinner suggested they should each have about 20 minutes for 'lead-off papers', which both parties would see in advance. After that, each would have ten minutes to rebut the other's case. Rogers agreed but, as a canny and experienced debater, made it a condition that Skinner should go first; so Rogers would have the last word. The terms of this gladiatorial combat were set, and in the next nine months, both men were polite to each other but, also, nervous. Much was at stake, and it was more than personal. It was a battle for the very soul of psychology.

In January 1956 Helen and Rogers went on holiday to St Vincent's in the West Indies. He used the time to scribble a first draft of his presentation. There were distractions, however. One morning Rogers surprised a girl in the nude and said 'that seemed to start the day off in a suitably primitive style'. He noted they were not being overcharged as they were paying $9 a day for their room. They met an amusing aristocratic British couple. The holiday felt like a good start to a big year.

By 2 March 1956, Rogers was back in Chicago. He wrote to Dr Richard Solomon explaining that the subject for the debate with Skinner was the control of human behaviour. Rogers put a number of young researchers to work on preparing his paper, including his son-in-law, Larry Fuchs. The correspondence concerning the debate was marked confidential and 'to be read only by the person whose name follows'.

By 8 May, Rogers was sufficiently confident to invite publicity without clearing it first with Skinner. Rogers wrote to Edwin P.

Morgan, a radio broadcaster, after Morgan had mentioned one of Rogers' papers in a report about a Unitarian minister who was frightened people could be brainwashed. Psychologists claimed, Morgan reported, to know how to disintegrate a human personality 'dissolving his self-confidence' – and, therefore, they needed political supervision. Rogers planned to make sure Morgan would give the debate with Skinner air time, so he told the broadcaster of their plans.

On 30 July 1956, Rogers wrote to Skinner at Harvard with the first draft of his paper. He said he was showing it to a few members of his staff for comments. He also wanted Skinner's reaction to the idea of letting Morgan have copies of their papers in advance so that he could produce a radio programme about their debate. Rogers also let it drop that *Time* magazine had been in touch to do a piece on the Chicago Counselling Centre; they, too, wanted advance copies of their debate presentations. 'I don't know how you feel about this but I favour such steps,' Rogers wrote to Skinner, adding, 'I don't crave publicity but I think it would be good to get the public thinking and I believe it would be good for our profession in that it presents psychologists as a definitely significant group.'

Rogers was aggressive but fair. He noted that in his first draft Skinner used the word 'choices'. If human beings were conditioned, as Skinner claimed they were, how could they have choices?

Skinner replied on 9 August that he liked Rogers' paper and felt sure the symposium would have something to offer. Skinner suggested a small change in the timing of their papers; they should each spend 25 minutes on the 'lead-off' paper and then have 15 minutes for rebuttals. Skinner invited Rogers to meet him two days before the debate to clear up certain points. 'The main thing is to get our points of view straight,' so neither of them would be tempted to score mere debating points, or misrepresent the other's position. Rogers had got Skinner's position on the nature of 'happy accidents' wrong, Skinner noted.

Skinner may have been sensitive because Rogers was one of three people to get a medal at the convention. The American Psychological Association was honouring him with the first Distinguished Scientific Contribution Award. Rogers always said this was the award he prized above all others because he had been so dedicated to trying to bring empirical methods to bear on the problems of psychotherapy. In his acceptance speech, he did not mention the inconclusive nature of his research in that area.

On 2 September the two men met and ironed out some basic misunderstandings. They agreed there would be no cheap point-scoring. On the 4th, the debate, billed as the battle of the scientists against the humanists, attracted a large audience. Rogers went out of his way to say he found Skinner likeable and not sinister. This personal testimonial mattered, given the unfair reputation Skinner had acquired as a result of the Skinner box rumours and the critical response to *Walden Two*.

One phrase – 'the prediction and control of behaviour' – keeps on recurring in the debate. The phrase can be traced back to a paper of 1913 written by John B. Watson, 'Psychology as the Behaviourist Views It'. Watson argued psychology could not hope to use introspection to understand the workings of the mind and should concentrate instead on the study of observable behaviour. Rogers did not question the goal of predicting and controlling behaviour but wanted to know who would be in charge of the control and for whom.

Skinner first argued that, until recently, a true science of human behaviour seemed impossible because it was assumed either that people were 'free agents' or that predictions in psychology were just statistical. Of those brought up in a particular way, 53 per cent would develop personality trait P 64 per cent of the time. Such statistics 'would always leave room for personal freedom'. As psychologists discovered better techniques for predicting and controlling behaviour, traditionalists got scared and raised 'the spectre of the predictable man', Skinner said. But they had a hidden agenda. If human beings were predictable they were machines with no free will. That called into question the practice of punishment. The murderer or the thief could hardly be blamed personally if his crimes were the result of poor conditioning. How could it be right to lock up or execute a person who was not morally respon-sible? In education, the dilemmas were less dramatic but as real. How could it be right to penalise students who failed if it wasn't their laziness that ruined their work but the incompetence of their parents and teachers, who had never given them the 'right' reinforcements? They were victims, not sinners, Skinner suggested. And the world likes to punish sinners. Old religious habits died hard.

The illusion of free will also suited American capitalism. The gullible consumer thought he, or she, bought brand Y toothpaste or brand X car out of free choice. Not so. Behind every decision to buy, behind every choice for brand X and against brand Y, there was always a history of conditioning, Skinner said. That history made Bloggs buy X, Black buy Y and Briggs buy nothing at all.

The argument that unscrupulous men would control those who knew how to control behaviour had to be seen in context, Skinner said. 'Man has got himself into some pretty fixes and it is easy to believe that he will do so again,' he added. Those who resisted new techniques of behavioural control often had 'heavy investments in the old'. The status quo made them richer and more powerful. Skinner also believed psychology would allow individuals to live better, fuller lives. He ended on an optimistic note, 'No one wishes to develop new master–slave relationships or bend the will of the people to despotic rulers in new ways. These are patterns of control appropriate to a world without science' (see *Scientific American*, 30 November 1956, for a published report of the debate). But conscientious scientists had to explore new techniques of control because the world did so often get in a fix.

Rogers started his 25 minutes by outlining the areas of agreement between them. 'Men have always endeavoured to understand, predict, influence and control human behaviour – their own and others',' he said. The behavioural sciences were making 'increasingly rapid progress'. But Rogers worried that psychologists would misuse the enormous power of the new behavioural science. Robert Oppenheimer had compared psychologists with physicists in charge of the atom bomb; Rogers did not argue against that comparison.

Forty years on, it is clear both Skinner and Rogers were too optimistic about the future. Psychology has yet to deliver ways of rehabilitating offenders or of improving the skills of students. New drugs rather than new psychological techniques have revolution-ised the treatment of mental illness. (The drugs cause problems, of course, but controlled studies do prove they usually help.) In fact, psychology's main success has been unexpected: it has taught a new language. Studies at prisons such as Grendon Underwood in Britain, a prison that is a therapeutic community, show that 'graduates' of its intense rehab programmes reoffend as often as other prisoners but they learn to explain how the stresses and psycho-social pressures make them do it. They have become recidi-vists with insight and a good grasp of psychobabble.

In 1956, however, the new techniques such as operant con-ditioning and 'token economies' seemed to guarantee success. In his reply to Skinner, Rogers asked who would control these tech-niques and who would set the goals for this new social engineering: this was a great ethical issue. Skinner, Rogers sniped, had decided people should be happy, well-behaved and productive, but it was Skinner who defined happiness and good behaviour and he didn't even realise he was doing it. He may also not have realised the subtle changes between his drafts. In his first draft, Skinner had talked about using psychology to achieve 'improved' educational practices and 'wiser' government and had spoken of 'choices' but, in the final draft, Skinner avoided even these 'value-laden terms'.

They may have banned cheap point-scoring but Rogers was not above poking some good-natured fun. Skinner himself had not been very well conditioned. He was too unruly. Rogers added, 'I would hate to see Skinner become "well behaved" as that term would be defined by most behavioural scientists' and 'the most awful fate I can imagine for him would be to have to be constantly happy' in the behaviourist utopia. The real Skinner was clearly unhappy about many things and that made Rogers prize him.

Skinner was not amused, however, when Rogers likened *Walden Two* to Orwell's *1984* (1949) as being much the same 'at a deep philosophical level'. In *1984*, Big Brother uses punishment to con-trol people while Skinner always argued that proper conditioning techniques would do away with the need for punishment. Indi-viduals would be shaped by rewards.

Rogers' positive recommendations relied almost exclusively on his experiences as a therapist. Rogers asked four key political questions. Who will be controlled? Who will exercise that control? What type of control will be exercised? To what end will that control be used? The German rocket scientists who had developed the V bombs were happy to work either for the United States, to help destroy the USSR, or for the USSR, to help destroy the United States. Their loyalties were governed by who had happened to capture them in 1945 – not by ethics. Rogers fretted that Skinner's vision would allow control to pass to an elite of brain scientists who would 'serve the purposes of whatever individual or group is in power'. It was not good enough to say vaguely, as Skinner had done, that the scientific control of behaviour was desirable because it would lead to a 'far better world for everyone . . .'

Achieving a far better world involved making ethical choices. Learning to make responsible personal choices is 'the most essential element in being a person', Rogers said, and one 'which exists prior to any scientific endeavour'. He described ways in which the techniques of therapy made it possible to learn how to make such ethical choices. He wrote, 'it is possible for us to choose to value man as a self-actualising process of becoming; to value creativity and the process by which knowledge becomes self transcending.'

Secondly, science could 'discover the conditions which necessarily precede these processes'. The only 'authority' needed was the authority 'to establish certain qualities of interpersonal relationships', for when people were in good interpersonal relationships, they changed for the better. Rogers argued that such relationships create the conditions in which men and women become more responsible, more flexible, more creative, more self-actualising and, therefore, more ethical. Free men would tend to be good; the more free they were, the better they became. *Walden Two* was too closed, rigid and predictable for its citizens to flourish. Rogers never claimed Skinner was exaggerating what conditioning could achieve – merely that he ignored the ethics involved.

Skinner was stung by some of Rogers' points. In interviews in 1971 and 1974, Skinner told me he often felt an unfair image of his ideas was presented – and that applied to Rogers to some extent. But Skinner was no mean debater. He countered that Rogers' values were transitional, the product of a particular time and culture. What was the evidence clients really became self-directing? Did what they learned in counselling apply in the real world? Skinner wanted individuals to understand how their behaviour was shaped by outside forces. Given the inconclusive research on the outcomes of therapy, Rogers was lucky Skinner did not concentrate on a fundamental question. How could Rogers erect an ethical system on the basis of his therapy when his research had failed to prove clients got better and became more responsible?

It is hard to say who won the debate. In a sense both Rogers and Skinner did because it confirmed their reputations as stars who spoke for their particular kind of psychology. The debate received considerable media attention. On ABC Radio, Edwin. P. Morgan complained that the differences between the two titans were 'vague if not downright baffling to the layman'. The baffled Morgan found it reassuring such debates were going on even if they were rather obscure.

Rogers enjoyed the debate and it was something of a model for others over the next 20 years. He had similar dialogues with the theologians Paul Tillich and Martin Buber, the psychiatrists R. D. Laing and Rollo May and the anthropologist Gregory Bateson. None of these other confrontations, however, had the drama of the encounter with Skinner. Never again was so much at stake, the future of a discipline. Rogers and Skinner agreed to continue their discussions and they had two other public dialogues, in 1958 and in 1962. Both were much less intense, and Skinner scored at least one bull's-eye. He learned of a story where Rogers and another man were out duck hunting. Only one duck was shot. Both men made for the dead bird but by the time Rogers got there, the other hunter had picked up the duck. Rogers did not lose his cool but observed in his best therapeutic manner, 'You feel this is your duck?' This was enough to persuade the hunter to hand over the bird. Rogers was amazed Skinner had heard this story and insisted it hadn't happened quite like that.

## Plans to leave

A week after the debate, on 13 September 1956, the board of trustees of the University of Chicago minuted that Rogers had received $350,000 from the Ford Foundation for a five-year programme of research into psychotherapy. Ironically, almost as soon as he had the money, Rogers started to consider leaving Chicago. The decision was due to a number of factors. Rogers was certainly beginning to resent the terms of his contract. It had been one thing to hand over to the university all his fees and royalties when he had not been well known, but his books were selling in thousands, and he could now command considerable fees for lectures.

There was also the continuing problem of his relationship with Billings. Rogers was still offering therapy to its patients. The psychiatrists were unhappy about some of his methods, and on 24 October 1956 there was a huge row between Rogers and a Dr Aldrich. Aldrich accused him of violating the code of ethics of the American Psychological Association – of which Rogers was president – by giving treatment without the help of doctors. Rogers was practising illegal medicine, Aldrich said. He intended to complain to the university. Rogers was furious. He felt slandered. He pointed out that he had just been approached on a very secret Department of Defense matter as one of the five leading 'mental health men in the country'. As well as citing Wolff, Rogers wrote to the Vice-Chancellor of the university enclosing a copy of a letter from Seymour Kety, a leading neurologist who praised Rogers' work. Rogers said he could hardly be both a danger by practising illegal medicine and one of the 'leading mental health men'. This row further soured the atmosphere at Chicago. It also made it very hard for Rogers to continue working at Billings.

That winter Rogers and Helen went on holiday to the British West Indies with David, Corky and their children. On his return, Rogers took up a position for the spring term at the University of Wisconsin as the Visiting Knapp Professor. The local paper played up Rogers' ancient connections with the university. The faculty was excited by Rogers' arrival and the university decided to offer Rogers a deal that might lure him permanently away from Chicago. Virgil Herrick, the professor of education, was chosen to try to fix the appointment.

One reason why Rogers had so many difficulties at Billings was that he had no official standing in Chicago's department of psychiatry. Wisconsin offered the possibility of a joint appointment in both psychology and psychiatry. Rogers would no longer be an outsider who had to beg doctors to let him near their patients. It was tempting and Rogers started to discuss terms with Herrick. While these negotiations were beginning very confidentially, Rogers also agreed to stage a second debate – with the Jewish theologian Martin Buber, who was deeply influenced by existentialism.

Rogers had not read much of Buber's work, so this dialogue involved far more preparation than the duel with Skinner. Students were set to read Buber. Rogers ploughed his way through his masterpiece *I and Thou* (first published in German in 1923) and, on the basis of this slightly feverish homework, he produced some notes that highlighted their differences and throw light on Rogers' basic philosophy; 'I have puzzled over the nature of man as I have discovered it in deep therapeutic relations. Have come to some negative and some positive conclusions.'

Rogers did not find man to be basically hostile or destructive as did Calvinists or Freudians and others 'who would control'. He did not, like Rousseau, find man to be 'a perfect being sadly corrupted by society'. He did not discover man to be 'completely neutral and without a nature, a tabula rasa . . .' Rather, he found 'man to have the basic characteristics inherent in the human species and these seem to be basically trustworthy characteristics which make for his own enhancement and those of the species.'

The clash with Buber brought Rogers into contact with a thinker whose ideas were heavily influenced by the Holocaust. In Chicago, Rogers was on the same campus as Bruno Bettelheim, a concentration camp survivor who ran the Orthogenic School for autistic children. Like Rogers, Bettelheim started to win a national reputation in the late 1940s. He wrote much about the Holocaust, as did another existential psychiatrist, Viktor Frankl, whose work

Rogers knew. Yet in his preparation for the debate with Buber, Rogers seems to have ignored the Holocaust completely. Just as in his work on creativity, Rogers stubbornly refused to face the issue of rejection and insecurity, now he refused to look at evil and the reality of human destructiveness. These were hardly novel topics; Freud had discussed them in *Beyond the Pleasure Principle* in 1920, but the Holocaust gave them special urgency.

The dialogue with Buber was less exciting than the Skinner debate, though it allowed Rogers to ask what he admitted in his notes were 'impertinent questions'. How had Buber, who did not practise therapy, come to have such a close and sensitive knowledge of relationships? He asked whether the moments of revelation in Buber's I-Thou relationship were like the peak experiences in therapy when there was perfect empathy. One exchange nicely sums up the differences between the two men. Rogers insisted that fundamentally 'man is good', to which Buber responded by saying 'yes, man is good – and evil'.

Rogers was certainly not anti-Semitic; he was certainly not lazy intellectually. So it is perhaps surprising that he ignored the issue of the Holocaust.

## The schiz project

In 1957, Rogers summed up 15 years work in the paper 'The Necessary and Sufficient Conditions of Therapeutic Personality Change' (*Journal of Consulting Psychology*, 21). As the title suggests, he was still trying to find a mathematical formula that would express what happened in therapy. Rogers suggested the formula was truly simple. If the therapist achieved unconditional positive regard and so created empathy with the client, then it would follow that the client would experience catharsis. Catharsis would lead to insight; insight would lead to positive changes in behaviour. Entering into non-directive therapy was like getting on a train. As long as the driver knew his job, you were bound to reach your destination. This 1957 paper was the high-water mark of the claims for the success of therapy. Rogers allowed no doubt that if the necessary conditions were achieved, cure would follow. The paper never mentioned all the problems with the actual research on the outcome of non-directive therapy.

The visiting professorship at Wisconsin worked out well and Rogers was offered the chance of a permanent chair. He was sorely tempted. Helen was fed up with Chicago. In Wisconsin, his outside earnings would be his to keep. But, most of all, Rogers felt there was no prospect of resolving the impasse with the psychiatrists at Billings. So, for the second time in his life, a quarrel with psychiatrists was part of his motivation for moving to a new position.

The details of the research into the use of non-directive therapy with schizophrenics – the schiz project – were eventually published in 1967 in a book that is probably the least read of all Rogers' works, *The Therapeutic Relationship and Its Impact: A Study of Psychotherapy with Schizophrenics*. It was a project that was plagued by problems from the start and that has been attacked by Jeffrey Masson in *Against Therapy* (1989).

Rogers' basic idea was to study 40 psychotic patients, to offer them non-directive therapy and to see if that helped them. His hypothesis was, of course, that it would. Masson claims the research at the Mendota State Psychiatric Facility allowed Rogers to act as a benevolent despot. Mendota was a grim-looking institution which had been built in the 1890s. It housed up to 2000 patients. The doctors were happy to accept Rogers' ideas as long as it did not interfere too much with their routines.

Rogers was to encounter new problems. In Chicago, most clients were motivated and functioned well enough to study or hold jobs. Billings housed many students who broke down. Long-term psychiatric inpatients such as those at Mendota were a very different population. Many were apathetic, many were hostile. Some situations were exasperating. Non-directive therapists didn't usually have to deal with male clients who ran into the women's washroom. Or patients who tried to hang themselves in isolation cells. At Mendota, some patients just wouldn't speak. The challenge was fascinating.

Once he had agreed the terms with the University of Wisconsin, Rogers faced the problem of how to break the news to his colleagues in Chicago. It was a shock for them. Rogers wrote to his co-workers admitting they would be hurt and surprised by his move. It was not a question of anything they had done wrong, he reassured them, but Wisconsin would give him the chance to work with psychologists and psychiatrists. He would be part of the faculty that trained 33 young psychiatrists at the start of their careers. He could convert them to the non-directive way of thinking. Rogers compared himself to a frontiersman again. It was time for the cowboy to saddle up and ride towards the next frontier and the next insight. The Ford Foundation were a little concerned that the professor to whom they had just awarded $350,000 was suddenly decamping.

By the autumn of 1957, Helen and Rogers were packing up their house and on the move again. They found a house near a lake in Madison in a beautiful setting, and Rogers started to focus on the 'schiz', or schizophrenia, research. In February 1958 Rogers framed a formal proposal for the Mendota project, which drew some inspiration from a scheme he had seen in a southeast Louisiana state hospital. He also gathered together his team, which included Eugene Gendlin, John Schlien and a young graduate student, Charles Truax. The first year in Wisconsin was marred, however, by a number of personal problems. The very frank evidence Rogers left in the Library of Congress reveals that many of these family difficulties were an interminable saga that seemed to end only with death or divorce. The troubles included the breakdown of his sister-in-law and the ever-worsening marriage of Corky and David.

As early as 1951 David criticised his parents for not coming to see them in New York when Corky was ill. (Just as Walter and Julia had not come to see Rogers when he had to be operated on for his ulcer.) As the 1950s progressed, Corky took to drinking more and to taking barbiturates. David felt angry, hurt and worried. Sometimes he was so upset that he felt totally uncreative. He wrote to his father, 'I realise once again how uncomfortable it makes me to discuss my unhappiness with you.'

Paradoxically, David was often on the phone to his father complaining of migraines and depression. He was 'in a hell of a rush going I know not where'. He found it hard to unbend. He admitted that he was no longer 'as personally tortured by Corky's unhappiness'. His father kept many notes of these fraught conversations;

Rogers also spent hours listening to Corky on the phone. Her side was that she felt inadequate, having 'married into a family that is so goddamned creative it kills me.' She thought she could write to prove herself worthy of their high standards.

In his spidery handwriting, Rogers also kept notes of conversations with his sister-in-law, Ruth, who was married to his brother John. Ruth was frequently distraught. She heard voices. She claimed to have been in love with another man for 12 years, though she no longer saw him. She had sexual fantasies that made her feel ashamed. She was taken to hospital late in April 1958 and Rogers complained that she was immediately given ECT. She had not even seen a neurologist – and she might have been suffering from some organic condition. In a letter of 29 April 1958, Rogers wrote that Ruth had been treated like a guinea pig.

After she came out of hospital, Ruth was supposed to receive treatment on an outpatient basis at St Luke's Hospital but Rogers was concerned about the quality of her care. Ruth had fantasies of her home burning down and feared imminent death by cancer. She also seemed to think her husband was trying to kill her. On 6 June 1958 Rogers wrote to her doctor, Robert C. Macmillan, at St Luke's. If Macmillan was not intending to see Ruth in therapy during the summer, Rogers could suggest possible therapists. It was not wise to leave her with no help for two months. By the following week Rogers' letter was irrelevant as Ruth had had to be rehospitalised. She felt oppressed by an evil presence and had run away from her house in her night-dress, which caused a lot of local comment.

In the circumstances, with three family members in crisis and a large project to start, it is perhaps not surprising Rogers began to develop stomach problems. In the winter, the drama of Ruth only got worse – and more socially embarrassing.

On 24 January 1959 Ruth was hospitalised again after an episode at a swimming pool when she started making passes at the lifeguards. Again, Rogers wrote to St Luke's demanding better care. John wrote to Rogers a few weeks later to say he hoped and believed she was now getting better. Ruth left hospital and went to stay with Margaret in Daytona Beach, but the positive interlude was short. In March Ruth had to be rehospitalised and given frequent courses of ECT. Her doctor noted 'we'll have to keep giving her shock treatment till she snaps out of it' – a comment that outraged Rogers. He reassured John that Ruth's breakdown wasn't his fault. He had not made any serious mistakes in his marriage. As Rogers' relations careered from one crisis to the next, he seems to have been at their beck and call. And sometimes they even had the temerity to complain.

In July 1959 David wrote a long and very self-absorbed letter to his father. David told Rogers there were many resentments and problems he had not dared admit before. During his internship he had been at the end of his tether. He wrote, 'I was pretty dreadfully upset during the first part of internship . . . I don't think that I ever really vocalised it to you – I was afraid I'd blow apart.' David added that though their contact had been infrequent, his father had been of tremendous help to him more recently.

After the son, the son's wife. On 17 October 1959 Corky was yet again on the phone complaining bitterly about how depressed she was. Then came the physical illnesses. In December, Helen went into hospital. Rogers noted his own health was not good. He now had high blood pressure and was sweating a lot.

With so much to worry him, it is not strange Rogers found it hard to concentrate on the Mendota project, and the project needed great attention to detail, particularly as Rogers was unsure in his dealings with psychotics. A letter (30 May 1959) from a client called Ann focuses on the fact that in one session Rogers had mentioned how rejected a therapist can feel when talking about trying to deal with psychotics. Ann wrote to him linking this with her own experience of him as a therapist.

In their session Rogers had offered Ann an extra 20 minutes and she felt that this was his response to his feeling that she was never able to get enough of anything, neither love nor time. She added that in those 20 minutes 'everything went wrong'. His offer made her feel she was making unreasonable demands. 'Anyway I felt pretty confused and upset at the end of those 20 minutes and after I managed to get my world right side up again – which took some doing – I was hurt and angry at your participation in what happened.' Ann guessed that she had landed on 'a particularly troublesome area for you'. She was writing as they sometimes bumped into each other – she was clearly also working in the psychology department – and she was quite willing to be friends. Rogers replied on 10 June coolly; he had not found her unduly demanding though he did accept her description of what had happened.

This rather inconclusive experience with Ann, as well as the constant family crises, pushed Rogers to take stock. By the end of 1959, he was thinking more than ever before about the impact on him of years of practising therapy, of offering rapport, of being the perfect listener.

## Personal insights

In a lecture called for some reason 'The Last Lecture', written round 1959–60, Rogers began to analyse his own negative reactions in certain situations. I have argued he had paid little attention to the stresses of therapy for the therapist. As he started to confront this self-inflicted taboo, Rogers began to write in a more personal and confessional way than ever before.

In preparing for this lecture, Rogers said he had been 'amused' by this invitation for a variety of reasons. First, he no longer believed in giving lectures, which seemed to him to be the worst way of teaching. Helen suggested he confine his words to saying that he didn't lecture. Then he could invite questions from the audience. 'Had appeal,' Rogers wrote. Then, what was the meaning of that gloomy word, 'last'? Was this to be the last lecture before 'I shuffle off' or before 'I retired' or before 'I stopped lecturing'? For all these reasons, Rogers decided he wanted to say 'something very personal'. In the 1950s, Rogers' style had become more relaxed but essentially he had remained an academic author. It was only now as he neared 60 that his writing would become much more homely and accessible, a quality that would make his work appeal to a larger audience than ever before.

In the lecture Rogers finally faced up to some aspects of hostility. Some clients were hard to accept; therapists disliked them. Rogers wrote, 'It does not help, in the long run, to act as though I were something that I am not. It does not help to act calm and pleasant when I am actually angry and critical.'

It did not help to act confident when he was frightened. Façades could be destructive. His children complained they were expected not to be angry. Rogers admitted he did not find it easy to stick to the rule of expressing his feelings. His education had taught him reserve, the polite mask, the limits of what was acceptable to say, the dangers of feelings. Often, he said, he behaved in one way on the surface while, below, his feelings ran the opposite way. He found it specially hard to express anger. Paradoxically, he found it 'of great value' when he could allow himself really to understand another person. Real understanding was subtle. It took effort not to say, 'That's fine', to go beyond the appearance of listening and, instead, to try to see what something meant to another person. 'To test whether you have understood the preceding statement of the other, rephrase it or summarise it in a way that is satisfactory to him,' Rogers advised his readers. The exercise would show how hard and rare it was to achieve empathy.

Every time we really understand someone we risk being changed by that experience, Rogers argued. And change is unsettling. American culture made it hard to air dissenting views either in families or in politics. 'On a national scale, we cannot permit another nation to think or feel differently than we do.' Yet these differences, the separateness of individuals, were one of 'the most priceless potentialities of life'.

Rogers went on to formulate a dramatic proposition. 'Neither the Bible nor the prophets, neither Freud nor research, neither the revelations of God nor man can take precedence over my own direct experience.' Rogers said he felt a subjective need to perceive order and meaning, and that had attracted him to research. He was now willing to question some of his sacred cows. He admitted that much as he loved the phrase, 'the facts are friendly', the facts did not always feel like that. The phrase was perhaps a little glib, even misleading. He added, 'I still hate to readjust my thinking, still hate to give up old ways of perceiving and conceptualising.' But he claimed he could cope with it now, adding, 'yet at a deeper level I have . . . come to realise that these painful reorganisations are what is known as learning.'

In his experience, Rogers said, people 'have a basically positive direction', but he did not want to be misunderstood. 'I do not have a Pollyanna view of human nature.' Human beings could be vicious, selfish, anti-social, despairing and suicidal but it had been one of the 'most invigorating parts of my experience' to work with such individuals and find in them 'positive directional tendencies'. Rogers briefly contemplated evil and destructiveness but decided the sinner could always repent, the good therapist would always bring out the good in a person. It was hardly a serious response to such a fundamental issue and, peculiarly, Rogers offered an animal comparison. The lion had his nature as king of the jungle. Human beings also had their nature – and it was not to growl, but to grow, to develop towards self-actualisation, to become more authentic.

Rogers brooded over his differences with Karl Menninger again. He said, 'So when a Freudian such as Karl Menninger tells me that he perceives man as "innately evil" or more precisely "innately destructive" I can only shake my head in wonderment. It leads me to all kinds of perplexing questions.' Rogers did not ask them, however. He just wondered how two men who saw distressed individuals could have such different responses. Rogers had no answer and said, a little facilely perhaps, that maybe it didn't matter too much as long as the therapist cared for his client.

Rogers was facing less theoretical problems. He wrote (23 June 1960) to his son-in-law, Larry Fuchs, saying he was dismayed they had made little progress in devising a method of measuring openness to experience. There were also problems in the research at Mendota and some of these suggest Rogers was losing enthusiasm for the project. One of Rogers' achievements in Chicago had been to establish a democratically run Centre. It could survive when he was absent because he had trained his staff to cope with crises and encouraged the leadership skills of a number of senior staff. In Wisconsin Rogers aimed for the same management style but he did not devote the time needed to nurture the individuals involved. The result was something of a disaster.

From the start no one quite knew who was in charge of what at Mendota and, in that vacuum, Charles Truax, the youngest of the main researchers, started to behave in bizarre ways. Truax saw an opportunity to take over large areas of the project. Rogers initially did nothing. He was busy, he trusted Truax and he was less comfortable with psychotic clients.

The situation at Mendota was not something Rogers liked to discuss. On 9 May 1960, Lester and his wife came to dinner in Madison. Lester was determined not to be accused of 'doing all the talking'. He wrote later, 'I arrived with the firm intention to listen. I humbly apologise for my failure.' But Lester did not think it was entirely his fault. 'I asked Carl to tell me about his research at Mendota. He passed the buck to Will who looked into space and dodged answering.' Lester seems to have unintentionally raised a thorny subject and was left feeling frustrated and even a little guilty. Lester asked if he could come back one day and listen. In his letter, he also congratulated Rogers and Helen on the real estate they were developing; they had always had a shrewd eye for a property deal.

During the winter holiday of 1961, Rogers wrote most of what would become his most popular book, *On Becoming a Person*. It threaded together essays and papers he had written before. The book traced his own personal evolution, the evolution of non-directive therapy and outlined his hopes for using its techniques to help resolve social and political conflicts. Rogers summed up the inconclusive research results but added he was convinced they were on the right track. The reviews recognised the book was important. Its success would give Rogers financial security and much pleasure. He got hundreds of letters from readers who felt the book spoke to them – some were from the ends of the earth.


## Out East again

Rogers' work had attracted some interest in Japan (there is an interesting study to be done on why Rogers had managed to appeal to such an apparently conformist culture). He had built up a small following in Japan at Ibaraki Christian College and he had one devoted admirer, Logan Fox, an American who had lived in Japan. Fox raised the funds for Rogers to visit Japan and arranged his schedule. The trip was to be both exciting and frustrating. Rogers and Helen got shots for typhoid and cholera on 23 May 1962. They embarked on 8 June in Yasushima Mar and got to Japan a week later. They would stay out east till 21 August.

Logan Fox had set up a crowded programme comprising a series of workshops including one for 30 upper managers in Tokyo, a separate one for 49 probation officers and psychologists who worked for the Ministry of Justice and more workshops in Kyoto and Osaka. Rogers was struck by the beauty of Japanese women and their reserve. Few of them talked in public to men. Helen, on the other hand, was often harassed. She was very tall compared to Japanese women and she was stared at and, sometimes, even stopped in the street.

In the workshops, Rogers found the Japanese were less formal than he had expected. 'The industrial men got bold enough to express their scepticism and ended by learning a good deal. One man spoke up and said he could finally express his feelings.'

Rogers enjoyed many of the ceremonies of the visit. The Ministry of Justice gave him a meal at a restaurant in a formal garden which had been the property of a feudal lord. In the grounds, there were 30 to 40 remarkable bonsai trees, some of which were 700 years old. Rogers loved the setting. He was less comfortable at a traditional Japanese inn because a maid wandered into the bathhouse when he was totally naked.

They travelled to Osaka and Kyoto. Kyoto was more fun than Tokyo but there was the problem of compulsory sight-seeing. Everywhere their hosts wanted to take them to temples and shrines and, soon, one shrine seemed much like the next. They were bored but didn't want to offend. When Bruno Bettelheim, whose view of human nature differed totally from Rogers', visited Japan, he had the same complaint—too many shrines—but at least Bettelheim had no illusions about having understood the Japanese. For all their attempts to be Western – and that included flirting with therapy – Bettelheim had no idea what made them tick. Rogers felt less alien and that Japanese reactions to him were gratifying. It was perhaps the first proof that his ideas were of interest outside America.

Back in Wisconsin, the situation at Mendota had not improved. Rogers' enthusiastic therapists moaned about the apathetic patients who were 'probably more unpromising as clients than any group which has ever been studied in psychotherapy research'. One of the team felt hopeless as there was no prospect of finding enough therapists 'to clean out the back wards of state hospitals'. They were all terrified – and perhaps a little insulted – by the patients' passive acceptance of the status quo. The ungrateful lunatics didn't realise who was treating them, the *crème de la crème* of psychotherapy. Despite their elite status, the therapists were often powerless. When a patient was denied ground privileges or kept in restraints for a long time, they couldn't do much. The therapists didn't run the hospital, the medical staff did. Doctors and ward attendants were sometimes annoyed when patients became more independent after therapy. The staff often saw that as impertinence rather than improvement.

The research project ran into more personal problems. These centred on Charles Truax, who committed suicide a few years after the project finished. Truax stole the analysis of some of the data and threatened not to return it unless he was given a very prominent role in the write-up. At first, Rogers thought this was all a misunderstanding. The other authors felt Rogers was too soft on Truax and were outraged that he did not stand up to what they saw as the young man's blackmail. Truax wouldn't return all the data, so much of the work had to be repeated and rechecked. Rogers then tried to resume the traditional role of leader and started to make decisions on his own but his colleagues refused to accept his sudden autocratic behaviour. Three senior staff threatened to sue if Truax got too prominent a credit. Rogers was upset by all the fighting. He had never known a research project that was so unhappy.

Then, for the first time for 20 years, a journal rejected a paper by Rogers. In 1963, he submitted a brief piece to the *American Psychologist*. It outlined his bitter critique of graduate work. It was sparked by the very rigid programmes graduate students in Wisconsin had to follow. The university seemed to believe students could not be trusted to pursue their own scientific research and that passing examinations was the only mark of success. 'Education was evaluation', Rogers accused, and evaluation was education. Nothing else mattered. 'The truths of psychology are known,' he wrote with irony and 'method is science.' This orthodoxy implied that 'Creative scientists develop from passive learners. Students were best regarded as manipulable objects rather than as persons.'

The paper was a radical *cri de coeur*. When it was rejected by the *American Psychologist*, Rogers got his own back smartly by writing a letter which the editor had to publish. The letter said that rumours of this paper had aroused intense interest and Rogers would like to let his fellow psychologists know that if they sent him 50 cents they could get a roneoed copy of it.

After so many problems, Rogers was glad to accept a year as a Fellow at Stanford University in the Institute for the Advanced Study of the Behavioural Sciences. His absence did nothing to cure the problems at Mendota where the research was now running into conceptual difficulties worse than any he had encountered in 1949, 1951 or 1954. As they started to look at the results of a sample of 38 patients, it became clear the facts were not friendly at all.

In his contributions to the book that summarised all the findings, Rogers had to salvage some optimistic results. He admitted they had believed giving schizophrenics unconditional positive regard would lead to cure. There was evidence schizophrenics could experience a process of change like other clients and that they valued the therapeutic relationship. 'Though this fact shows up in no specific way,' Rogers had to admit, 'it pervades all our data.' But there were some very disturbing results as well, which he did his best to confront.

Perhaps what was most worrying was that both psychotics and 'normal' clients shared a similar view of what was going on in therapy but the odd ones out were the therapists. 'It is a sobering finding that our therapists, competent and conscientious, had over-optimistic and in some cases seriously invalid perceptions of the relationships in which they were involved. The patient, for all his psychosis, or the bright young college student with no knowledge of therapy, turned out to have a more useful (and probably more accurate) perception of the relationship' (Rogers 1967, p. 92). Rogers accepted they had only 'inched' forward. In his summing-up he redefined the research as being a study neither of schizophrenics nor of psychotherapy but 'most importantly a study of relationships' (p. 546).

Rollo May, the well-known humanistic psychiatrist, had been asked to act as one of 12 independent consultants on the project, and he pointed out that one thing struck him after listening to many hours of tapes of sessions. The therapists seemed to pay little attention to negative feelings the patients expressed. Rogers' team couldn't stand hostility and so did not see it, report on it or act on it.

All the squabbles set back publication by almost three years. At Stanford, Rogers was in a much less fraught environment. While he was there he met a British philosopher of science, Michael Polanyi, who was a formidable scholar. The two men liked each other enormously and Rogers was a little in awe of Polanyi's learning. Polanyi had developed a theory of tacit knowing and was interested in the spiritual. It was the place to think large thoughts.

Being away did not solve family problems, though. In April 1963 David was troubled again because Corky was taking too much Seconal. Then she had to go to hospital. Rogers' son-in-law Larry was also going through an upsetting period.

Coming back to Wisconsin late in 1963, Rogers must have been aware that the results of the Mendota study had yet again failed to demonstrate scientifically that psychotherapy works. It was 23 years since he had started to record sessions as part of his research programme. He began to contemplate leaving Wisconsin. Again, it would be wrong to suggest Rogers left his post for this one reason. He had enjoyed his time at Stanford; California was exciting but it is hard to escape the conclusion that the failure at Mendota hurt badly.

Rogers no longer needed a conventional job. He was not far off retirement age. His books were bringing in a decent income; he had some investment income and he didn't want to have to administer a department. When Rogers resigned his professorship at Wisconsin, he got a pained letter from the university president in which he regretted that they had not been able to provide their distinguished colleague with the opportunities he needed. It was their fault the great man was leaving.

Rogers, for the first time in his life, was not leaving for a recog-

nised university job. In 1959, he had helped set up a radical institution, the Western Behavioural Sciences Institute. Its outlook
would be humanistic but also scientific. Much of the finance for
setting up the Institute came from a rich physicist, Paul Lloyd,
who had attended one of the first groups that Rogers had been
involved in running. Lloyd had poured $700,000 into the Institute,
which by 1964 was doing well and was attracting government
research projects. It would provide Rogers with a base, good colleagues such as Richard Farson and a chance to explore new fields
– especially those of encounter groups and education.

For the last time, Helen and Rogers set out in 1964 to a new
home: in Torrey Pines Road in La Jolla. But the new setting did
not mean an end to old problems. Soon after they moved to La
Jolla, Rogers received a rather sad letter from David; he complained there was too much pressure of work so that he doubted
if he would ever have 'the guts or the discipline to step back and
decide what I really want to be myself.' David's marriage was in
a worse mess than ever, and Natalie's and Larry's marriage was
also beginning to show strains. The crises in their lives now
coincided with a major change in Rogers' career.

Since 1939, Rogers had worked as an individual counsellor.
After the failure of the Mendota project to prove the value of
psychotherapy, Rogers started to concentrate much more on
groups, especially short-term groups. Now, as never before, he
caught the mood of the times. There was a tradition of group work
in psychoanalysis. One pioneer analyst, William Bion, argued it
would be impossible to provide psychoanalysis for all those who
needed it. They needed cheaper, quicker methods. Treating people
in groups made sense. After the war, the social psychologist Kurt
Lewin had set up and studied T groups or sensitivity groups.
Rogers had, in fact, studied some of Lewin's research. But no one
was prepared for the enormous and sudden interest in encounter
groups that mushroomed in the early to mid-1960s.

The encounter group, Rogers once said enthusiastically, might
be the most important social development of the 20th century.
From 1964, he acted as the facilitator for many different groups.
For a shy and reserved man, it was an unlikely role but he brought
into groups all that he knew of counselling and of trying to create

democratically led organisations. The groups also gave him a great deal as a person – a sense of being in touch with people and at the cutting edge of what he called a quiet revolution. In this revolution, uptight Americans would finally learn to share their feelings and find out who they really were. Rogers seemed to love this new freedom. He kept notes on many of the groups that he facilitated and these allowed him to publish one of the seminal works on encounter groups (Rogers 1970).

The group work also allowed Rogers to pick up an old enthusiasm. He hoped that group techniques would offer a way of teaching people in conflict to resolve their political differences. Oddly enough, one of the first places where Rogers would try to do this was a temple of technology, Caltech. This is an episode worth examining in a little detail because it was such a clash of cultures – humanistic psychology and hard science.

## Caltech

In 1964, after he had moved to the Western Behavioural Sciences Institute, Rogers decided to spend two days a month at Caltech. With so many university campuses being taken over by students, the Provost of Caltech, Robert F. Bacher, thought it might be wise to investigate what the feelings and dissatisfactions among students and faculty might be. Rogers, who was working in La Jolla, was an ideal choice. He was credible to many of the faculty and to all the students. Bacher invited Rogers to do some consultancy for Caltech – a job that was to occupy Rogers regularly for the next four years. There was no definite brief. Rather, Rogers was to take the emotional temperature of the campus. He was undoubtedly flattered to be recruited by such a famous institution.

The Caltech faculty included Roger Sperry, who did much of the pioneering work on the right and left hemispheres of the brain, and Richard Feynman, who eventually won a Nobel Prize for physics. Feynman was a very down-to-earth genius, given to practical jokes, but he never regarded Rogers as a real scientist. Sperry, however, was intrigued by some of the softer sides of psychology.

Soon after he arrived, Rogers started to work with the so-called

Honker Group, a talking club for 24 senior members of the faculty. In his capacity as facilitator, he kept the minutes. Rogers found there were at least two visions of Caltech. Traditionalists did not care about the questions the sixties counter-culture raised. They wanted Caltech to train world-class imaginative scientists and did not worry about what these 'boffins' were like as people and whether or not they related creatively, harmoniously or authentically to other people. Had Newton 'related'? The progressives, however, felt that Caltech was too narrow and needed to change. Creative scientists had to be socially responsible and they couldn't ignore human relationships. Science couldn't duck social problems and take refuge in ivory towers and pristine equations. The traditionalists countered they were not in the business of making value judgements. They were worried they would spend years on worthy projects which might be politically important but which couldn't be resolved by the scientific approach. (It could be argued that these hard-nosed scientists were more realistic than Skinner and Rogers had been in their debate, which was so optimistic about the future of psychology.)

Students also had problems. Though Caltech's students were among the brightest, a fifth of those Rogers talked to complained the demands on them were so great they became obsessed with exams. The progressives suggested Caltech was not looking ahead. 'We need to dream,' Rogers quoted one of them as saying. What would education be like in 1980? He felt stimulated by the arguments.

Rogers was also excited by the prospect of another long trip. Helen and Rogers booked a cruise to the South Pacific for Christmas 1964 and then travelled to Australia and New Zealand, where Rogers gave a series of lectures. He was interested in the attempts to develop culture-free tests for Aborigines. By 30 January 1965, Rogers and Helen were in New South Wales. They were the guests of the Australian Psychological Society which showed a film of a patient treated both by Rogers and by Fritz Perls. It was possibly the first example of something Rogers would increasingly do as he got older – demonstrations of therapy. He remained an acute social observer: Australia struck him as interesting because people could satisfy their basic needs. There was little poverty – yet people seemed smug, not very happy and dull. Clearly people needed more to their lives.

By 18 February 1965 Helen and Rogers were still far from the States, sunning themselves in Samoa. They knew that back home there were family problems. Rogers got back to find a letter from his daughter saying that despite his skills in individual therapy and in running groups, he was 'bad at talking'. In June Natalie was angry with her parents, including her 'great psychologist father'; her experience was that they rewarded with love those who kept their angry feelings to themselves. Rogers and Helen took the easy way out and called her selfish. Helen, for her part, felt excluded because Natalie was telling her father about her own experiences in therapy.

By March, Rogers was back in Caltech. His minutes of the meeting of the Honker Group on 11 and 12 March reveal many petty tensions. Rogers said that in deference to Richard Feynman he would not use first names in reporting contributions. The minutes also testify to deep differences among the faculty. One group felt that Caltech ought to be involved in 'all three great mysteries – the interior of the atom, the outer reaches of spaces and the nature of life and mind'. Others thought this would risk lowering their scientific standards. The most outspoken views came from Richard Feynman, who was worried that under social pressures Caltech would have to compromise with all kinds of pseudo-sciences. Sperry, on the other hand, had a vision of Caltech broadening its courses and would have liked to recruit an experimental psychologist, such as Donald Hebb, and a philosopher, such as Michael Polanyi, who 'would help discover the meaning and implications of what we are doing'. Many Honkers, however, did not think they needed philosophers to tell them what they were doing.

Feynman offered an interesting definition. Biological science could concern itself only with matters 'under the skin'; mind, morals and metaphysics were interesting but not the stuff of science. He launched into an impassioned speech which Rogers wished he could reproduce. Caltech existed to solve scientific problems, not other kinds of problems, however interesting they might be. 'Science should be separated from the importance of the problem. Science starts from curiosity.' Feynman rejected Freudian psychology as not being remotely scientific and had no wish to bring in inappropriate subjects such as art as part of the curriculum.

Rogers made a passionate reply of his own. He wanted Feynman on his side. Behavioural scientists might be inadequate in their conceptions and crude in their outlook but as long as they were open to the evidence, they were scientists. 'We simply cannot expect the behavioural sciences by one leap to be at the same level as physics.' Rogers said psychology was an infant science. He started to campaign for Caltech to introduce it as a major subject. He made a list of all the members of the Honker Group in which he judged how open they were, how influential and how easy to reach. Feynman scored one, i.e. top, on influence.

On 19 March Rogers talked to Sperry and, as he analysed Sperry's views and feelings, he began to see he had something of an ally. Sperry seemed discouraged by how conservative the administration was and suggested a division of behavioural sciences would be useful. It would soon introduce courses in clinical psychology. But Sperry's attitude was complicated. He was proud of Caltech and loyal to it but he was also frustrated by its resistance to change. Sperry respected Rogers but he was also very sceptical about one of Rogers' enthusiasms – learning through interpersonal experiences.

Late in May, Rogers complained to Bacher that while in theory Caltech welcomed new ideas and 'infant science', in practice it was very different. 'I doubt very much that Caltech has ever nourished or provided a climate for an infant science. Sure once he has shown he can run a hundred-yard dash, read books, makes noises like a scientist, Caltech is glad to adopt it. At that point you're betting on an almost sure thing. But, damn it, an infant is not a sure thing.' Early physicists would probably have not been made welcome at Caltech, Rogers carped. He thought Feynman got so enraged partly because the discussions in the Honker Group easily became confused. They were focusing on two issues – should they encourage the development of some sort of human sciences in the institution, and how could they improve the interpersonal relationships among the faculty? These were separate questions but somehow they were getting muddled. Rogers ended his letter to Bacher saying he was mad. 'At you, at me, at us, at Caltech', and signed off, 'Your consultant (this is a consultant??)'.

On 3 June 1965, by way of reply, Bacher wrote to Rogers to say that people like Richard Feynman very much doubted that Rogers' work was remotely connected with science. They deeply resented Rogers' claim to be something of a scientist. But Bacher was emollient. He said it seemed to him quite wrong to describe psychology as an infant science. He was looking forward to lunch with Rogers so that they could discuss some of these issues.

It was after this lunch that, on 11 June 1965, Rogers proposed a weekend for the Honker Group, where everyone could let their hair down and discuss the crucial issues. He planned to surprise what he saw as over-rational types with something close to an encounter group; its effects could be revolutionary. 'The total climate of the institution might gradually be perceptibly altered,' he suggested. Norman Davidson objected that their problems were not interpersonal but intellectual, and so were the solutions. Sperry said the morale would be helped by having a set of meaningful goals for Caltech rather than by introspective soul-searching. Another Honker argued that student concerns about mathematics courses would not be helped by having a watered-down encounter group.


## Scientific encounter

Finally, on 11 and 12 November 1965, Rogers managed to hold the intensive group experience for the Caltech faculty. It took place in the house of a friend and turned into an attack on Bacher. Bacher was told he made speeches that were too expository. But the group did not lead to any magical changes, almost certainly because many of those who took part had no intention of sharing their deepest feelings.

A new zeal was perhaps making Rogers push too hard. For years his colleagues had praised him for being tolerant and always interested in their point of view. For the first time, in the autumn of 1965, Rogers attracted bitter personal criticism. People close to him started to accuse him of being dogmatic and, ironically, of being completely unwilling to listen. One possible reason was that Rogers, under so much stress, was drinking more and becoming more irritable and impatient.

Soon after the Caltech 'encounter' Rogers received letters from both Natalie and Larry which suggested their marriage was close to the end; in her letter Natalie made a telling observation. She said the hardest thing she ever did in her life was to walk into a therapist's office and ask for help. 'I notice you, too, seldom, if ever asked for help. How fortunate someone on your staff offered to help you after your runaway trip.' Clearly, however, Rogers had not discussed it much because Natalie added as a PS: Was it Ollie Bown who offered the help? She also complained she found it hard to be critical or angry at her mother without being made to feel guilty. Helen's whole life had been as a wife and mother. She could not let herself think she had failed at that.

Larry wanted to maintain good relations with his father-in-law, so he sent Rogers an essay on Protestants, Jews and Catholics for comment. But Rogers objected to what he claimed was a personal statement being dressed up as an objective one. Then Larry accused him of having 'a strong resistance on your part to hear ideas which are not congenial to your own. It seems to me that your total response can be summarised something like this; I can accept all kinds of feelings from Larry but I don't want to discuss his ideas unless he puts them explicitly in the context of feelings and emotional preferences' (18 November 1965).

Larry complained he was being accused of being dishonest just because Rogers did not care for some of the arguments. He added, 'But I lately detect a new kind of reductionism in your approach. I object to this attempt to reduce thought to feelings.' Larry said he believed strongly thoughts and feelings were interlinked and that it was important to understand those links, but he found it useful to read Marx, Max Weber and de Tocqueville, 'without being aware of the feelings that went into their thinking.'

Larry wrote, 'It matters to me in my relationship to you that I often find you closed to ideas, styles and people who just don't happen to fit into your experience.' Human beings had reasons as well as feelings. Rogers had forgotten the need for sound arguments. Larry would pay for his impertinence in pointing this out.

Though the weekend of 11 and 12 November did not lead to a fundamental breakthrough at Caltech, Rogers continued to work two days a month there. He complained he was 'increasingly despairing' as to what to tell students who wanted to do graduate work in psychology. He took part in a debate with Fritz Perls and Albert Ellis and sniped that Ellis was 'terrible as usual'. Rogers stayed at Caltech till 1967 and the experience made him more radical about education. But it's important to keep his radicalism in proportion. Much could still shock and dismay him. In April 1967, he read a survey of student use of LSD and marijuana and noted that things had changed since his University of Chicago days.

## Family problems again

The end of the 1960s was a paradoxical period. On the one hand, Rogers was being lionised as a hero of the counter-culture. On the other hand, close to home, Rogers was acutely aware of failure. Helen was beginning to be resentful. They also had very different attitudes to the sexual revolution. As she was well into her sixties, it did not seem very relevant to Helen, but Rogers started to suggest their marriage should move with the times. Did it have to be so closed and exclusive? His groups were full of attractive women; he was still a good-looking man. It was frustrating. He was preaching the joys of sexual freedom without much chance to practise it.

Rogers also had regrets about his role as a father. He had left much of the parenting to Helen and he reproached himself for not having been warm enough. That was changing but his closeness to Natalie itself created tensions. Helen felt excluded. In one letter (13 September) Natalie complained she felt her mother was very cold towards her. After Natalie had taken part in a workshop in Hawaii that made her focus on all her dissatisfaction with Larry, she confided in her father. To Helen she said nothing, and Helen hated that. It was as if Rogers was now robbing her of something that had been central, her role as the main parent.

Rogers also had to cope with Larry's feelings. Larry was becoming very critical. In May 1967, Larry wrote an angry letter to Rogers. He was upset about an article by Richard Farson which compared Caltech to Auschwitz and stated that all its students were 'niggers and slaves'. Rogers felt the article had some validity for it expressed Farson's true feelings. Larry thought the comparison between a concentration camp and a university, however oppressive, sloppy. It offended him that Rogers believed a paper Larry had written about 'the appeal of stranger groups' was less valid because it pretended to be a set of facts. By stranger groups, Larry meant groups where people who did not know each other got together – encounter groups. One reason for their appeal, Larry sniped, was that they gave people the chance to form 'deep relationships' with no responsibility. You could fall madly in love in a group and go home three days later to the comfort of your wife. It was escapism.

Peevishly, Larry also griped that Rogers seemed always to have been bored by his ideas. Once when Larry was trying to say something crucial, the great listener thumbed through *Newsweek*. Larry accused his father-in-law, 'Do you really care? Is truth something you care passionately about?' Larry added that Hitler was no doubt one of the most genuinely angry men of the 20th century but the strength of his anger did not make him right or reasonable. 'For a humanist to constantly deride reason, as I find you doing, in order to make your point that people hide their feelings and are therefore less human seems not only unnecessary but harmful.'

Larry was also offended by Rogers' snide remark that, as he had never experienced 'the caring, the feedback, the confrontation, the honesty which occurs in such groups', his views on such issues were limited. Larry countered, 'Am I wrong in detecting what I have never seen in you before – a certain smugness in your statement "after you have had such an experience then I would be much more intrigued in knowing what you think about it."' Rogers did not take Larry's attack very seriously, it seems, perhaps because he saw Larry essentially as an academic; in February 1968, Rogers, reflecting on a California workshop, said he realised how hard it was 'for academic people to express feelings and how suspicious they are of that part of themselves.'

Natalie dispelled any doubts her father might have had. She told him that for all his accomplishments in the world, Larry felt he was inadequate as a man and that she had been forced to be too much of a mother to him. The relationship between Larry and his father-in-law got worse in the next few months.

The grandchildren were easier to deal with. In October Rogers wrote the Dean of Admissions at Swarthmore College a recommendation for Anne saying she was an intense scholar. Rogers mentioned a story she had written about a date where it slowly becomes clear she is describing a date between a white boy and a black girl. Frederick Haragon replied he hoped his own children would get as 'open and as appreciative an appraisal from their grandparents by the time they are ready for college.'

On 12 December 1967, Larry acknowledged he had not written because of the tension between them. Rogers called it an 'estrangement'. Larry was obviously feeling vulnerable and conciliatory. Maybe it was all his fault and maybe it was the result of jealousy. It was hard to be the daughter of such a famous man and also hard to be his son-in-law. Natalie worshipped her father and just mentioning his name could bring a glow to her face. Larry admitted it made him envious. Moreover, Rogers was always preaching self-sufficiency and independence and yet he seemed to be more dependent on Helen than he, Larry, had ever been on Natalie. As his son-in-law saw it, Rogers could always count on Helen to compensate for his weak points.

Rogers had to cope with an even more serious crisis. His son had a coronary. Rogers felt scared, guilty and powerless. It was a frightening reminder of mortality. In his files Rogers kept a letter that had been sent to David who in turn sent it to his father. It's both a historical curiosity and a model of good advice. Its author was Lyndon B. Johnson when he was the Democratic Leader in the Senate. Johnson had himself suffered a heart attack and had written to the Supreme Court Justice, Felix Frankfurter, after Frankfurter had a heart attack. Somehow, the letter had reached a friend of David Rogers, who passed a copy on. Johnson wrote that after he had his coronary, he had made certain concessions to his heart so he now worked only 16 hours a day instead of 18 as in the past. He had also modified his eating habits and made food less important in his life. Johnson warned Frankfurter he was likely to suffer from depression. To Rogers it seemed a wise letter.

His son's heart attack meant Rogers had to reassure Corky. She needed to talk and he was the great listener. But he found it impossible to be detached because he blamed her for much of David's unhappiness. Corky complained that Rogers was angry with her. He was, but he was also frightened because he could see his son needed a stable loving wife – and Corky had never been that.

Rogers wrote that 1968 had been a dreadful year. It was all the more difficult because he didn't have enough to do, and one person he could let off steam to, his brother Walter, had gone off to Ceylon to work on a birth control programme. Rogers missed him. The turmoil around the 1968 presidential election also made Rogers gloomy and, with Nixon's election, he fretted there might be a repeat of the Crash and Depression of 1929.

On 8 March 1969, there was a sudden change of atmosphere between Larry and Rogers. Natalie had come to stay with her parents and, while she was there, Helen received an anguished letter from Larry. Rogers replied to him. Larry was wrong to think they were on Natalie's side and against him. Rogers assured him that much as he loved Natalie, he valued Larry too. And Larry had a case. Rogers had seen Natalie be bitchy to Larry as he had also seen Larry at an evening 'when you treated me as tho I didn't exist'. It was then that Rogers realised why Natalie was so critical of her husband. Rogers also acknowledged the intellectual differences between Larry and himself, but that was no tragedy. Rogers did not know who was right and who was wrong 'but I just like the growing independence of your thinking.' It was a generous letter.

On 18 April 1969 Rogers also got a letter from Leslie, David's mistress. She was desperately worried because David was saying that his life was a mess and he was 'withering inside'. Obviously he was desperately unhappy. She was yet another person turning to Rogers as if he could find a solution. Leslie wrote with grace and diffidence but, still, the letter made him realise how appalling his son's plight was.

Most of Lyndon Johnson's advice was to live a calmer life. There was little hope of David doing that after his coronary. He was depressed, chronically anxious and torn between two women. Rogers was acting as confidant to his son and, perhaps, hearing more of his reality than ever before. Notes of two phone conversations, on 13 and 16 July, deal with the fact that David felt he was drying up inside. He was holding too much and didn't seem to be able to stand anything. Rogers told him that he wished he could be in a group and loosen up. He suggested David and Corky come on holiday with them in November or go to Palm Beach in January, but that was too far off. Meanwhile he suggested that David 'blow off to me via tape.' He promised to keep the tapes from Helen if that was what David wanted but his son 'needed a safety valve'. On 16 July David was feeling he was screwing up life in general. He was making himself unhappy, making Corky unhappy and making Leslie unhappy. He no longer liked Corky but he felt terribly responsible for her. Not surprisingly, under so much stress Rogers' blood pressure went up.

On 24 July Rogers got another letter from David, who said he could no longer stand his marriage. He had tried what Rogers recommended, telling Corky about his feelings and his need to spend time with another woman but the 'explosions' were so momentous that he cancelled his planned trip with Leslie. David felt he was being asked to be responsible for Corky and that 'we make life crappy for the other'. They also discussed the moon landing, and Rogers made a brief note which said 'sweating'. David was hostile to his father at times. All this talk about feelings was crap. He had also said to Leslie that he was not going to marry her.

Rogers faced problems on every side. Helen's arthritis got much worse and she had to be hospitalised. Her ill health also meant one of the pleasures Rogers had long enjoyed – travelling – would be restricted because he would have to be at home to look after her; there was no one else. Beset by all these 'life events', Rogers turned to the consolations of drink, especially vodka. It was a way of coping that he, as a therapist, would not have recommended, and booze may have contributed to his erratic judgement when the Western Institute faced a crisis.

Ever since he had left Wisconsin, Rogers had not had to bother with academic politics. Now, there were serious difficulties at the Western Behavioural Sciences Institute. Dick Farson had resigned as its director. The Institute was losing its radical edge. The board was proposing to spend $120,000 on hiring business managers and bookkeepers to bring in new research. The final straw was an attempt to censor the weekly bulletin the Institute produced. The rich physicist, Paul Lloyd, had stepped in as director. Rogers protested vigorously to the board and said the present atmosphere had become so authoritarian it made 'the Divine Right of Kings look like a weak-kneed sissified theory.' Rogers expected his fame would force the board to reconsider the decisions that had led Farson to resign. Rogers pointed out that Jonas Salk, a friend and the inventor of the polio vaccine, had praised the Institute for showing the way in terms of establishing democratic ways of doing research.

The board did not, for all Rogers' fame – and *Time* magazine had called him 'the elder statesman of encounter groups' – listen to his protests or react to his threat of resignation. So he resigned and immediately set about finding a new home for himself at a centre he helped set up.

Rogers was one of the founders of the Centre for Studies of the Person. This was much more a group of friends and like-minded people than a formal institution. It is a measure of Rogers' increasing radicalism that he had few qualms about leaving the WBSI for something so improvised. There was no money, so only the secretaries got paid. Rogers, in fact, often met their salaries out of his own pocket. Everyone would be at liberty to pursue his or her own projects. Rogers was now a completely free agent as far as his work was concerned. At home, he felt rather trapped. But there was no one he could talk to about that truthfully, even in the encounter groups, and also no one to challenge his thinking. Yet Rogers needed challenging.

In 1969, as Rogers moved to the Centre, Stanley Milgram at Yale published a classic study of obedience. The subjects were told Yale was doing a study of the impact of reward and punishment on learning. Their job was to give electric shocks when students seemed to be lazy. Milgram showed that decent human beings were likely to follow orders even when these seemed to involve inflicting pain on innocent people. Milgram's subjects were easily made to ignore the screams they heard: students who didn't learn had to be punished to encourage them to work. Milgram's study was hailed as a masterly demonstration of social situations where the darkest aspects of human nature took control. The study got enormous publicity. It was said to explain why so many decent people in Nazi Germany had blindly followed orders. It was years before anyone criticised this interpretation (Harre 1983).

I dwell on this because Rogers had changed enormously since he had left Chicago. He had loosened up, become an expert on encounter groups and enjoyed a new career as a popular author. All these changes, including all the experiences in encounter groups, did nothing to disturb his faith in the basic goodness of persons, however. He showed no signs of taking any critique seriously. In 1969 he published *Freedom to Learn*, which repeated his attack on rigid education, reliance on exams and other educational conventions. Some reviews were acid. Edgar Friedenberg (who wrote the Fontana Modern Masters book on R. D. Laing) said that 'Like another American philosopher, Huckleberry Finn, Carl Rogers can get in anywhere because the draught of his vessel is so terribly shallow.' The review said he had no sense either of the tragedies of life or of the complexities of human choices. R. S. Peters, a British philosopher of education, was also scathing because the book seemed to suggest students could make up their truths as they went along. It was dangerous nonsense from a rather silly man, Peters suggested. Rogers dismissed these critics as reactionary.

Few things could be worse in the late 1960s than to be reactionary. At the beginning of 1970, Rogers went to see *Bob and Carol and Ted and Alice*, a film about two couples in California and their 'wife swapping'. Rogers, as he reached 68, was beginning to be much more interested in sex than he had been for many years. The sexual revolution was showing him that he had led a very narrow, repressed romantic life. It was time to make up for that.

HAROLD BRIDGES LIBRARY
S. MARTIN'S COLLEGE
LANCASTER

8

---

# The Old Wounds of an Old Pioneer, 1970–1980

Rogers did not resign from the Western Behavioural Sciences Institute and lick his wounds. He put his energies into making the Centre for Studies of the Person a lively base. Humanistic psychology had to put down foundations outside the universities because the academics were so hostile and sneering. The Centre would provide Rogers with an intellectual home for the rest of his life. He could research, write and campaign from there. The informal set-up gave him the freedom to explore ideas that might have seemed too bizarre or too radical on a university campus. There was a drawback, however. At the Centre, no one had the status to challenge him or his ideas. As a result, he was never nagged into attending to 'unfinished business', such as the issue of human destructiveness.

The informality meant Rogers could often work from home. Helen needed constant attention as her health was getting worse. She had hernia problems and walked less and less. In 1970, Rogers spent only 70 days away from home compared to 142 in 1966. After 1970 he travelled even less. His own health was far from good. He had an eye infection as well as the high blood pressure – and he was still drinking a great deal.

Given all that, it is hard not to admire Rogers' sheer energy. On his 70th birthday, he jotted down for family and friends an account of how he spent his day. It was ceaseless activity, answering phone calls, replying to letters, dealing with publishers and fitting in a spot of gardening. At 8 a.m. the day started with an urgent phone call from a woman who had been to a workshop in 1955 and now desperately needed to see him. She would be in La Jolla in two days. He had to make time for her. He couldn't say 'no' to her or to many others, a failure he found troubling.

On a typical day, the mail brought letters from the Fiji Islands requesting his latest ideas on education, an offer to become president of a Midwestern college, a letter from Randy Davis, an offender he was helping, and other fan letters. He approved the cover of *Carl Rogers on Encounter Groups*, which Harper & Row were going to publish and had discussions about changes in the film *A Conversation with Carl Rogers*. Then he went into the garden where the work ethic still ruled. He had a horticultural project and was trying to grow a moosehorn fern. At present, the fern wasn't thriving but it soon would show personal growth and, anyway, his begonias were blooming.

In the evening Rogers and Helen went to a movie and dinner. When they got back at 11 o'clock Rogers took a phone call from a young man who had just finished reading *On Becoming a Person*. He wanted the author to know how excited he was by it. Far from being annoyed at being rung so late, Rogers was delighted this student had stayed up to 2 a.m. to share his enthusiasm.

As Rogers worked from home that day, the list did not include one of his most significant activities in the 1970s – facilitating encounter groups. Throughout the decade he led groups which were often televised and, on occasion, he would do sessions of demonstration therapy with volunteers in front of an audience.

There was enormous popular interest in semi-serious psychology. By 1970, the magazine *Psychology Today* had a circulation of well over a million and Rogers' books were very much in demand. Helen began to worry that all the praise was going to his head. He was getting more adulation than he deserved, she felt, and that contributed to the bitterness of their last years together. Rogers kept a sad and frank journal of some of their quarrels. Natalie became so worried about her father's drinking that at one point she suggested he should follow Betty Ford's example and book himself into a de-tox clinic. He should kick the vodka before it kicked him.

Despite the problems, Rogers still produced a stream of learned articles and chapters for serious books. He was on the editorial board of, and a frequent contributor to, the *Journal for Humanistic Psychology*; he also wrote for a variety of other publications. Rogers reflected on the social and political turmoil of the early 1970s in such papers as 'Some Issues that Concern Me' (1972), but he did not lose his basic optimism. In that paper, he outlined the dangers of overpopulation, of the relentless growth of cities and of the failure of American parents to look after their children well. But human beings were still deep down good.

Rogers also became more interested in the spiritual and, particularly, in counter-culture approaches to religion. He liked the work of Carlos Castenada, who got his anthropology doctorate by studying the Indian magician Don Yaqui. Yaqui, the perfect model of the magus, could levitate, summon up the spirits of his ancestors and probably live in two universes at the same time. At least while on mescalin. Rogers was never cynical enough to suspect (as some did) that Yaqui was a fictional character.

Rogers was also fascinated by the parapsychological studies of individuals who had come back from clinical death and claimed to have seen a light in the tunnel, white-robed figures and soft-spoken voices that seemed to be the welcoming committee for the after-life (Moody 1976). In his debates with Buber and Tillich, Rogers had explored similarities between religious experiences and therapy, but he had not been much concerned with the question of whether religious experiences were 'true'. Rapport and revelation were both peak experiences. Now, faced with the problems of his own ageing and of Helen's serious illness, he began to ask more practical questions about reincarnation and other paranormal phenomena. Maybe death was not final?

Most academics at 70 slow down and are apt to repeat their favourite ideas. In the last 15 years of his life, Rogers managed to avoid this. He not only liked to work but he seemed to need to work. He thought it was because he was so bad at having fun, but work also offered a break from all his personal difficulties. There was something more obsessive, too. At 70 despite being world famous, Rogers kept on having to prove how productive he was. He counted lists of his publications. At one point, he totted up he had published over 120 articles in Japanese-language journals. He marvelled but didn't have the ability to laugh at himself for having to keep score.

For someone so imbued with the work ethic, it is extraordinary that Rogers approved of the hippies, the sexual revolution, the student sit-ins, flower power and even the use of drugs. They all inspired rather than disturbed Rogers. He was influenced by the historian Laurence Whyte who wrote that such 'perturbations' usually preceded great changes in society. The world was never the same after the First World War, Whyte wrote. At the end of the 1960s, Rogers sensed a similar dislocation, another historical shift, but this time for the good. As antique inhibitions dissolved, as people made love not war, a 'new person' would emerge. This counter-culture super-hero/heroine would slash his/her way gloriously to a brave new world of authentic relationships. Out would go the greed of Wall Street and the oppression of the military-industrial complex. In would come insight, love and harmony.

Rogers did not see – but then few did – that the counter-culture was also deeply narcissistic and that it would turn out often to be selfish. For many people being 'open to experience' would mean being utterly absorbed in themselves, the favourite hobby of the 'Me' generation. Rogers never admitted the self-obsession partly because the counter-culture seemed to him so liberating; he was shedding his constrained past and constrained self. Moreover, like everyone else, he had nothing against which to compare the sheer energy of the rock, the riots, the drugs, the pill, the sex and the anti-war protests.

Sometimes, Rogers' enthusiasm for radical ideas was uncritical and even naive – an old man trying new tricks. The easy theory, of course, is that he was seduced by these freedoms to make up for 70 years of inhibitions. That may be true but his passion for radical ideas was also touching and admirable. He was, of course, not as free as he pretended and he was wrestling with many demons in the 1970s. But he was much more open than most old men – open and, sometimes, vulnerable.

As the problems between Dave and Corky were coming to a head, Rogers showed none of these endearing traits, however. In a letter written in August 1970, Rogers told his son he had gone to see a lawyer on his behalf. The lawyer's advice was that David should come out to California on professional grounds. David had already resigned from Johns Hopkins after his heart attack. If he were a California resident for six months, he would be able to sue for divorce there, so the smartest thing to do was to 'cool it' and to pretend he was committed to make the marriage work. That would put Corky off her guard. David should not try to have Corky committed but he should establish his residency in California. If he sued for divorce from there, he might able to stop the house going entirely to her. Rogers told his son to keep this letter in a very secure personal file. It was a Machiavellian plan and, initially, it worked.

In the middle of 1970 Rogers went to Pittsburgh where he was asked to facilitate an intensive two-day group organised by the Pittsburgh TV station WQED. The group included high-school students, narcotics officers and a man who had been convicted of drugs-related offences – Randy Davis. Davis was actually on bail while the group was taking place and it was only at the very end that he revealed that he was facing trial for an offence committed before he had entered rehabilitation. Rogers tried to get Randy's sentence reduced.

By October Randy Davis was inside and wrote to Rogers. 'Carl don't feel bad about me being here' because, in the end, he had done this to himself. Rogers replied he was saddened by Randy's sentence and felt 'awful about it'. He offered to write to Randy's Congressman and Senators on his behalf. Randy was grateful for the offer. The WQED show had been a great success. A studio executive told Rogers it was exciting and meaningful; when he and his wife watched it, they nearly cried.

On 11 November 1970, Rogers told Randy he had asked publishers to send on three copies of his books. At Christmas time, Rogers promised to talk to three more influential people to see if anything could be done to help. He also gave Randy a little personal information. Rogers loved gardening and had been married 46 years. He encouraged Randy to make use of the time inside to educate himself and perhaps also help some of the other inmates. In January 1971, Rogers wrote to Gladys Costock, a member of the Board of Parole of the Western Correctional Centre, and asked her to see to it Randy was recommended for parole as soon as possible. His efforts failed, however.

## The politics of psychology

After leaving the Western Institute, Rogers came into contact with a graduate student, Alan Nelson, who asked him one day about the politics of therapy. Rogers was startled by the question and even more so when Nelson pointed out that non-directive therapy altered the balance of power in the counselling room. The therapist no longer had total control. Rogers claims this was a revelation and compared himself to the man who had been speaking prose all his life but did not know it. He had been practising politics ever since he left Rochester without knowing it. (The character is Molière's Tartuffe but Rogers either did not know or did not care to cite the source.) There were other forms of political education. Natalie made him see the importance of feminist ideas. Remarkably for a man of his generation, he started using 'she' as the generic pronoun in many of his works.

Rogers concentrated on three themes for most of the 1970s. The first was the value of encounter groups. *Carl Rogers on Encounter Groups* was a publishing success the moment it hit the bookshops. Encounter groups offered a means of introducing a new approach to personal and social conflicts. He travelled all over the world with that message. Tony Merry, a lecturer in social work who met him towards the end of his life, was impressed that Rogers continued to have the patience to listen to people. Rogers ran groups in South Africa, Brazil, Italy, Poland and even the Soviet Union. He arranged to fly a number of Protestants and Catholics from Ulster over to the States to see if his approach could make people see beyond their stereotypes of the Papist and the Orangeman as eternal enemies. The sessions of this group were made into a film – *The Steel Shutter*.

The participants from Ulster started out full of hostility towards one another. One woman said that if she came across an IRA man lying injured on the street she would step over him and leave him to die. The IRA were less than human. Slowly, however, the Catholics and the Protestants came to see that they had a lot in common, that beneath the prejudices and hatreds they were all human. When members of the group got back to Belfast, some remained friends. But like many psychologists before him, Rogers minimised the social issues and over-estimated the importance of persuading people to get on with each other. The experience of the Ulster men and women suggested to him that Northern Ireland needed 2000 such encounter groups. Perhaps, but he never asked whether the individuals who agreed to take part in the group were typical. Wasn't it likely that though they could huff hate with the best bigots, they were at least a little more open-minded than most?

Five years later, Rogers likened Camp David to an encounter group, with President Jimmy Carter as the facilitator between Begin and Sadat, sworn enemies who hugged at the end of their negotiations just as if they had been in Esalen!

Rogers continued to write, lecture and campaign about his second theme, the need to reform education. He remained true to one of his early enthusiasms. Fifty years after he had studied the works of John Dewey, he was still insisting the educational system was too rigid and unimaginative. Prizes went to those who could parrot information back and did not ask troubling questions.

The third theme in Rogers' work was more personal – observations of himself and of the process of ageing. As he reached 70, then 75, 80, 85, Rogers reflected on what it meant to be growing older. He was very sensitive to the loss of physical skills as his eyesight failed and he found it harder to play tennis and harder 'to get it up' – a phrase used in his jottings, not in a learned journal. He wrote movingly on the frailties of age, even if he ignored one of his main handicaps, his drinking.

Remarkable though Rogers' achievements during this late period of his life were, the public accounts do not reflect many agonising private traumas – as tensions in his marriage finally erupted. He left some very frank, very bitter and very sad notes in the Library of Congress. They show he was unhappy and, paradoxically, for one who taught people how to express their feelings, that he didn't know what to do about his tendency 'to clam up'. The therapist had never been able to heal himself. In a little corner of his mind, he was still that shy little boy who wandered in the woods and who preferred books to people – and he wanted people to know it.

## Encounter group guru

Rogers had spent most of his life accepting the decencies of middle-class American life. You were supposed to be polite; you were not supposed to be too emotional or angry. Now, suddenly, it was almost compulsory to talk about feelings, to reveal the inner self. If one looks at *On Becoming a Person* (1961), it is perhaps not bizarre that Rogers should have been so ready to enter the spirit of this experiment because he talked in the book of the bliss of dropping the façade and of hunting the authentic 'I' to find one's true self. Encounter groups seem to have made it easier for him to do that, and whatever Larry Fuchs' reservations, Rogers himself felt he experienced a sense of liberation in the groups that he had never had when doing therapy.

The problem was that he did not find it easy to use his 'learnings' from encounter groups in the most intimate relationship in his life – his marriage. Rogers never seems to have asked the subversive question: what did that mean in terms of what encounter groups could really achieve?

The many groups he ran brought Rogers face to face with a sad reality, he said. Individuals were probably more aware of their inner loneliness than at any other time in history. When people had to fight to make sure of their next meal, they had no time 'to discover that one is alienated from others in a deep sense' (Rogers 1970, p. 110). The conditions of modern life, the destruction of old communities, the impersonal nature of the contemporary grind, made individuals feel terrifyingly alone. Rogers spoke 'of the loneliness that exists when the person feels that he has no real contact with other persons.' Too many people were scared to drop their façade. Let the mask slip and what was left? Only ugliness. No one could accept them for what they were. It's an old neurosis. Groucho Marx joked that he refused to be a member of any club that would have him; Rogers cried that deep down he was unlovable. If people knew what he was really like, they wouldn't love him, admire him or, even, buy his books.

All that could change in encounter groups. An ordinary person could discover his or her self and realise others were not turned off by that self. The encounter group was a magical oasis where American capitalist obsessions didn't kill all joy, all feeling, all hope. You didn't have to worry about what your job was or whether you were successful. Rogers knew research showed that if individuals were asked 'who they are', men replied by first giving their occupation: I am a plumber, a policeman, a psychologist. Work was the basis of their identity. No wonder so many felt empty and insecure. Groups opened new horizons; people saw how shallow it was to 'be' your job.

Rogers gave many case histories from his groups, snapshots of moments of pain and moments of transformation. Yet again, his skill at picking quotes made *Carl Rogers on Encounter Groups* vivid. Many group members felt lonely, trapped and frightened. They had no friends and did not know who they were. One young man confessed to his diary that at one point he was so tired and despondent at the end of a group that all he wanted was for someone to walk into his room and show him kindness. But he ached with needing that. Others talked of feeling naked in the encounter groups and of being terrified of seeming not to be 'cool'. The group taught them to be comfortable when they were not pretending and taught them they could unpeel their masks without getting too bruised. Their naked self wasn't ugly.

In his studies of individual therapy, Rogers had meticulously plotted the stages as clients developed insight and, finally, changed. It took months, occasionally, years. But in encounter groups, it was quick, a matter of a few days, sometimes a few hours. Rogers did not ask why that should be, or whether people were pretending. He had once cited Solomon Asch's work on the social pressure in groups. Encounter groups put immense pressure on those who took part to say they were growing, changing, actualising and that it was 'far out'. But in his enthusiasm, Rogers never raised the critical issue of the effect of group pressure or of how lasting these transformations might be.

In encounter groups Rogers could be proactive. He didn't have to wait for the client to 'grow'; as facilitator, he could make things happen and take risks. He described one case where he had gone over to a woman. She looked calm. Deceptively calm, his intuition told him. He sat by her and asked her how long she had been crying. It was a risk, for there were no tears. She said she had not been crying.

'No, I mean, how long have you been crying inside?' Rogers asked. The sage had hit the mark.

'Eight months,' she said.

He held her like a little child until the sobbing stopped. How had he known she was crying? she asked.

Rogers did not ask himself if this was real, or theatre, or whether his status as a guru provoked effects among the 'groupies'. Some of his pleasure came from the fact that he felt he was changing and becoming less uptight. His main 'learning' was that there was nothing to be frightened of. When he dared to drop the armour, when he made no effort to embellish his real self, he enjoyed life the more. Drop the façade and be happy.

The case histories in *Carl Rogers on Encounter Groups*, he wrote, 'make clear that in an intensive group experience it is possible for a person to peer within themselves and see the loneliness of the real being who lives inside his everyday shell or role.' Rogers defended encounter groups strongly in a letter to the *New York Times* in 1971 after a piece claimed that many people came out of groups traumatised. He recognised the dangers of such techniques as EST, which tried to demean people and lower their self-esteem, but, on the whole, groups were very positive. He even persuaded Helen to go along but, after two experiences, she never wanted to try a group again.

In five years, 237,000 copies of *Carl Rogers on Encounter Groups* were sold. At home, however, one of most frequent accusations was that he never told Helen what he really felt. He didn't seem to her to be much more open than before.

## The inward eye

There was also no sign that his relationship with Lester mellowed as they got older. In fact, the opposite. Their letters suggest Rogers was under such stress that he was starting to be irrationally angry – and quite unable to take a joke.

The brothers were corresponding more than usual through 1970 and 1971. Rogers seemed still to want his brother's approval, though he appeared to deny the fact to himself. On 29 July 1971, Lester wrote a letter in which he marvelled that Carl had not known for decades 'how far apart our philosophies were. I have, ever since in Rochester you took the word of a workman that his foreman was unjust and terrible and counselled on that basis without ever checking with the foreman as to how industrious and willing the bird was.' Lester pointed out that when Rogers went West he dealt largely with 'worshipful admirers'. Like Helen, Lester wondered if fame were not turning Rogers' head. Lester explained that his own work at Bates & Rogers had not consisted of giving orders to employees but of teaching, because each construction job presented different problems. Lester stressed he did not like 'yes' men. He always encouraged discussion and debate but, in the end, it was up to him to take the final decisions for the company. That was life. This was by way of introducing a thorny subject. Lester went on to say the reason he did not like *On Becoming a Person* (and the reason their sister Margaret did not like it either) was 'you apparently felt the strict but honest and in so many ways very wise upbringing you had . . . was most unfair to you.' Lester rejected this idea and said he so loved and respected his parents that he 'didn't kick' and that it didn't seem to him so terrible they had been forbidden to dance and to smoke. Lester added a final blow; he didn't finish *On Becoming a Person* because it was wordy and repetitious.

Curiously, Rogers replied that it seemed the 'mildest letter I had gotten from you in years.' They were entitled to their different views. Rogers appreciated Lester's reaction to the encounter group book. He would send Lester *Freedom to Learn* to read but warned his brother to be careful because it would make his blood boil as he'd disagree with all its ideas. Rogers also told Lester that Corky was in hospital – again.

Lester replied it was 'strange that as an experienced psychologist you should feel I am "hostile" whenever I differ with your perspectives or try to ask questions'. He denied he was bitter. He joked he might cancel his subscription to the Centre's newsletter. This stung Rogers more than one might expect. In October 1971 he wrote to Lester informing him he was having his name taken off the mailing list for the Centre for Studies of the Person. Rogers then got in a wounding blow. In the envelope he enclosed Lester's contribution of $15 in cash since that meant Lester would be able to lie to the Internal Revenue Service. 'I think it should appeal to you to be able to take $15 of tax deduction which you don't really deserve,' Rogers said. It was one of the last phrases he would ever address to his brother.

Rogers added he had shown a friend of his Lester's latest letter and his reaction had been, 'Why the hell do you continue to try to communicate with him?' Rogers told Lester he had tried to communicate with him because they were brothers but now communication was impossible. He suspected Lester was so hostile because he was jealous. And with good reason, Rogers pointed out. Lester was not, after all, a best-selling author whose views hundreds of thousands of people from Cape Town to San Francisco wanted to hear. Rogers listed his sales figures. That wordy, repetitious book Lester could not be bothered to finish had sold 180,000 copies; *Freedom to Learn* had sold 81,000 copies; *Client-Centred Therapy* had sold 112,000 copies. Rogers was speaking to people's needs and confusions.

Lester replied he was sorry he had hurt his feelings and he had been making a joke about possibly cancelling his subscription. He added he was proud of his famous brother. It was all too late; Rogers does not seem to have ever forgiven him.

## A marriage manual

We know a good deal about Rogers' marital problems because of his papers in the Library of Congress. These include notes titled 'What I Want for Myself' (1975) and 'What I Want to do for Myself' (1977), written at Carmel. They also include jottings of a series of conversations between himself and Helen. Some reveal a much darker, despairing persona than Rogers ever allowed to be glimpsed in public. This was the man who was consuming 12 oz of vodka a day – and insisting all was well.

The dramatic difficulties started when Helen had a hernia in 1972. There were anxious weeks in hospital when she was close to death. Rogers kept notes of her condition and her mood. When she got home, she had to struggle to recover physically and to ward off depression. Rogers was her main carer and many of his resentments came from being forced into this role. He could not leave her at home without making arrangements for her.

Psychologists are rarely discouraged by their life experiences. Erich Fromm had been married five times when he wrote *The Art of Loving*. So it is not odd that Rogers started to write a book on marriage. He said the counter-culture made it timely to look at the whole range of relationships between men and women, but he also seems to have wanted to write a little about his own marriage. Certainly the book mentions some personal problems. Helen must have agreed to their publication, but in 1972 she was still the dutiful wife.

In *Becoming Partners*, Rogers repeated the story of the sexual difficulties he and Helen had had in the 1920s in their innocence. Rogers skirted over their more recent difficulties. The most it said was that she resented a little the fact that he got all the recognition and awards – trophies that mattered to him or he would have prevented Kirschenbaum ending each chapter of *On Becoming Carl Rogers* with a list of honorary degrees, awards and medals received. Rogers never admitted Helen was getting more bitter as she felt she had lived her whole life in his shadow.

In January 1972, Rogers discussed the manuscript of his book

*Becoming Partners: Marriage and Its Alternatives* with Donald Cutler at Stirling Lord (Academic Division) Inc. Rogers wanted the book to reach a wide public and insisted it had to be published in paperback after only six months. As Cutler was keen to keep Rogers, he agreed.

Rogers said he had permission from all the people he had included in the book and he attached a copy of the relevant letters. The book included a history of the marriage of a couple called Jennifer and Jay. Jay was a brilliant academic who had spent much of his life abroad. When his wife, influenced by feminism, started to become more independent and to complain Jay might not be the man for her sexually, Jay could not understand. 'For such a brilliant man', Rogers said in a surprisingly judgemental comment, this was a 'marked lack of insight.'

On 4 February 1972 Larry Fuchs, who was now divorced from Natalie, was surprised to hear from friends that a portrait of his marriage formed a crucial part of *Becoming Partners*. Larry was recognisable as Jay and Natalie as Jennifer. Larry's friends were amazed he should have agreed to the publication. Their children would see that it was an analysis of their parents' marriage – and they would find that rather difficult to handle. Larry was shocked and told his friends he knew nothing about the book or the portrait. Certain of Rogers' integrity, he replied, 'Nonsense, Carl would never invade my or anyone's privacy without permission.' When Larry got hold of the book and started to read it, he was stunned. One of the longest chapters described his and Natalie's marriage in intimate detail. Anyone who knew would recognise them.

Larry wrote a furious letter to his ex-father-in-law accusing him of betraying trust and confidences. Rogers does not appear to have replied, which provoked another letter. Larry said that he had no wish to cut communication but he did want an explanation of what seemed totally unethical conduct.

On 9 February 1972 Lester died in Palm Springs. Rogers would not go to the funeral. His brother John wanted him to give the funeral oration, however. Finally Rogers consented to write it but he would not attend. It had to be read out for him. The eulogy was perfectly decent, praising Lester's work in building up Bates

& Rogers and his co-operation with the International Labour Organisation. It also acknowledged that the brothers had gone their different ways and it ended, conventionally enough, by remarking that Lester died while he was still an active man who could enjoy himself. It would have been a day's travel by plane from San Diego for Rogers to attend. But he would not go.

## Divorce and cunning

By the summer of 1972 Helen's health was deteriorating. From 23 May 1972, she had to have a wheelchair, and the daily routine of care fell almost totally on Rogers. Ironically, he had to take on the role of carer at the very moment when his encounter group work was bringing him into contact with many lively young people – and lively young women. A consistent theme of the next few years is Rogers' resentment of Helen's illness. He was bitter that it stopped him travelling and exploring new experiences. It was perhaps also easier to be angry with her than to face up to his own ageing. Even worse, they had such different wishes they couldn't grow old in peace.

By 1972, David had put into action the plan he and his father had hatched. He filed for his divorce in California, and there was nothing Corky could do to prevent it. On 2 January 1973 Rogers had a long phone conversation with her. She could not stop crying. She belonged to one man. She now knew the divorce plot had been hatched by her father-in-law as well as her husband and she would never forgive either of them. She was bitter that the children loved Bobbie, who would become David's second, wife, and she wanted to know what she, Cora, who had known David since they were 15, was supposed to do with the rest of her life.

On 5 February, a relative called Corky and then warned the family she was suicidal. She was found dead the next day. She had indeed committed suicide.

These difficulties did not affect Rogers' growing eminence as a radical social commentator. *Becoming Partners* had been published and was well received. Rogers illustrated many different forms of 'relationships' – marriages, cohabitation, communes. The message was that traditional marriage was only one of a number of ways in which men and women could live together. In South Africa, the book was banned because one chapter explored the marriage of a black man and a white woman. Len Holstock, who had studied under Rogers between 1960 and 1963, told the *Sunday Times* of South Africa that it was a scandal the government was preventing South Africans reading one of the great psychologists of the century. Rogers also started working on his autobiographical book with Kirschenbaum, a respectful work that tiptoes around almost all of the personal crises.

As he reviewed his life, some paradoxes became very clear. Increasingly, it seemed to Rogers that he had lived his marriage in a deadly conventional way. Of course he had loved Helen; of course he still loved Helen. But the moral standards of Walter and Julia had meant he had virtually no other sexual experiences. He had been tediously faithful for nearly 50 years. For over ten years, he had been one of the prime advocates of being open to experience, of making love not war, so it was a not very pleasing irony that he had always made love to the same wife. In her wheelchair, Helen was less than sympathetic.

When Rogers raised the idea of an open marriage and of having some sort of relationship with another woman, Helen first sulked and then became possessive. Her continuing ill health made her feel especially vulnerable. Early in 1973 she had a hip joint operation.

Rogers' sudden interest in seeking new sexual partners was perhaps also a way of denying his fears of ageing. On 30 July 1973 David wrote to his father saying tests showed Rogers had senile macular degeneration. His eyesight would inevitably get worse, though a regime of vitamins might help a little.

By the summer of 1974, Rogers felt under such stress that he took ten days away at Simson Beach to be by himself. He made sure Helen had help and he rang her every night but he felt he had come to the end of his tether. He enjoyed the solitude and it did something to restore him in time for their 50th wedding celebrations on 4 September 1974. Dave and Bobbie and Natalie came to spend some time with them at a motel in the California Valley. Rogers said that it was a happy time.

In public Rogers continued to take workshops and to press for educational reform, and he was now more willing than ever before to get mixed up in campaigns. On 20 January 1975 he wrote to Jay D. Michael, the Vice-Chancellor of the University of California, to complain that Michael was working to prevent the election of John Vasconcellos to any position where he could influence university policy. Rogers found the opposition 'mind boggling' because it suggested the university saw no need to innovate. He believed 'educational institutions to be among the most outdated and rigid of our cultural organisations.' He picked out as a typical university product Robert McNamara, who was one of the most brilliant men of his generation, but who did not understand that 'little men in black pyjamas who believed passionately in a cause' could defeat the mighty USA. Academics could not grasp passion. 'McNamara is a prime example of the kind of learning you are advocating – a blindness to the feeling aspects of life'. Rogers added he had just been selected by the journal *Education* as one of the Gold Medal Educators of the 1970s, so perhaps they should listen to what he had to say.

One of the initiatives Rogers had encouraged in the late 1960s was bearing fruit. Humanistic psychology was beginning to develop its own institutions. The Centre was surviving. The *Journal of Humanistic Psychology* was successful and, often, very lively. It even ran a piece by Woody Allen. By 1975, there was also a network of seminars and conferences where humanistic psychologists could discuss ideas and research. That year Rogers attended a conference in Tucson where they discussed the future of humanistic psychology.

## The love of his life

The tensions in his marriage left Rogers rather vulnerable and, finally, that showed. Not long after the Tucson conference, in August 1975, Rogers met and fell in love with Bernice Todres during an encounter group. She was a divorced woman who wanted to be a therapist and a writer. They first met on Saturday 2 August 1975 at 9 a.m. They were with a group of other people who would be taking part in the 'intensive'. Later Rogers wrote that his intuition told him, 'I would like to hug' her. Bernice responded very spontaneously so they embraced for the first time within minutes of meeting. For the next eight days, they both took part in many group sessions. I have relied heavily on the correspondence and the notes that Rogers made in describing what happened.

There is something moving and pathetic in the spectacle of the love – and lust – of an old man for a much younger woman. The relationship with Todres was to be tremendously important for Rogers but he was always at a disadvantage with her. He wanted her more than she wanted him, and that did not change from their first date to their last row.

It was not until 10 August, a Sunday, that Rogers had the courage to invite her to his room. He noted, 'I feel so good about myself. Yesterday I asked if she would come to my room. Yes. Suggested 8.30. I have had so many vivid fantasies about being with her, caressing her, loving her. I have felt it would be so enriching to me if I could.' As 8.30 drew near, 'I was so nervous I could hardly contain myself.' His heart beat 'like a triphammer'. When she did come into the room, he felt 'like an adolescent all over again.' Rogers opened up to her. He wrote that he told her about his fantasies and 'I shared my incredibly straight and naive sex experience.' He told her about the sexual side of his marriage and that he had not had sex for two and a half years. He confessed he had occasional desires for an outside relationship and how Helen felt threatened by that.

Bernice Todres told him about her divorce. Rogers then felt she wanted to channel the conversation back to safer professional topics so they talked about the group and other subjects. But by 11 o'clock, 'I pulled it back to the sexual aspects. I told her I'd like to share my crazy fantasies about her and I did – the whole bit'. Today, of course, that could provoke accusations of sexual harassment. In the mid-1970s, it was part of sexual liberation. She said, according to Rogers, that his desires were very natural and she could feel 'the vibes' between them. She too wanted to be physically close when she felt so close emotionally. 'I felt so relieved', he wrote. 'Then we parted with a long loving embrace and the best tongue kiss and lip kissing I ever had.'

Rogers admitted he gloated for the next hour over his semi-conquest. But he was determined not to crowd her. He seems to have injected the experience with deep meaning from the start. This was not a fling but a truly great love. He wrote that night, 'But that a woman I love loves me is still something that seems a bit of a miracle. I still ask "Who me", but it is not as incredible as it used to be.'

Eight pages of notes then deal with the emotional ups and downs of the next few days. When Rogers found that Todres felt as he did, he wrote, 'Far out!' Love affected his work, though. Throughout one group session, he felt depressed, which he shared with them, 'weeping, of course' until Bernice came over and held his arm. She let him hold her leg which he could feel was 'nice and bare'.

At 3.30 that afternoon Bernice came to see Rogers. He was not the only man in the intensive who was attracted by her: she felt delighted because she had thrown a man out of her bed the night before and she had defended Rogers against the vituperative attacks of a male behaviourist. (In a published account of the group Rogers disguised her name and his feelings. He said she was pleased with herself because, after dinner, she decided her escort did not have the right to go to bed with her just because he had bought her a steak dinner.) It would have been uncool for Rogers to object to another admirer, especially when Todres had given him the push. Rogers wrote, 'We sat and lay on the bed – lovely warm kisses.' They didn't last long. Todres had to go to a four o'clock meeting. Rogers mooned she felt deliciously soft and added wistfully, 'I don't suppose I do.'

The intensive encounter group had to keep going through all the romancing. On the Thursday morning, Rogers had to deal with a 50-year-old woman who was discovering her sexuality. In the afternoon, Rogers whispered he hoped to see Bernice one last time. Then during the group, 'I started out feeling lonely and sad but wound up dancing slow a lot. Others joined me.' Again, there's something admirable and comic about a 73-year-old man gyrating and weeping because he was finally getting in touch with his feelings.

When Bernice came to see him that evening, she said she was

too tired to stay long so they just exchanged a kiss. She explained to Rogers she had had a severe rejection from a man and was very uptight about sleeping with anybody. So before it went beyond kissing, she was off again out of the bedroom.

The next drama concerned a picnic on Friday 16 August. Bernice did not show up and that made Rogers dreadfully anxious. He had no idea what had happened to her and, after asking a number of people to look out for her, he went up to her room. There was no sign of her. Eventually she did turn up but Rogers wrote that after the evening encounter group session, he was very angry. All this 'needless churning' had made him bite two blisters on his lower lip. He was quite determined to tell her how furious she had made him.

On Saturday at breakfast, Rogers told Bernice how bad she had made him feel. She explained she was going through a crisis of her own, had run into a man she trusted and spent hours sobbing on his shoulder. Rogers was relieved it had been only on his shoulder. He was very nervous and frightened she did not care for him. 'She gave me a sad farewell and a long loving deep kiss. Her lips are so soft.' Bernice hoped to come to La Jolla soon. And then she was gone again.

Over the next three years they had an episodic and obviously unsatisfactory relationship. Rogers could not leave Helen and Bernice Todres never seems to have asked him to. In La Jolla, they had a brief, tense evening together. Then, in November, they spent some time in New York, which Rogers found frustrating because she would not sleep with him. In New York he also experienced a completely illogical fear of her. Perhaps it was the guilt he felt towards Helen, he noted. They saw each other next in Boston in April where for a moment Rogers thought he was about to succeed in seducing Bernice. They had an intense, romantic meal in a restaurant. In the end, however, there was no sex.

Between April and August, it was just letters and phone calls. Rogers had to be careful not to upset Helen while Bernice often promised to send letters which never arrived. The ups and downs of the relationship made Rogers more and more unhappy. By May 1976 Rogers had still not managed to persuade her to sleep with him. He was beginning to wonder if he found Bernice's body so desirable because it reminded him of Helen's 'lovely long-limbed body' when she was young. One afternoon Rogers found himself sobbing on his patio and saying, 'I want a woman to love, I want a woman to love.' While Bernice loved him in her way 'it was not enuf' (his spelling). Her refusal to sleep with him hurt. He admitted he had few illusions about his sexual prowess because every year 'I find it harder to get it up. I'm not even sure I want to try intercourse.' But he did want to pleasure her sexually and for her to pleasure him 'but why is that so important that I feel totally rejected when she draws the line there?'

Rogers added that one weekend of passion might be enough. As it became obvious Bernice would not sleep with him, Rogers' notes make it clear that he started to seek out other sexual partners. And one had left him with very erotic memories. 'But my one night – hell two hours – with that other woman has given me delicious memories.' He remembered 'her nude body as we made up the bed together afterwards – the miracles she could work with her lips and tongue – and now we are good friends only.'

He was annoyed at himself for being over-emotional and annoyed because he was drinking 'much too much and that frightens me too – and makes it likely I wouldn't be much good sexually.' He was putting away most of a bottle of vodka a day; Natalie had the sense to tell him that this did not make him very attractive.

Rogers felt Bernice could be cruel and he was hurt that she had never acknowledged how much help he had been to her. 'It reminds me of the Lao-tzu saying that, with the good leader, people say "we did it all ourselves".' It was he who had helped her be more open in her relationships with men; it was he who had stood by her when she felt depressed and hopeless. It was he who had encouraged her in her dreams of being a therapist and a writer. Rogers scribbled a whole litany of what he had done for her.

The relationship also forced Rogers to confront his feelings about Helen. On 25 May 1976 at 7.30 in the evening, he wrote that he had casually said to a therapist friend that he wanted to see him in the next few days. The reality, however, was that he wanted immediate help. 'I want to see him now. I always underestimate my need for help and get desperate before I call for it.' He took a Valium and a drink before going for counselling. Rogers was aware of how ridiculous his position was. Hundreds of people loved him; Bernice loved him in her way. But logic had nothing to do with it, as his therapist pointed out. 'I feel deprived and that is my reality. I feel deprived of all the sexual relationships I might have had outside of marriage which Helen's feelings prevented.' He realised he had never been monogamous at heart. He added, 'Part of my sadness is my deep sadness over Helen. I'm living with a person wasted in body, depressed in spirit and clinging in her relationship. This is not the woman I married or loved and the strain of being with her gets too great. I'm reconciled to her dying, feel it would be a mercy all round if she could.'

The therapist helped him clarify his rush of feelings. Bernice Todres had opened up a 'vast reservoir of love that I want to give and give and give.' But she lived far away and 'her strange (to me) feelings about sexual contact' made it impossible for him to act on the flood of feelings she released in him. Also she put him 'in a begging situation which I hate myself in'. Begging someone to let him love them 'would turn anyone off'.

He added that Bernice was 'kidding herself' because their relationship was not non-sexual but then, he had to admit, that was her reality. He had to respect that, even if it hurt. But he was completely smitten so he was willing to deceive Helen 'my wife of 52 years' and a dying woman if he had to in order to keep his 'affair' with Bernice going. He justified his behaviour easily; he did not love Helen as he had done before. He was even quite proud of his ability to pretend. 'I realise I've been getting more competent in deception and can do it even though it's a lousy way of maintaining a good relationship.' Nothing, however, would make him deceive Bernice because he really loved her.

Rogers was waiting on tenterhooks for a letter from Bernice. He noted acidly that he found it hard to separate the person and the body but that Bernice found this remarkably easy.

Despite his adoration, Rogers was again making alternative plans and 'quite cold-bloodedly compiling a list of women who might accept me sexually and whom I like and respect' if Bernice still resisted bed. Some of these second-best women were eager to have sex with him but, unfortunately, the two women he fancied most already had relationships. Despite that, his plan would be to go for these two first but if they were not willing 'perhaps I could learn to enjoy sex with some of the others'. In this confused and distressed state, he was not managing to do any creative work, he complained.

In August 1976, Rogers wrote to Bernice celebrating their anniversary. He did not mention the fact that she had not been willing to sleep with him. He said again he wanted to spend time with her and, inevitably, that provoked problems with Helen, problems that led to ugly scenes at the end of the year.

On 30 December 1976, Rogers and Helen quarrelled. Helen decided to accompany him to a workshop at Sagamore, but Rogers did not want her to come. Natalie was going to be there – and it may have been that he hoped to get away to see Bernice. Upset, Helen said that she would never mention Sagamore again, never stand in his way. But the next day, she was depressed, saying she had nothing to look forward to in the New Year and that she hated seeing it arrive.

After dinner, Helen went to bed. As Rogers helped her, she began crying and complaining and Rogers jotted down her sharpest words. She said, 'You just always put me down.' She knew he didn't love her any more and that she was just a burden to him. He helped lots of other people but 'you're just a stone image'. People thought he was a god but why didn't he help her? He was always making her feel small.

Rogers said that he did not have the answer. Helen told him, 'Stop saying you don't have the answer. None of us have the answer for anything. It makes me angry to have you say that. Stop it.' Helen felt she should have died when she was so ill. 'You wouldn't miss me a bit if I were gone.' He had already withdrawn from her. 'You don't love me,' Helen said, 'I don't contribute anything to your life. All I have is memories. You just clam up.' She accused him of no longer respecting her. When he kissed her or they snuggled it was just out of his sense of duty.

Rogers admitted the nature of his love for her had changed. But hers, Helen insisted, had not. She said, 'I try so hard and it's not worth it. I wish I could die tonight.' By the end of the evening

Helen was very angry. She wanted him to promise something that he did not specify but he refused. It would depend on his feelings. He told her he liked her when she was angry and that he didn't know 'how to scrap'. He finally realised how hurt she had been when he didn't want her at Sagamore.

They did not see the New Year in together. Helen was in bed by 7 o'clock. Rogers tried to sleep around 8.30 but then he woke up. The next day they resumed their conversation. She told him that nearly always when she explained how she felt, he did not respond. He said he felt so useless when he started to express his feelings and 'I wasn't understood.' Everything Helen said sounded so utterly definite. She could never be wrong. 'This last set her off,' Rogers commented.

'I'm not judgemental, I'm the most open-minded person I know. Don't you ever . . .' Helen snapped.

That evening Rogers wrote, 'What do I feel about all this. I feel confused and upset. I'm a bit scared by the truth of what she is saying. She is right in almost every respect. I don't think I do love her. I respect her abilities with people. I have known that my life would be simpler if she was gone . . . I do clam up . . . I do keep things from her.'

He felt unable to help Helen find a life of her own and he admitted he was concentrating on his other relationships. In the end, Rogers always felt guilty that he and his daughter, Natalie, had been to Sagamore leaving Helen ill, 'a dying woman', on her own, as Natalie later put it.

But there were brief moments of hope when Rogers thought his life might be magically transformed. On 10 January 1977 Bernice wired him to say that he had no idea how much he meant to her.

Sometime in February Rogers and Helen had a huge row; 'she called me all the names in the book in a quite bitter way and talked of "perverted sex and feeding on adulation"'. But her accusations had also made her think. Later, on 28 February Helen told him she had something important to say. As Rogers jotted down their conversation – and it has to be remembered that all this is based on his notes – Helen admitted she had been the first to break their sexual commitment by refusing to have sex with him any more. She had come to feel that it was unreasonable to ignore his need for a sexual life. She didn't understand, but if he wanted to pursue sexual contact with other women, she would accept it. Rogers told her she was a remarkable person to have made that decision and it made him feel 'more warmly' towards her.

'And perhaps you'll be less secretive,' she said.

He agreed with her he would.

'Because I won't disapprove so much.'

A little later she said, 'This is sort of what you've been trying to get me to understand for a long time.'

'I said yes,' Rogers wrote.

Rogers told her he appreciated very much what she was saying and he knew it was a huge change in her attitude. He would understand if she slipped back into her old possessive self from time to time.

Rogers obviously hoped for some domestic peace now, as well as some physical consolation. With neither Bernice nor Helen willing to have sex with him, Rogers developed a relationship with a third woman, Rachel. He was cynical about her: she loved him more than he loved her and so there were no difficulties in persuading her to go to bed with him.

A week after Helen had said she would allow him to have his incomprehensible flings – and clearly Rogers felt better once he had her permission – she started to tell her truth as she had never told it before. He never wanted to listen, she said. Rogers kept a note of this bleak exchange of 2 March. Helen had no intention of resuming her role as a good wife, she was too angry.

She told him that around 1962 she began to feel jealous and resentful towards him. Those feelings had become stronger over the years though it had taken her some time to realise how angry she was. Helen gave what Rogers would later call 'the whole catalog'. They had always had to move to fit in with his career. She particularly hated moving to Chicago. Rogers had always had his way 'in sexual matters'. He methodically listed her catalogue of acccusations:

'You are grateful for what I [Rogers] have done for you sexually but you resent very much the fact that I "laid down the rules" and forced a shift from sex in the evening to sex in the morning; that I refused to let you be aggressive or take the initiative; that

I had you lie perfectly still in the last years so that I could achieve orgasm.'

His rules about sex – when and how to have it – had done much to put her off sex completely.

But Helen was also bitter because she was so badly handicapped while Rogers could be 'bouncing around'. She resented more and more the adoration and adulation he received. Rogers noted her attack, 'People think I'm a guru, almost a god and you resent that. You know I am very human, have many faults and you feel that in this situation I am almost a charlatan.' He said that he had done nothing to deserve the latter. If people fantasised he was an all-powerful guru, was that his fault? He had never encouraged it; Helen was less sure.

Helen also complained Rogers never seemed to admit he was wrong. He had no lightness, no humour and, she added, their standards seem to have diverged. She was particularly hurt by his constant accusations that she was trying to control him. That was not fair. Rogers hit back that he had had to fight like a tiger to get away to San Francisco to see Bernice. Helen had done everything to stop him.

Helen told him she was afraid that if all these negative feelings continued she would end up a bitter, resentful old woman. Rogers tried to exclude her all the time and she was sad their marriage had come to this wrangling. They could continue to live in the same house and make the most of their relationship for as many years as they had left, but she wished it could be as it once had been. Rogers certainly kept one secret from his wife. He had sent $5500 worth of cheques to Bernice. The cheques do not seem to have been cashed but Rogers clearly was very worried his family would find out about this gift.

In the next few months, even though Helen had promised to be understanding about his need to explore sex with other women, there were more bitter arguments. Helen went into hospital for a blood transfusion on 19 April 1977. In a note dated 25 April 1977, Rogers rehearsed things he wanted to tell her (though it is impossible to know whether he ever said any of this to her). This was his catalogue of where she had gone wrong. She had to understand their biggest differences related to sex and 'men-women relationships'. Rogers wrote, 'I have sexual feelings and sexual needs. I don't know whether you can accept these facts. At present I keep such feelings and needs completely secret from you because I don't wish to be judged.'

'I care a great deal for Bernice – can't entirely explain why – and that is very likely to continue. I don't believe it harms our relationship.'

'I enjoy being loved by Rachel though she loves me more than I her.'

He said he wanted to feel 'OK' about keeping portions of his life and his relationships separate and private from Helen. He admired Helen's strength so he had to be careful not to be overwhelmed by her. He had never mentioned it before, so this smacks of trying to win marital brownie points, but he now said he understood her resentments. It was unfair that she did not get a share of the praise heaped on him. This sudden concern for her ego came too late. Helen didn't believe a word of it. She told him 'fame had gone to his head'. And he was ungrateful. He didn't love her. She loved him 'more than life itself'. When Rogers tried to comfort her, she yelled, 'Don't touch me. You're evil.' She had never had such a thought or feeling before. Both of them were shocked by her outburst.

It was a comfort to get a letter from Natalie in which she told Rogers that he gave her great courage to continue. She was glad he was taking better care of himself as 'the inner stress you put on yourself causes a lot of physical strain. You would do your body a real favour if you could stop drinking.' She added, 'I am glad you are more open to intimacy.' Natalie told him that now that Helen was better, he was learning to deal with the anger and frustration he had repressed when she was close to death. She sympathised. He had to live in an atmosphere where Helen gave little support and the support she did give was of the 'I live for you' type which Natalie found 'really a drag'. But Rogers should acknowledge the miracle that Helen had recovered.

There are no further notes until August 1977 when Rogers listed what he wanted for himself and for his relationship with Helen. First and foremost, Rogers wrote that he wanted to initiate more contacts with other people. He made a long list of the individuals to get to know, including a man with a boat and a person marked as 'Gurdieff'.

'Take an afternoon to do something special with someone other than Helen.'

'Try to begin writing more personal things.' He listed love and intimacy, shyness, the risk of being out in front and the vexed question of 'liking myself'.

'Try to organise my priorities so that things I want to do come first and responding to the demands of others comes second.'

'I want to spend more time with Bernice as a friend which is the only way she will accept me.'

In addition, Rogers wanted to try meditating and promised himself to take at least an hour's exercise a day. Tennis and bowling were out. He added he wished he could learn to play 'just for fun'. He had never been much good at that and he was 'worse now'.

'Right now, I need to appreciate and like myself more. Then I wouldn't be such a sober sided withdrawn guy.'

A second set of notes addressed what Rogers wanted with Helen. He wanted to express his feelings as they occurred. 'I realise I have not been good at this. My way has been to withdraw, to clam up for fear of hurting.'

He repeated the imperative. He had to 'feel OK' about keeping a part of his life separate from his relationship with Helen. 'I don't want complete togetherness. It is not healthy or good for me.' Helen could 'bring about guilty feelings in me by a word, an inflection.'

Unfortunately for Rogers, his passion for Bernice was not making him happy either. He didn't believe she tried to get close to him, except once. He sent her a birthday gift of a necklace with a note that said, 'I seem to have woven you into my heart ... when you wear it I hope you will feel my embrace.' The wrapping was clumsy because Rogers was very bad at ribbons and bows.

There was one high spot through all these difficulties. In 1977 Rogers went to Brazil where he took a number of large workshops. Up to 800 people attended and they had a wonderful sense of community. In the halls Rogers radiated wisdom – he was still the perfect professional listener. He believed passionately in the need to take his ideas outside America. And he could forget the problems at home.

Later in 1977, Rogers wrote a paper on ageing. He claimed he had learned to be more intimate with people through his experiences in groups, and that this new gift had made it possible for him to have a number of close, loving but platonic relationships with women. This was, of course, not wholly true: his notes make plain that at least two of the relationships were not platonic, but to admit even platonic friendships caused Helen some anguish and she would not allow him to publish the paper. She was no longer the dutiful wife but an angry old woman. Rogers honoured her wish and the paper did not appear in her lifetime. (It was published in 1980; see below.)

Keeping going was an effort. In June 1978, David Rogers noted that Natalie was worried about how much their father was drinking, his shakiness and his tendency to repeat stories, his nasal stuffiness and his froggy voice. As a doctor, David was sure that most of these problems were due to Rogers drinking too much vodka. It was this that made him feel he wanted to jump out of his skin. David guessed his father had become so soaked in alcohol that he now felt awful when he was sober. If he could quit drinking he would feel much better.

A few days later Rogers got a letter from Natalie which was prompted by her reading an early copy of the Kirschenbaum book. She said she felt 'estranged' from her father and sad about him. She was aware he was gaining too much weight and was depressed 'with a thin foggy veil around you so I can't get very close to you.' She was frightened about his forthcoming trip to China and realised that he was nervous in case he could not get his hands on alcohol there.

Miraculously, through all these crises, Rogers began to find the energy for serious writing again. In 1978, he wrote a paper on reality which was a turning-point in his personal thinking. It argued that psychology needed to accept there was no such thing as objective reality and that there were as many realities as there were persons (Rogers 1978). The text showed Rogers was speculating about the possibilities of parapsychology. He cited the work of Robert Monroe on out-of-the-body experiences, of Carlos Castenada and of the dolphin expert John Lilly, and suggested that any account of reality had to take into account 'mysterious and currently unfathomable "separate realities" incredibly different from an objective world'.

The next year, he was back on far more familiar ground with the publication of *Carl Rogers on Personal Power*, in which he examined the person-centred approach to psychotherapy. He had a powerful vision of what the brave new youngsters, who were not repressed by old codes and conventions, could achieve. Rogers spoke of them as 'emerging persons'.

'I find these persons to have a deep concern for authenticity. Communication is especially valued as a means of telling it as it is.' They rejected the 'present hypocritical culture' and 'the guile and falsehoods of Madison Avenue'. They were open about sexual relationships instead of being secretive or leading double lives.

Rogers ended the book with an effective device. He summarised conventional positions such as that 'education is about evaluation' and counterpointed these official slogans with terse 'word bites' of his own, counter-aphorisms, as it were. For example, he claimed research showed that 'the most creative students were the ones who set their own agenda'.

At the end of 1978 Helen Rogers started to fail. They had gone together to a medium and Rogers had been very moved by the experience. Helen started to have visions of a white light beckoning her and was increasingly sure there would be some form of survival 'on the other side'. Rogers acknowledged he was surprised. He knew Helen was regurgitating what Moody had found but he did not mock her experience. This seems to have been a key factor in reconciling them, so that one day, as she lay in her hospital bed, he told her how much she had always meant to him and how much he still loved her. It was suddenly as it had been when they were happy. He was so sincere it blew away years of bickering and bitterness. He described what he went through at her bedside as an 'internal frenzy'. He had always loved her. She didn't have to carry on living with all that pain because she thought other people needed her. She could die if that was what she wanted. Helen seemed at peace after this. She died the next day, and Rogers fervently believed that his sudden empassioned declaration made her death easier.

The night after Helen died, Rogers and some friends met with the medium the two of them had seen together. The seance was soon in contact with Helen, he said. She told them her dying was very peaceful, that she now had the form of a young woman again and was in contact with her family. Rogers said that all this made him even more interested in parapsychology.

Not surprisingly, Helen's death provoked a final crisis in Rogers' relationship with Bernice Todres.

By 17 March, Natalie was concerned about her father. She told him she knew this was a difficult time for him but she was worried about his drinking. He was concerned he was putting on weight but there was no mystery about that. He was drinking 12 oz of vodka a day which she had calculated meant he was gulping down 1440 calories. The drink didn't only damage his waist-line. He also complained about his poor balance and that he walked like an old man. He showed Natalie how hard he found it to put one foot in front of the other. She pointed out 'Dad, that is a sobriety test.' But when she brought up these points in person, she complained 'you put up a wall between us.' He just didn't listen.

On 11 May 1979 at 6.30 a.m Rogers drafted a letter to 'my dear, dear, incredibly provocative Bernice'. It was an attempt to sum up their relationship. The letter veers constantly between the positive and the negative. He faced his frustrations in the relationship and, by now, they were not just physical, but one gets the feeling that he would have forgiven her anything if only she had made love to him once.

He had decided to write down some of his feelings towards her as he became too nervous when he was around her and was bad at saying what he meant. The letter was written after he had been to a week-long group that she was facilitating. On Monday, they had a good time 'made blissful by the understanding that you liked to touch and be touched by me.' But then she spoiled it by insisting she had not said that and by her behaviour which made it plain she did not want a physical relationship with him.

On Tuesday night, alone in a restaurant, Rogers had wept into his fish chowder. On Wednesday in a group session, she had made it clear she felt disgust and contempt for him. Her 'aura of dis-approval was so thick' he felt he 'could cut it with a knife'. But he had reasons to criticise her, too. She was much too defensive. She wanted to keep her own concerns, her real self, out of the workshops she ran and that reminded him of his 'purist days in Chicago when I was so determined to keep myself out of the interaction because I was sure the client had it within him/herself to achieve insight'.

He also confided to her some of the paradoxes of his position. Hundreds of people wanted to get to know him but how could they do that in one evening? He knew he made mistakes but he could not stand being in a relationship where everything that he did was judged to be 'stupid, wrong or insensitive'. He had called Bernice an unmitigated liar and he accepted there was no excuse for that but he did have good reasons for wishing that she was 'more truthful about factual matters'. He blamed her for not hav-ing said at the start of the week how busy she was going to be. That was typical. She had often let him down. Away from her, he had some balance; he knew he was not wholly to blame. Bernice's constant criticism had brought back ulcer pains he had not had for 40 years.

It wasn't as if Bernice were clear about her emotions either, he pointed out. Example, she had told him to 'fuck off'. Even he couldn't have the insight to realise that she didn't mean 'get lost' but that 'fuck off' meant she wanted to see him within the hour – and that she was waiting just two doors down the corridor for him to appear. He was a guru, not a psychic.

Rogers said he had been sustained by things Bernice had told him, such as that she wanted him to be part of her life and that he had spoiled other men for her but, he added, 'I realise from your way of touching me – with one exception in the restaurant in Boston – that probably you can never love me with spirit, mind and body.' He underlined 'body'. He hoped she realised that much of what he had written was written through tears, though he made some effort to stop them dripping on the paper. He knew she had a marvellous future. 'I wish I could share it with you.'

On 20 June 1979, Rogers roughed out, but did not send, a letter to Bernice from Rome. He felt he needed to write her one more letter 'to get you out of my system – to end any thought of a continuing love'. He had a few final ironies for her to think about. She was so unjust; Rogers listed all the faults she blamed him for. He did not love her in an adult way. He had committed the crime of 'encouraging you and helping you – therefore treating you therapeutically'. So he would be a therapist and hypothesise she had some sort of deep conflict which meant she had to throw him out of her life violently. She was able to love her children but not him, not 'freely, now or later. That thought does toxic things to my feelings for you and I am not willing to risk further offering my love to someone who totally rejects it. I feel badly wounded but I am sure that some day my wounds will recover.'

A few months later the relationship was finally over. On 7 December 1979, Rogers confided to his notes that his four-year platonic relationship with Bernice Todres had come to an unpleasant and hurtful end. He wanted a continuing loving relation with a woman but 'I would certainly want – need – a woman who would enjoy being pleasured by me sensuously and sexually'. His own needs were less important, as his sexual capacities were declining but 'I would however get enormous satisfaction out of satisfying her physical needs.' He did not think he wanted a marriage 'certainly not for a good long time'. Age differences didn't matter to him but he just happened to be drawn to younger women.

In 1976, Natalie had told Rogers he seemed to going through the kind of battles she had gone through in establishing her identity after leaving Larry. Helen's death and accepting that Bernice would never give him the love he craved were traumas but they also freed Rogers. He vowed he would recover from Bernice, and he did so. Perhaps, privately, he realised that he couldn't explain why he had wanted her love so much and came to see he had made a bit of a fool of himself. Certainly, the last seven years of his life were much calmer. This calm helped restore his health somewhat and gave him the energy to continue to publish and travel. His relationships with his children were now very warm, as David had settled into a much happier marriage.

Rogers had been through a stormy decade. The only wonder is that he never seems to have used the material – painful as it was

– to enrich and deepen his ideas. He had survived his wife's death, rejection, and a drinking problem. But rather than look inward, in the last years of his life, Rogers looked outwards. It was bleak there – but easier perhaps to deal with than his inner landscape. Psychologists have never been that good at learning from their own problems.

# 9

## Dying Young,
## 1980–1987

Rogers sometimes told friends that his parents had warned him that he was so sickly he would die young. As he got older he liked to repeat the phrase but he gave it a new meaning – he would die with a still-young attitude. Physically Rogers was in reasonable shape. His worst problem was his eyesight but he could still walk along a beach and he had every intention of enjoying his fame and his freedom.

He celebrated his 78th birthday in California with a party he very much enjoyed. He was now able to explore sexual relationships without the guilt that had dogged him while Helen was alive. He was to have a number of female companions over the next few years – some platonic, some seemingly not. He left no further introspective, despairing jottings or notes.

As he facilitated workshops over the next seven years, Rogers was astonished by the degree of interest there was in his work in Europe, South America and the Far East. He was amazed his ideas had had such an impact on so many different people. His travels also made Rogers more and more interested in the political uses of therapy. He had a sense of urgency. He wrote on nuclear war, started the Peace Project and helped organise the Rust workshop, which was an experiment in bringing decision-makers from 17 different countries together. In all this, Rogers moved far away from being an individual therapist and, when he did demonstrations, those who were his transient clients were so over-awed by his fame that their responses were rather peculiar, as Susan Slack described when she said he just sat there and knew her (Slack 1985).

In 1980, Rogers finally published his paper on ageing in the *Journal of Humanistic Psychology*. He included the material Helen had vetoed. Rogers allowed himself to be fairly explicit about sex. Despite his age, he had now found relationships where he could express his sensuality and his sexuality. He could report he was 'older and growing'. He said nothing about Bernice and the traumas she had caused him.

He also published *A Way of Being*. In it he tried to understand why he was still so determined to work. He compared himself to the historian Arnold Toynbee, who had said he still worked at the age of 80 because he felt he would be conscience-stricken if he did not. Rogers thought he had a different reason for working and he described it with nice modesty. He felt that, like most people, he had had only one idea in his life and he struggled to communicate it. There was a more personal need, however, it seems. He still worked because he wanted to get through to people. He still felt he was the shy little boy who could not express himself properly, who found it easier to write love letters than to be a lover. He still did not sit well in his skin. 'I do not feel I quite belong,' he wrote. Writing was his 'message in the bottle'.

In January 1982, friends gathered to celebrate his 80th birthday. It was quite a party and it included an imaginative cabaret in which on stage there was a discussion between two Carl Rogers. Rogers enjoyed the humour, and some of it was an extremely affectionate way of poking fun at him. At one point the performers demonstrated the famous Rogers techniques of listening. One way was to 'Listen to 127 clients and the mother of one of them using this method of listening.' To demonstrate, the performer leant forward and put his finger on the cheek. This was the posture of total empathy. 'And then I listen to 188 clients and three gypsy moths using the second method,' said the second Carl Rogers.

'And what's the other method?' asked the first Carl Rogers.

The second Carl Rogers put a finger in each ear. Make yourself deaf – the perfect way to listen.

There were some more serious aspects to the celebrations.

Rogers read a paper on his Secret Life with Plants. Having talked endlessly about psychological growth he now wanted to talk a little about his interest in plants. It recalls his passion as a teenager for Morison's scientific agriculture. He took his party audience on a brief and amusing tour of his begonias, his ferns, his orchids and his camellia bush; he compared personal growth and plant growth. 'I think it began with the wonder of the growing seed thrusting up through the soil becoming something new and strange transcending itself.' He was still very capable of a graphic phrase and said that 'perfection without continuing growth is boring to me'.

On 10 January he sent a message thanking all those who had made the party wonderful. 'Great food, too much of it and best of all,' he said, the statements from so many people, 'tributes deserved and undeserved, tender poems ... It is a very precious thing to me to be so loved and to have had a significant part in so many lives.'

Yet the year brought its difficulties. Later in 1982 the *Journal of Humanistic Psychology* carried a sharp exchange between him and the humanist psychiatrist Rollo May. Though coated in politeness, the exchange shows that Rogers' critics were still irritated by his failure to face up to the problem of human destructiveness. May accused Rogers of misquoting him by saying he insisted on the 'demonic' aspects of man. May said that he wrote of the 'daimonic' which was not the same; 'daimonic' meant having the will to affirm and had nothing to do with evil. It was rather typical of Rogers to confuse the two. May quoted a famous saying of the German poet Rilke that highlighted the twin-sided nature of human beings. Rilke wrote, 'If my devils are to leave me, I am afraid that my angels will take flight as well.'

May asked what Rogers made of the fact that in 30 years, years in which therapy had become more and more popular, the suicide rate had risen by 171 per cent. He said Rogers had always had problems in honestly facing up to negative emotions. May had first discovered that when he had been an adviser on the Mendota project. Rogers had ignored not only the work of Milgram, which showed people were all too willing to follow immoral orders, but the famous experiment of Philip Zimbardo reported in 1971.

Zimbardo got volunteers to act the roles of prisoners and prison guards to see how the situation would affect them. As Rogers well knew, the experiment had to be stopped because the people playing the guards became violent to their charges. It was as if, when given a licence, ordinary people suddenly acted out enormously aggressive impulses. The whole history of the 20th century, May said, was a history of destructiveness. But somehow Rogers had not engaged with these aspects of the human psyche. He had swopped the Id for Pollyanna.

Rogers drafted a rather defensive response. He pleaded he was pressed for time as he was about to go on one of his international trips. Rogers repeated that he found that clients, when they met empathy and acceptance, turned out to have a fund of good in them. He clearly was not to be shifted on this point and had less and less interest in discussing such questions as the roots of destructiveness.

Rogers wrote to his brother Walter on 1 June to say that his eyesight was deteriorating. The vitamin regime that had combated macular degeneration was now failing. He could not read without a magnifying glass. His peripheral vision was still good so he could drive, but when he focused on something, it became a blur. Despite this, his schedule for the summer of 1982 was heavy. He was lecturing in Texas; then he would be in Mexico at an international forum of the person-centred approach. Then he was going to South Africa to give two workshops and to have meetings with people of all races and even with witch doctors. Rogers told Walter, 'the man arranging it is a former student. He thinks I can have some impact on the racial situation there.' This prospect pleased Rogers because he still believed his techniques of therapy might make it easier to resolve political conflicts.

Before leaving on his travels, Rogers wrote a waspish letter to a graduate student, Curtis Graf, who had sent him an outline of a project that compared Rogers' work with that of a well known psychoanalyst, Heinz Kohut. Rogers complained what Graf had sent him was just an exposition of Kohut's work and his own. 'I don't quite see where your own creative effort comes in.' Rogers attacked Kohut as one of those European thinkers, like Freud and Marx, who were not interested in checking their theories against the facts. He contrasted these armchair slouches with himself who had always taken care 'to define my terms as precisely as I could and then state every aspect in such a way that it could be translated into operational terms and tested by research.' Nothing in the letter admitted that his efforts to prove the effectiveness of psychotherapy had, in fact, ended in failure. Rather piously, Rogers wrote, 'It has never been clear to me why other theorists are uninterested in having their theories tested.'

In the summer, Rogers made his trip to South Africa. The tour was a great success and introduced hundreds to his style of therapy. He particularly enjoyed a demonstration therapy session in which he discovered that the 'client' was sad because she had lost touch with her 'naughty little girl self'. Rogers, who liked to believe there was still a lot of the timid child in him, warmed to her. Politically, he could not have much impact.

In 1982, Rogers published a paper on nuclear war and repeated that it would be very helpful if politicians on both sides of the Iron Curtain could express their deepest fears about the other side. That was the only hope of avoiding Mutually Assured Destruction. He was drinking less and, apart from his eyes, he seemed in better health, but in 1983, Natalie wrote to him to suggest she and David needed some instructions from him on what to do if he should fall gravely ill. She imagined he and Helen had some agreement between them on what to do if either of them lost their mind.

In 1984, Rogers officially launched the Peace Project, the aim of which was to explore ways to bring people from different cultures closer together. He hoped to do this by staging a conference for officials, politicians, diplomats and other decision-makers. They would see how therapeutic techniques could cut through the usual suspicions that dogged international relations. It was a noble aim and Rogers got a lot of local help. Two San Diego residents, Mary Van Dyne and Jane Cremer, started to raise the $300,000 needed to fund the conference. Rogers approached a number of Hollywood stars for help and activated many of the contacts he had made during his 'missions' to South America.

Rogers might be worried about the state of the world but he was quite pleased about the state of psychology. In his paper 'Towards a More Human Science of the Person' (1985) he pointed out that in the 1970s academic psychology had dismissed humanistic psychology as too vague and idealistic. He sensed that was changing. He was impressed by *Human Inquiry* (1981), edited by two British psychologists, Peter Reason and John Rowan. The book reported empirical studies that tackled real human problems. The scientific model that had ruled in 1956 when he debated with Skinner was now out of date. Psychology was less obsessed with aping physics, and physics itself was becoming distinctly quirky. Rogers was struck by the work of John Polkinghorne, a physicist with an interest in religion, and that of Fritjof Capra, author of *The Tao of Physics*.

By the middle of 1985, Rogers' plans for the international conference were making only slow progress. The problem was money. However, Rogers and his co-worker, Gay Swenson, had a lucky break. A Viennese bank agreed to allow delegates to stay at a hotel they owned. Suddenly, the whole project was feasible.

By 30 October 1985, Rogers could outline to the *Los Angeles Times* details for the Vienna Conference that would be held between 1 and 4 November. The reporters were introduced to the moosehorn fern which, after 17 years, had grown to a massive size. Rogers told them just as plants grew, he hoped the Vienna Conference would lead to personal growth. Three things gave him pleasure now – 'my love relationships, the opportunity to try out a dream that everyone had said was impossible and the satisfaction in watching my big moosehorn fern grow.'

Rogers flew to Vienna for what should have been something of a triumph. The conference brought together a number of well-known politicians, including the vice-president of Costa Rica, three former vice-presidents of Latin American countries and senior civil servants and academics. The discussions were frank, and Rogers believed it was useful for normally constrained men and women to be in a setting where they could express feelings and be rude, undiplomatic and human. It became evident that many of the Latin Americans were angry about the United States' insistence on controlling Central America. For many participants it was a positive experience. Two Palestinians called for a similar conference to be held for them and Israelis. But the conference did not have a specific agenda. It had no problem to solve so that, for all the glamour of those who attended, when one reads accounts of it and talks to those who attended, it remains unclear just what was achieved. In any real negotiation, the stakes – and the atmosphere – would have been very different.

Back in California, Rogers started to plan a trip to the Soviet Union. He was 84 years old and it may be unkind to be overly critical; nevertheless this trip raises major questions about Rogers' political judgement. He arranged to give a series of workshops to psychologists and mental health workers in Moscow and in Tbilisi, Georgia. Many were attended by large numbers who had absolutely no experience of group work. There were some interesting cases as Rogers revealed in the account published by the *Journal of Humanistic Psychology* after he died. For example, one old Soviet military man who had devoted his life to Communism constantly complained to his daughter and mocked her interest in psychology. The high rate of divorce caused many problems, Rogers noted.

By 1985, the campaign against psychiatric abuse in the Soviet Union had gathered momentum. Cases such as those of Vladimir Bukovsky and Major-General Grigorenko had caused an outcry all over the West. These were sane men who had been diagnosed as mad because they were fighting against Communism. To the Soviets, Rogers was a godsend. He would help establish their respectability. The World Psychiatric Association had forced the Soviets to resign because of abuse at such institutions as the Serbsky. But Rogers obviously felt it was more important to offer the Soviets the chance to learn about non-directive therapy than to stand up for human rights. It is likely that some in his audiences were members of the KGB.

It was a usual ploy of the Soviets to spring sudden invitations on well-known guests. Once he was in Moscow, Rogers was asked to address the Scientific Council, part of the Soviet Academy of Sciences, which backed Soviet psychiatrists. Interestingly, one psychiatrist who attended said he did not come as a psychiatrist but as a psychotherapist. Rogers did not want to offend and possibly believed that he could teach something to his hosts. His accounts of his speeches do not suggest he mentioned the fate of the dissidents once. The only mention of the politics of the Soviet Union was a small paragraph headed 'Below the Surface' in which Rogers said that a very small number of people complained about the 'system'. He went on to say 'Because they fit the American stereotype of the Russian situation, it is probably easy to overestimate their importance.' He went on to add that participants felt 'very free' to discuss professional issues. Rogers' ability to behave as if there were no issue about dissidents or about the use of psychiatry in which psychologists were implicated is extraordinary. It was the personal, never the political that mattered. He ended the paper with rhapsodic quotes from those who took part on how they had all shared 'this great emotional experience.'

Yet Rogers was astute, despite his age, about many aspects of Soviet society. He marvelled at the fact that people from such a different culture could be inspired by his ideas and understood that its bureaucracy was unwieldy but he focused totally on his workshops – and not at all on the wider political issues.

In these international workshops, Rogers often did demonstration therapy sessions. A series of papers in the *Journal of Humanistic Psychology* in 1985 gives some insight into what this was like. The person who took the role of 'client' felt touched by an aura because Rogers was so famous. A 40-year-old therapist, Susan Slack, described her feelings when she was invited to be the demonstration client. She devoted five pages to the wonder of being treated by Rogers. 'I felt a compulsion to reveal all. It amazed me that he was able to sense my needs and to respond to me in so short a time.' When Rogers suggested a second interview she felt honoured, as if she were being invited on a television chat show. On stage Rogers told her, 'You are nervous and I accept that.'

When he read what she had written in the *Journal*, he admitted that 'it is perhaps typical of me that I do not remember the contents of the interview at all.'

One can forgive that, given his age. He had spent much of his life making notes because his parents and siblings had teased him for his poor memory. The paper that he wrote 'On Reaching 85' was much shorter than his earlier writings on old age and far less personal. It gave a brief résumé of his recent work in Vienna and Russia but it still had a nice touch of humour, saying he now understood Oliver Wendell Holmes when he said, 'Oh to be 70 again.'

The end was sudden. Early in 1987, Rogers was hospitalised. He died on 4 February. His death was mourned by literally hundreds of colleagues as well as by his family. The obituaries were respectful. The *Journal of Humanistic Psychology* mourned the passing of a man who had changed the nature of therapy. The more conservative *American Psychologist* ran an obituary by his old colleague, Eugene Gendlin. He suggested that Rogers' greatest contributions were those of the middle years of his career – the development of non-directive therapy and the attempt to show that therapy worked. It was a generous tribute and glossed over the saga of the inconclusive research findings.

Rogers tried to find a way between the narrows of behaviourism and the obscurities of psychoanalysis. Since his death, however, it has become clear that his enduring impact has been more on counselling practice than on psychological theory. For example, a recent plea for psychology to be more open to people's experiences cites hundreds of authorities, but not Rogers (Henry *et al*, 1997). In social work his influence is strong, though it would be exaggerating to claim that there is a school of non-directive therapy or of the person-centred approach. Rather, Rogers' philosophy – listen to the client, treat him or her with respect, use empathy, try to get the client to find his or her solutions – has become part of the fabric of therapy.

Thorne (1992) has traced the various controversies among those who still believe in person-centred therapy, among 'purists and modernisers'. He refers to the work of R. F. Levant and J. M. Schlien who conclude that as far as client-centred therapy is concerned neither research methodology nor outcome evaluation has much to be proud of (*Client-Centred Therapy and the Person-Centred Approach*; New York, 1984). The facts were anything but friendly; the high ambitions, the equations that would give the necessary and sufficient conditions for people to change were never fulfilled. But therapy is more of an art than a science and, just as the Impressionists changed painting, Rogers changed therapy by offering new ways of doing it.

He made therapy friendlier, more accessible and he took some of the controls out of the hands of therapists. He helped popularise the idea that therapy was not just for the 'sick' but that it could help anyone to be happier and find his or her real self. In the developed West, therapy has become part of the culture, partly owing to Rogers' influence. Despite his many and very human failures, therefore, he remains one of the most important psychologists of the twentieth century.

# Bibliographical Notes

The extensive collection of Rogers' papers in the Library of Congress runs to over 140 boxes of material. They remain an invaluable source for any study of the development of his ideas and in particular the clashes between private and professional ideas. The Library of Congress papers include not only the family correspondence, drafts of papers, correspondence with publishers but hundreds of Rogers' jottings of conversations and ideas. Rogers usually kept copies of letters he sent, so that the manuscripts provide a rounded picture of some of the important correspondences of his life, such as that with B. F. Skinner about their 1956 debate and with his brother Lester. The collection even includes his old bank book, which records his early savings from the Chinese crafts he imported into the United States, hotel bills, drawings made by his children and a card advertising the Hotel Jayhawk, where Rogers stayed. It is a remarkable treasure trove. It is to Rogers' immense credit that he declared all the material in this collection to be in the public domain.

Primary source material – though much of it is of far lesser import – also exists in the archives of the University of Wisconsin, the archives of the University of Chicago, the archives of the University of Ohio and the archives of Columbia University as well as those of Rochester Public Library.

Rogers was a prolific and successful author. In the back of *On Becoming a Person*, he himself provided a bibliography of his work from 1930 to 1960, but that is far from complete. A full bibliography would also need to include such film and television documentaries as *The Steel Shutter* and audio cassettes that Rogers helped make because, even though he did not direct them, he was often the key 'author'. Kirschen-baum (1979) did not attempt a full bibliography, and I have not attempted to provide one either.

As I have tried to show the context in which Rogers worked, I have often referred to other material. I list his books, articles and other materials as they occur in the chapters rather than alphabetically. When Rogers was co-author of material he placed in his collection at the Library of Congress I have done my best to trace his co-author.

**General**
Rogers, C. R. (1965), in Boring, E. and Lindzey, G., eds, *A History of Psychology in Autobiography*, vol. 5, Appleton Century Crofts, New York
Kirschenbaum, H. (1979) *On Becoming Carl Rogers*, Delacorte Press, New York

**Introduction**
Rogers, C. R. (1942) *Counselling and Psychotherapy*, Houghton Mifflin, Boston
Buber, M. (1937) *I and Thou*, Clark, Edinburgh (original German edition published in 1923)
Laing, A. (1994) *R. D. Laing*, Peter Owen, London
Thorne, B. (1992) *Carl Rogers*, Sage, London
Cohen, D. (1977) *Psychologists on Psychology*, Routledge, London
Skinner, B. F. (1983) *Matters of Consequence*, Knopf, New York
Sutton, N. (1996) *Bruno Bettelheim*, Duckworth, London
Elms, A. (1994) *Uncovering Lives*, Oxford University Press, Oxford
Evans, R. (1978) *Carl Rogers: The Man and His Ideas*, E. P. Dutton, New York
Gendlin, E. (1988), obituary of Rogers, *American Psychologist*, 43, 127–8

**Chapter 1**
Rogers, M. (date unclear), unpublished document on family history in the Library of Congress collection
Cohen, D. (1985) *The Development of Laughter*: unpublished Ph.D thesis, University of London
Erikson, E. (1972) *Youth, Identity and Crisis*, Faber & Faber, London
Rogers, J., unpublished notes prepared to assist Margaret Rogers in her family history, Library of Congress collection

Rogers, C. R. (1977) 'Personal Growth' in *Twelve Therapists*, ed. Arthur Burton, Jossey Bros, San Francisco

McClelland, D. (1964) *The Roots of Consciousness*, Van Nostrand, Princeton, NJ

McClelland, D. (1977), interview in Cohen, D. *Psychologists on Psychology*, Routledge, London

Rogers, C. R. (1913) 'The Chickville Times', unpublished MS in Library of Congress

Rogers, C. R. (1915), essay on Rogers' schoolboy trip, unpublished MS in Library of Congress

Morison, J. (1909) *Feeds and Feeding*, Lippincott, Philadelphia

Rogers, C. R. (1922), report on the trip to China, *The Intercollegian*, vol. 1, 21

Latourette, K. S. (1938) *The Chinese, Their History and Culture*, Yale University Press, New Haven

Renan, E. (1909) *Life of Jesus*, Macmillan, London

**Chapter 2**

Fosdick, H. E. (1943) *On Being a Real Person*, Harper & Row, New York

McGiffert, A. C. (1946) *A History of Christian Thought*, vols 1–2, Macmillan, New York

Freud, S. and Bullitt, W. (1967) *Thomas Woodrow Wilson*, Weidenfeld & Nicolson, London

Rogers, C. R. (1927), outline of dissertation research on children's tests, unpublished MS in Library of Congress

Rogers, C. R. (1931) 'Measuring Personality Adjustment in Children Nine to Thirteen', Teachers College, New York

**Chapter 3**

Masson, J. (1984) *The Assault on Truth*, Collins, London

Rogers, C. R. and Carson, C. W. (1930) 'Intelligence as a Factor in Camping Activities', *Camping Magazine*, 3, 8–11

Rogers, C. F. (1933), notes on tests used in camp, unpublished MS in Library of Congress

Rogers, C. R. and Rappoport, M. (1931) 'We Pay for the Smiths', *Survey Graphic*, 19, 508ff

Rogers, C. R. (1933) 'A Good Foster Home: Its Achievements and Limitations', *Mental Hygiene*, 17, 21–40

Rogers, C. R. (1936) 'Social Workers and Legislation', *Quarterly Bulletin*, New York State conference on social work, 7, issue 3, 3–9

Taft, J. (1933) *The Dynamics of Therapy*, Macmillan, New York
Allen, F. (1934) 'Therapeutic Work with Children', *American Journal of Orthopsychiatry*, 4, 193–202
Rogers, C. R. (1934), essay on children who bully, unpublished MS in Library of Congress

**Chapter 4**
Rogers, C. R. (1937), draft proposal for Guidance Clinic, unpublished MS in Library of Congress
Rogers, C. R. (1938), notes for a study of Rochester youth, part of the programme funded by Rochester Community Chest, unpublished MS in Library of Congress
Shaw, C. (1936) *Delinquency Areas*, University of Chicago Press, Chicago
Thurston, H. (1930) *The Dependent Child*, Columbia University Press, New York
Healy, W. and Bronner, A. F. (1937) *New Light on Delinquency and Its Treatment*, Yale University Press, New Haven
Baker, H. and Traphagen, V. (1935) *The Diagnosis and Treatment of the Problem Child*, Macmillan, New York
Benney, M. (1936) *Low Company*, reissued by Caliban Books, London in 1974
Thurber, J. (1936) *Let My Mind Alone*, Hamish Hamilton, London
Rogers, C. R. (1939) *The Clinical Treatment of the Problem Child*, Houghton Mifflin, Boston
Rogers, C. R. (1938), book review in *Mental Hygiene*, vol. 22, 132
Fenton, N. (1940), review of *The Clinical Treatment of the Problem Child* in *Journal of Consulting Psychology*, 4, 37
Roe, A. (1953) *A Comparative Psychological Study of Eminent Psychologists and Anthropologists and a Comparison with Biological and Physical Scientists*, Genetic Psychology Monographs, vol. 67, no. 352
Rogers, C. R. and Bennett, C. C. (1941) 'Predicting the Outcomes of Treatment', *American Journal of Orthopsychiatry*, 11, 210–21
Snyder, W. U. (1945) 'An Investigation of the Nature of Non-directive Therapy, *Journal of General Psychology*, 33, 193–223
Rogers, C. R. (1940) 'The Process of Therapy', *Journal of Consulting Psychology*, 4, 161–4
Rogers, C. R. (1942) *Counselling and Psychotherapy*, Houghton Mifflin, Boston
Darley, J. (1943), review of *Counselling and Psychotherapy* in *Mental Hygiene*, 27, 222

Murray, H. (1943), review of *Counselling and Psychotherapy* in *Journal of Consulting Psychology*, 7, 156–8

Hacking, I. (1995) *Rewriting the Soul*, Princeton University Press, Princeton, NJ

Rogers, C. R. (1942) 'A Study of the Mental Health Problems in Three Representative Elementary Schools' in Holy, T. C. *et al*, *A Study of Health and Physical Education in Columbus Public Schools*, Ohio State University Bureau of Education Research Monographs, no. 25, 130–61

Covner, B. (1942) 'Apparatus for Recording Therapeutic Sessions', *Journal of Consulting Psychology*, 6, 175–82

Rogers, C. R. (1944) 'The Development of Insight in a Counselling Relationship', *Journal of Consulting Psychology*, 8, 331–41

Sargent, H. (1942) 'Non-directive Therapy Applied to a Single Interview Case', *Journal of Consulting Psychology*, 7, 183–92

**Chapter 5**

Napoli, D. S. (1979) *The Architects of Adjustment*, Kennikat Press, Port Washington, New York

Rogers, C. R. and Muench, G. A. (1943), unpublished case history of Cadet JL, MS in Library of Congress

Rogers, C. R. (1944) 'A Study of Returned Combat Gunners and Their Utilisation in the Flexible Gunnery Training Programme', unpublished MS in Library of Congress

Rogers, C. R. (1944) 'The Psychological Adjustments of Discharged Service Personnel, *Psychological Bulletin*, 41, 689–96

Rogers, C. R. (1945) Volunteer pamphlet, United Services Organisation, New York

**Chapter 6**

Rogers, C. R. (1951) *Client-Centred Therapy: Its Current Practice Implications and Theory*, Houghton Mifflin, Boston

Bryant, P. E. (1972) *Perception and Understanding in Young Children*, Methuen, London

Laing, R. D. (1961) *The Divided Self*, Penguin, Harmondsworth

Rogers, C. R. (1946) 'Significant Aspects of Client-Centred Therapy', *American Psychologist*, 1, 415–22

Rogers, C. R. (1947) 'Some Observations on the Organisation of Personality', presidential address to American Psychological Association, *American Psychologist*, 2, 358–68

Grummon, D. L. and Gordon, T. (1948) 'The Counselling Centre at the University of Chicago', *American Psychologist*, 3, 166–71

Rogers, C. R. (1948) *Dealing with Social Tensions*, Hinds, Hayden & Eldridge, Philadelphia

Rogers, C. R. (1949) 'Co-Ordinated Research in Psychotherapy: A Non-objective Introduction', *Journal of Consulting Psychology*, 13, 149–53

Seeman, J. (1949) 'A Study of the Process of Non-directive Therapy', *Journal of Consulting Psychology*, 13, 157–68

Snyder, W. U. (1945) 'An Investigation of the Nature of Non-directive Therapy', *Journal of General Psychology*, 33, 193–223

Haigh, G. (1949) 'Defensive Behaviour in Client-Centred Therapy', *Journal of Consulting Psychology*, 13, 181–9

Raskin, N. J. (1949) 'The Development of the Parallel Studies Project', *Journal of Consulting Psychology*, 13, 154–7

Raskin, N. J. (1949) 'An Analysis of Six Parallel Studies of the Therapeutic Process', *Journal of Consulting Psychology*, 13, 206–220

Laing, R. D. (1961) *The Divided Self*, Penguin, Harmondsworth

Brown, O. (1951) in *Client-Centred Therapy*, op. cit.

Eysenck, H. J. (1952) 'The Effects of Psychotherapy and Evaluation', *Journal of Consulting Psychology*, 16, no. 5, 319–24

Rogers, C. R. (1952), letters from holidays, unpublished MS in Library of Congress

Hebb, D. (1949) *The Organisation of Behaviour*, Wiley, New York

Rogers, C. R. (1952), notes on creativity, unpublished MS in Library of Congress

Rogers, C. R. (1954) 'Towards a Theory of Creativity', *ETC, A Review of General Semantics*, 11, 259–60

Peppiatt, M. (1996) *Anatomy of an Enigma: A Biography of Francis Bacon*, Weidenfeld & Nicolson, London

Eysenck, H. J. (1995) *Genius*, Cambridge University Press, Cambridge

Rogers, C. R. (1953), notes for presentation to Menninger Clinic, unpublished MS and hotel card in Library of Congress

Rogers, C. R. and Dymond, R., eds, (1954) *Psychotherapy and Personality Change*, University of Chicago Press, Chicago

Jenkins, R. (1955), review of *Psychotherapy and Personality Change* in *American Journal of Orthopsychiatry*, 25, 428–31

Tolman, R. (1955), review of *Psychotherapy and Personality Change* in *Journal of Abnormal Psychology*, 50, 407–9

Desai, M. (1956), review of *Psychotherapy and Personality Change* in *British Journal of Medical Psychology*, 28, 69–70

Shoben, E. J. (1955), review of *Psychotherapy and Personality Change* in *Journal of Consulting Psychology*, 19, 77

Rogers, C. R. (1958) 'A Process Conception of Psychotherapy', *American Psychologist*, 13, 142–9

Oppenheimer, R. (1955), paper presented to the annual convention of the American Psychological Association

Rogers, C. R. (1954), correspondence to and from Dr Wilff and to the Vice-Chancellor, letters in Library of Congress

Asch, S. E. (1953) 'Opinions and Social Pressure', *Scientific American*, 193, 31–5

Cutchfield, R. (1955) 'Conformity and Character', *American Psychologist*, 10, 191–5

Thomas, G. (1988) *Journey into Madness*, Bantam, London

**Chapter 7**

Broadbent, D. E. (1958) *Behaviour*, Methuen, London

Skinner, B. F. (1953) *Science and Behaviour*, Macmillan, New York

Skinner, B. F. (1955) 'Freedom', *American Scholar*, December issue

Rogers, C. R. (1956), letters to and from B. F. Skinner concerning setting up the debate, Library of Congress

Watson, J. B. (1913) 'Psychology as the Behaviourist Views It', *Psychological Review*, xx, 158–78

Rogers, C. R. and Skinner, B. F. (1956) Symposium held at the American Psychological Association convention at 7.30 in the Ballroom of the Sherman Hotel

Orwell, G. (1949) *1984*, Gollancz, London

Skinner, B. F. (1948) *Walden Two*, Macmillan, New York

Bjork, D. (1988) *B. F. Skinner: The Man*, Basic Books, New York

Morgan, E. (1956), programme on the debate between Carl Rogers and B. F. Skinner, ABC Radio, transcript in Library of Congress, Rogers collection

Minutes of the University of Chicago in Library of Congress, Rogers collection

Rogers, C. R. (1957), notes for the material re Buber, unpublished MS in Library of Congress

Rogers, C. R. (1958) 'A Process Conception of Psychotherapy', *American Psychologist*, 13, 142–9

Bettelheim, B. (1950) *Love Is Not Enough*, The Free Press, New York

Frankl, V. (1955) *The Doctor and the Soul*, Knopf, New York

Freud, S. (1922) *Beyond the Pleasure Principle*, International Psychoanalytic Press, London

Rogers, C. R. (1957) 'The Necessary and Sufficient Conditions for Therapeutic Change', *Journal of Consulting Psychology*, 21, 95–103

Masson, J. (1989) *Against Therapy*, Collins, London

Rogers, C. R., notes on conversations with his son David and his daughter-in-law Corky, unpublished material in Library of Congress

Rogers, C. R., correspondence with St Luke's Hospital concerning Ruth, unpublished material in Library of Congress

Rogers, C. R., correspondence with his brother re Ruth, unpublished material in Library of Congress

Rogers, C. R., 'Last Lecture' notes, unpublished MS in Library of Congress

Rogers, C. R. (1961) *On Becoming a Person*, Houghton Mifflin, Boston

Rogers, C. R. (1961), notes on his trip to Japan, unpublished MS in Library of Congress

Rogers, C. R. (1963), exchange of letters re C. Truax and the 'schiz' project at Mendota Hospital, unpublished material in Library of Congress

Rogers, C. R. (1964), paper on education, rejected by *American Psychologist*, published eventually on roneo, text in Library of Congress

Rogers, C. R. (1970) *Carl Rogers on Encounter Groups*, Harper & Row, New York

Rogers, C. R. (1964 and 1965), minutes of the Honker Group at Caltech, unpublished material in Library of Congress

Rogers, C. R. (1965), correspondence re New Zealand and Australia, unpublished material in Library of Congress

Rogers, C. R. (1965 onwards), exchange of letters with Larry Fuchs, unpublished material in Library of Congress

Johnson, L. B. (1959), letters to Justice Felix Frankfurter, unpublished material in Library of Congress

Rogers, C. R., Gendlin E., Kiesler, D. J. and Truax, C. eds (1967) *The Therapeutic Relationship and Its Impact*, Greenwood Press, Westport, CT

Milgram, S. (1974) *Obedience to Authority*, Tavistock, London

Harre, R. (1983), review of reprint of Milgram's book in *Psychology News*, no. 21

Rogers, C. R. (1969) *Freedom to Learn*, Charles Merrill, Ohio

Friedenberg, E. (1969), review of *Freedom to Learn* in *Harvard Educational Review*, 39, 217

Peters, R. S. (1969), review of *Freedom to Learn* in *Educational Research* vol. 11, 77

**Chapter 8**
Rogers, C. R. (1972) 'Some Issues that Concern Me', *Journal of Humanistic Psychology*, 12, 45–61

Moody, R. (1974) *Life after Life*, Bantam, London

Brown, R. C. and Tedeschi, J. T. (1972) 'A Rejoinder to Rogers', *Journal of Humanistic Psychology*, 12, 72–6

Rogers, C. R. (1969 onwards), correspondence re David Rogers' marriage, unpublished material in Library of Congress

Rogers, C. R. (1971), exchange of letters with his brother Lester, unpublished material in Library of Congress

Rogers, C. R. (1975) 'What I Want for Myself', unpublished MS in Library of Congress

Rogers, C. R. (1977) 'What I Want to do for Myself', unpublished MS in Library of Congress

Fromm, E. (1957) *The Art of Loving*, Allen & Unwin, London

Rogers, C. R. (1972) *Becoming Partners: Marriage and Its Alternatives*, Delacorte Press, New York

Rogers, C. R. (1973 onwards), exchange of letters between him and Len Holdstock concerning the possible visit to South Africa, unpublished material in Library of Congress

Rogers, C. R. (1975), exchange of letters with Vice-Chancellor of the University of California in Library of Congress

Rogers, C. R. (1975 onwards), notes and letters concerning his relationship with Bernice Todres, unpublished material in Library of Congress. These notes and letters occur for the next four years.

Rogers, C. R. (1975 onwards), notes concerning his marriage, unpublished material Library of Congress. As with the Todres material, these notes recur over the next four years.

Rogers, C. R. (1976) 'Do We Need a Reality?', *Dawnpoint*, 1(2): 6–9

Rogers, C. R. (1977) *Carl Rogers on Personal Power: Inner Strength and Its Revolutionary Impact*, Delacorte Press, New York

Rogers, C. R., exchange of letters with Natalie Rogers, unpublished material in Library of Congress

**Chapter 9**

Rogers, C. R. (1980) *A Way of Being*, Houghton Mifflin, Boston

Rogers, C. R. (1980) 'Growing Old – and Older', *Journal of Humanistic Psychology*, vol. 20, no. 4, 5–16

Rogers, C. R. (1982) 'My Secret Life with Plants', unpublished paper in Library of Congress read to his friends and family at his 80th birthday party in 1982

Rogers, C. R. (1982), notes concerning his 80th birthday party, unpublished material in Library of Congress

Rogers, C. R. (1982) 'Notes on Rollo May', *Journal of Humanistic Psychology*, 22, no. 3, 8–10

May, R. (1982) 'The Problem of Evil: An Open Letter to Carl Rogers', *Journal of Humanistic Psychology*, 22, no. 3, 11–22

Rogers, C. R. (1982), exchange of letters with Walter Rogers, unpublished material in Library of Congress

Rogers, C. R. (1985), exchange of letters with Curtis Graf, unpublished material in Library of Congress

Rogers, C. R. (1985) 'Towards a More Human Science of the Person', *Journal of Humanistic Psychology*, 25, no. 4, 26–43

Reason, P. and Rowan, J. (1981) *Human Inquiry*, John Wiley, Chichester

Capra, F. (1975) *The Tao of Physics*, Wildwood Press, London

Slack, S. (1985) 'Reflections of a Workshop with Carl Rogers', *Journal of Humanistic Psychology*, vol. 25, no. 2, 35–40

Rogers, C. R. (1986) 'The Rust Workshop: A Personal Overview', *Journal of Humanistic Psychology*, vol. 26, no. 3

Rogers, C. R. (1987) 'On Reaching 85', *Person-Centred Review*, vol. 2, no. 2, May 1987

Gendlin, E. (1988), obituary of Carl Rogers, *American Psychologist*, 43, 127–8

Thorne, B. (1992) *Carl Rogers*, Sage, London

Brazier, D. (1995) *Beyond Carl Rogers*, Constable, London

Nye, R. (1986) *Three Psychologies*, Brooks Cole, Monterrey, CA

Patterson, C. H. (1996), retrospective reviews of Rogers books in *Contemporary Psychology*, August issue, 8ff

Henry, J., Pickering, J., Stevens, R., Valentine E. and Velmans, M. (1997) 'Towards a Psychology of Experience', *The Psychologist*, vol. 10, no. 3, 117–120

# Index

*[Rogers' own publications are listed under Rogers]*